INTERIOR DESIGN Using Hand Sketching, SketchUp and Photoshop

Steven H. McNeill
Daniel John Stine

ISBN: 978-1-58503-686-8

PUBLICATIONS

Schroff Development Corporation

www.SDCpublications.com

Foreword

This book has been written with the assumption that the reader has no prior experience **hand sketching**, or using Google **SketchUp** or Adobe **Photoshop**. With this book, the reader will be able to describe and apply many of the fundamental principles needed to create compelling hand drawings, as well as develop SketchUp models and Photoshop imagery for presentations.

The content of this book is relevant to today's high tech design industry. You will learn what role architectural hand drawing has today compared to cutting edge computer design and rendering software; the two can be leveraged to create crisp, clean sketches with an economy of time!

The first two chapters cover computer basics, including managing files and knowing your way around the operating system. The next three chapters introduce the reader to SketchUp, an easy to use 3D modeling program geared specifically towards architecture. Chapters six and seven present the basic tools found in Photoshop, which is the industry standard raster image editing software.

Once you have worked through all the technology related introduction chapters, you will explore four chapters on various aspects of hand sketching. These chapters mainly focus on interior drawing concepts (see the authors' book *Chapters in Architectural Drawings – Hand Sketching in a Digital World* for more on architectural hand drawing).

The final four chapters work through the concept design process for an interior fit out project. The intent is that the reader would recreate these drawings as they appear in the book. The goal is to focus on understanding the process and developing the required techniques rather than getting bogged down in design right away; there will be plenty of time for that once you have the fundamentals down!

Although the book is primarily written with a classroom setting in mind, most individuals will be able to work through it on their own and benefit from the tips and tricks presented. ENJOY!

TO THE INSTRUCTOR:

As an instructor, you are strongly encouraged to request the *Instructors Resource Guide* for this book from the publisher. This guide will provide suggested solutions to exercises, additional exercises for some chapters, answers to end of chapter questions, as well as lecture suggestions for each chapter.

You may contact the publisher with comments or suggestions at: schroff@schroff.com.

ABOUT THE AUTHORS:

Steven H. McNeill is a registered Architect with 36 years' experience in the architectural field. He is the Director of Design at LHB (a 160-person multidiscipline firm; www.LHBcorp.com) in Duluth Minnesota. Mr. McNeill is involved in a broad array of project planning, concept development and design. His skills as a delineator were developed while working for such skilled architects as Duane Thorbeck FAIA and Dennis Grebner FAIA. He is a graduate of the University of Minnesota School of Architecture, has served as President of the American Institute of Architects (AIA) Minnesota, AIA Northern Minnesota, and has been an advisor to the Architecture Department at North Dakota State University (NDSU) and Lake Superior College (LSC) Architectural Technology Program. Steven has arranged sketching presentations for the AIA Minnesota Convention and is a co-founder of the Lake Superior Design Retreat, now in its 23rd year (www.aia-mn.org/lsdr). Steve has also written a textbook for the architectural designer:

- CHAPTERS IN ARCHITECTURAL DRAWING

Daniel John Stine is a registered Architect with nineteen years' experience in the architectural field. He currently works at LHB (a 160-person multidiscipline firm; www.LHBcorp.com) in Duluth Minnesota as the CAD Administrator providing training, customization and support for two regional offices. Daniel has worked in a total of four firms. While at these firms, he has participated in collaborative projects with several other firms on various projects (including Cesar Pelli, Weber Music Hall – University of Minnesota - Duluth). Mr. Stine is a member of the Construction Specification Institute (CSI) and the Autodesk Developer Network (ADN) and also teaches AutoCAD and Autodesk Revit classes at Lake Superior College for the Architectural Technology program; additionally, he is a Certified Construction Document Technician (CDT). Mr. Stine has written the following CAD/BIM textbooks (all published by SDC Publications):

- RESIDENTIAL DESIGN USING REVIT ARCHITECTURE
- COMMERCIAL DESIGN USING REVIT ARCHITECTURE
- RESIDENTIAL DESIGN USING AUTOCAD
- COMMERCIAL DESIGN USING AUTOCAD
- CHAPTERS IN ARCHITECTURAL DRAWING

THANKS:

The authors would like to thank their families for the encouragement and support provided during the months leading up to the book's deadline.

The authors would also like to thank their employer, **LHB** (www.LHBcorp.com), for its support of this project.

We are grateful to the various individuals who contributed architectural drawings for use in this book so that the reader might gain additional insight (please refer to the Index to find page locations):

- Anderson, Alan
- Booker, Darryl
- Poirier, Mark
- Porter, Anne
- Schneuer, Craig
- Thorbeck, Duane

This text has been greatly improved thanks to the following who meticulously reviewed draft manuscripts:

- Ashley Herstad
- Mike Matheny

A special thanks to LHB and Amy Rutten and Warren Schulze of Concordia College for allowing us to use sketches, created by McNeill, for the French Language Village.

Many thanks go out to Schroff Development Corporation for making this book possible!

Table of Contents

Notes:

Introduction to Computers Part I

Although many design students have some experience using computers, many do not have a good working knowledge of the parts of a computer and what they do. The goal of this chapter is to provide a solid foundation in basic computer terms and functions. This study will help ensure students are able to hit the ground running when working on the SketchUp and Photoshop sections in this book. The next chapter will cover the essentials of file management, including saving and backing up your files.

Section 1-1
Computer Basics: Terms and Functions

What you need to know

This study is not interested in the history or philosophy related to computers, but rather a more concise introduction will be presented. A person just starting to use a computer or learn a program, such as SketchUp AutoCAD, Revit or Photoshop, does not need to know everything about computers before being productive. This exercise will begin by presenting several computer terms and their functions. Many readers will be familiar with much of this information, but one will likely learn a few new things along the way.

Hardware

The next few pages will introduce various pieces of computer hardware, the portion of the computing experience on which a person can place their hands. This is in contrast to software and documents (covered later) which live electronically "within" the computer's hardware.

Computer

Some use the term "computer" in the all-inclusive sense – including the monitor, computer chassis, mouse, etc. Other times, the term "computer" is used to just describe the box to which the monitor and mouse connect. Either usage is valid. Finally, a laptop (see "Laptop" below) can be called a computer as well.

Computer: **Desktop Computer**

A desktop computer is most commonly used in the design profession due to the lower cost and additional "horsepower" when compared to a laptop. A desktop computer is modular; meaning the monitor, mouse, keyboard and speakers are separate components connected by wires (can be wireless). This allows for different hardware combinations depending on the needs of the user. CAD/BIM users typically need a larger, high resolution, monitor due to the large, complex drawings and amount of time spent looking at the screen in a given day.

Desktop computers are easier to enhance and upgrade than laptops as well. This is because of the large chassis (or box) in which the internal computer components are housed. An end user can easily add an additional hard drive, video card or RAM, for which most new computers allow room and connections. Depending on the age of the computer, however, it is often better to simply buy a new computer than it is to upgrade. For example, if a two year old computer were to be upgraded to a 64bit Operating System (OS), plus additional RAM, Video Card and a second hard drive installed to manage virtual memory, one might find that a brand new computer costs just a little more money and also has a better motherboard.

What kind of computer should a student buy?

When asking the question "what kind of a computer does a student need?" one might first consider if one is needed at all. Certainly a student may benefit from having access to their own personal computer but it may not be required. Some schools do require students to buy their own computer and software. Autodesk allows students to use their software for free (see website students.autodesk.com for more information), and Google offers a free version of SketchUp to everyone. But others do not, for example, there is no free version of Photoshop or Microsoft Office. Most schools provide computer labs that are accessible during class and at other times as well. Once the typical student is finished with school, their employer usually provides a computer to use while at work.

Most students who buy a computer get a laptop for its portability. It is very convenient to use your computer in class. Many schools provide wireless network access and internet connections throughout the school, and some also allow access to the printers via the wireless connection. Being able to work on CAD/BIM assignments and other homework can be especially convenient when students have jobs.

Although certain designs (i.e., CAD/BIM drawings) can become huge and extremely taxing on the computer and the software, most drawings done within the context of school do not demand the most powerful and expensive computers. Take a look at the manufacture's recommendations for computers for the software you wish to use. Many, such as Autodesk, provide "minimum" and "preferred" system specifications. The minimum specifications will likely be sufficient in a classroom environment. Of course, if you can afford it, you will have a better overall experience with the "preferred" system.

When considering options for a new computer, in addition to the minimum system requirements, you may want to prioritize as follows:

- CPU (and bus speed)
- RAM (total amount and speed)
- Graphics Card (including its amount of RAM)
- Size of high resolution monitor/screen
- Warranty (especially for laptops which are more prone to damage as they are mobile and easily dropped)

Computer: **Laptop Computer**

Laptop computers are becoming more powerful and less expensive every year. The once clear line between desktop computers and laptops is beginning to become not so clear (laptops used to be very expensive and slower). However, as stated in the previous section, a desktop computer is often a better overall value in terms of computing power. With that being said, the student would likely give up a little computing horsepower for the convenience of portability. Most projects worked on in school do not consume the kind of resources needed in a professional design firm.

As with most things, you get what you pay for. Extremely inexpensive laptops have low quality displays, low end graphics cards, minimal RAM and may not even have a CD/DVD drive. On the opposite end of the spectrum are high end desktop-grade laptops that have large, high quality displays, a fast CPU, the ability to house two hard drives and more.

Due to the compact nature of laptops, they are more difficult to upgrade. It is not too hard to add more RAM or replace the hard drive with a higher capacity unit, but rarely is a graphics card or display upgraded.

An extended warranty is a good idea for laptops given they are portable and more prone to damage. Some extended warranties will only cover parts that have stopped working under otherwise normal conditions, while better (and likely more expensive) ones will cover everything except it being lost or stolen, including the laptop being dropped or a soda spilled on the keyboard!

Computer: **Central Processing Unit (CPU)**

The CPU (aka *processor*) is the "heart" of the computer; this is where all the work is done. The speed and number of processors is a key factor in how a computer performs overall.

The speeds are measured in Gigahertz (GHz) and a higher number is better (i.e., faster). Dealing with the heat these things produce is an ongoing challenge for computer manufacturers – especially in laptops.

Until recently, the average computer on the market only had one CPU. But newer technology is shifting that trend toward multiple processors packed into one unit. These *Dual, Quad* and *six core* processors are becoming very popular; multiple cores cast into one die (i.e., CPU).

Multiple processors are useful for a couple of reasons.

1. When multiple applications (i.e., programs) are running, each can use a different processor and thus keep the overall system robust and working faster. One application might be AutoCAD or Revit *Architecture* doing a rendering, while the user is working in a spreadsheet or a word-processor with minimal delays.

2. A few applications, like Autodesk's 3DS Max have the ability to utilize multiple processors in order to complete a task sooner. Many applications can only use one processor at a time.

3. In the case of most software, multi-threading is accomplished by the computer spreading out work over multiple processors. The processors can run in parallel to shorten computing time.

Computer: **RAM**

The formal name, which nobody really uses, is Random Access Memory (RAM) – also called Temporary Memory (or just Memory). RAM is extremely fast memory that is only available and can only hold information when it has power, in contrast to hard drives (aka, permanent memory).

When a computer is turned on, the operating system (e.g., Windows Vista) is loaded into RAM from the hard drive. Then, when a user starts a program (e.g., Photoshop), that program is loaded into RAM. While using an *application* (program), the user opens a *document* (e.g., an image file), the file is then also loaded into RAM. In short, RAM allows multiple configurations to take place. For example, memory might hold an application one minute and then a video file, and then finally a Photoshop file. It is truly multi-dimensional.

Bits and pieces of the information in RAM are sent over to the CPU as needed to perform the additions and edits you are making to the *document* via the *application*.

> **WARNING:**
> *When working on a* document *(in any application, e.g., AutoCAD, Word, etc.) the user should* Save *regularly to avoid losing work due to a computer "crash" (i.e., software failure) or power failure. Any information in RAM is immediately lost when power is lost or the computer is restarted. Therefore, committing/writing the information in RAM to the hard drive (aka, permanent storage) using the* Save *command is very important. Some programs, like Word and AutoCAD, have an "autosave" feature that helps avoid losing large amounts of work. In most programs, pressing the* **Ctrl** *key followed by the* **S** *key causes the application to perform a* Save, *writing the information from RAM to the computer's hard drive.*

As one can guess, if too many *applications* and *documents* are opened at once, the space in RAM can reach maximum capacity. MS Windows has a backup plan in that event; the *operating system* begins to write information from RAM to the hard drive as *virtual memory*. This is good in that it keeps the computer from "crashing", but bad in the sense that the hard drive is significantly slower than fast-reacting RAM when sending data to the CPU. This slowness (or better, *slow access memory*) becomes a virtual bottleneck and the entire computing experience is degraded.

The cost of RAM continues to decline, but it still is far from free. A computer should meet the minimum RAM requirement stated by the software manufacturer, for both the OS and the application, keeping in mind these minimums are not likely taking into account additional applications being used concurrently. RAM is fairly easy to add for most computers. A student should buy as much as they can afford for a better computing experience.

One final note about RAM: a computer typically only has 4-6 slots for RAM and they usually have to be used in pairs. Thus, if all the slots are full, the existing memory may have to be discarded in order to upgrade. Generally, when it is time to upgrade, the cost of the on-board memory is so inexpensive, completely removing the old RAM and replacing it with all new RAM makes the most sense.

Computer: **Motherboard**

The *motherboard* is essentially a large circuit board within the computer. All the computer hardware connects directly to it: the CPU, RAM, graphics card (which then connects to the monitor), hard drive, mouse, keyboard, etc. There is a lot more that could be said about the motherboard, but we will save that for the computer science and engineering students!

Computer: **Graphics Card**

When the computer needs to display something on the screen, it does so through the *graphics card*. A graphics card has its own CPU (which is actually called a GPU, *graphics processing unit*) and RAM which are dedicated to displaying complex graphics. Some graphics cards are built into the computer's motherboard on less expensive computers and are not well suited for intense CAD/BIM programs (the RAM needed for the graphics card is usually taken from the computer's main RAM). A high quality graphics card consists of a separate card that inserts into a special slot on the computer's motherboard. One side of the card is exposed on the back of the computer so the monitor cable can be plugged into it. High end graphics cards can be made more powerfully by "teaming" multiple graphics cards. Some programs are designed to take more advantage of the power of graphics cards than are others. An application such as Autodesk's 3DS Max can use many of the features on a high end graphics card; the graphics card's software will even have special settings in it for 3DS Max (as well as other popular applications with which they have partnered). However, other applications do not use some of these special features.

AutoCAD has a special optimization utility that automatically runs when the program is first launched (and manually from the *Options* dialog). Autodesk Revit has a special setting within its *Options* dialog in which the graphics card's "hardware acceleration" can be used, as does SketchUp and Photoshop.

As one can see, the graphics card is an important part of the computer in the CAD/BIM world. When selecting a graphics card consider the following:
- Does the manufacturer's website offer regular software updates that can be downloaded?
- Does the manufacturer mention the CAD/BIM software you use in any of its literature or on its website? They are likely to mention widely used programs such as AutoCAD and 3DS Max, but may not mention other programs such as Revit or SketchUp.
- Does the CAD/BIM software manufacturer recommend a specific graphics card or manufacturer? Most will not "play favorites" and recommend one over another, but they may list minimum specifications (e.g., RAM) or list several cards that have been tested and found compatible with the software.
- What are the connection options to the monitor? See the discussion on monitors for more information.

Computer: **Drives**

Hard Drive
The computer *hard drive* is where all the software is stored: the operating system (OS), the applications (e.g., Photoshop, MS Word, AutoCAD, Revit) and the documents (e.g., drawings, letters, photos, music files, etc.). Most computers come with an adequately sized hard drive, especially in an office setting where all documents are stored on the server so they can be automatically backed up each night.

Given the fact that hard drives have moving parts, they are susceptible to failure. It is vital that important files are backed up. Several options are available for backing up data: tape drives (used on servers and some desktops), external hard drives (see the next topic on this), discs (CD, DVD, Blu-ray – these would be a manual process), and flash drives. Several internet backup companies have recently entered the market, offering both manual and automatic backup of data files over the internet; this has the added benefit of residing at a remote location in case of fire, theft or natural disaster.

Desktop computers and some laptops have the ability to house two (or more) internal hard drives. A high end CAD/BIM station might have a second hard drive dedicated solely to Window's virtual memory.

Again, due to the moving parts in a hard drive, they tend to be the bottleneck in speed, especially when opening and saving a file. Server hard drives are usually faster but much more expensive.

External Hard Drive

External hard drives come in all shapes and sizes. They typically plug into a USB port and sit near the computer. It is possible to carry one around but caution must be used so as not to damage it. A flash drive has no moving parts, which makes it better suited for portability. An external hard drive can have terabytes (2,000,000 MB) of space, whereas, at the time of this writing, a flash drive can have up to 64GB (64,000 MB) of space.

Some external hard drives come with software that can be installed on a computer which automatically backs up data from the main hard drive (e.g., emails, documents, photos, etc.).

Flash Drive

A *flash drive* is a "must have" for a student. It is a small portable data storage unit that plugs into any computer's USB port. Once plugged in, after a few seconds of configuration, a new drive letter shows up on the computer and one will have access to the data and any free storage space on it. Flash drives, which are solid state, are fast and tend to last a long time, compared to the moving parts of hard drives. These devices continue to get cheaper and hold more data. The larger flash drives, 64GB capacity, are larger than most students would need for school work; a 4 to 8GB unit would likely suffice.

A flash drive should be used to back up all school work, whether it is done on a school computer or at home. It is important to protect your data (i.e., documents) from loss or corruption. One does not need to back up software, just one's drawings, papers and photos for example.

> *TIP:*
> *AutoCAD, Revit and SketchUp create backup files that do not need to be backed up, they are the same size file as the primary file and would quickly use up all your available space. AutoCAD's backup files have a .BAK extension and Revit files have the same file name and extension, but have a suffix added to the file name, like "001", "002" and "003". SketchUp backup files have a .SKB file extension.*

Online Storage

It is now possible to save data to the internet (aka, *"cloud"*). Several companies are now providing "cloud" data storage space to which you upload files to a user account and can then download them from anywhere in the world, as long as you remember your user name and password. Some offer this service for a fee, offering perks such as guaranteed backup, redundant servers/locations, 24/7/365 access and software that will automatically backup user data files. Others offer free storage space with various limitations and may display advertising. Simply search the internet for "free online storage" to learn more.

Online storage is a great benefit to a student as it allows files to be safely backed up away from home and school, protected from fire, theft, etc. Also, as just mentioned, the files are accessible from any computer connected to the internet. When this process is used, the files are copied to the "internet" once the CAD/BIM program is closed. It would not be advisable, or even possible in most instances, to work directly in the file stored online.

Compact Disk (CD)

A CD is the original "disk" format that holds about 650MB of data. Most computers come with a drive that can read these, and many have the ability to write data to blank disks.

DVD

A DVD was initially created to store feature-length movies and then became a data storage option. A DVD can hold 4.7 GB (4,700 MB) of data (and more in some cases). Double-sided DVD's can stretch the storage to 8.5 GB of data and are readable by most DVD equipped computers. Many computers come with a drive that can read these, and many have the ability to write data to blank DVD disks.

Blu-ray Disk (BD)

A Blu-ray Disk (aka, BD) was designed to store HD movies. This format can store 25-50 GB of data (single layer vs. double layer). The most amazing thing is that the disk is the same size for a CD, DVD and BD. Most computers do not yet have the ability to read or write to a Blu-ray disk.

Computer: **Monitor**

Monitors come in many shapes and sizes. The older style monitor is the CRT; this is the deep, heavy monitor with a glass tube. The new monitors are typically LCD; they are approximately 1″ thick and are very lightweight.

In the world of CAD/BIM it is ideal to have a large monitor given the fact that the designer spends a large amount of time looking at the screen. A 20″-24″ widescreen LCD monitor capable of high resolutions is commonplace in the design industry. Note that computer monitors are capable of higher resolutions than 1080p HD televisions, so don't get confused. A widescreen 24″ monitor can have a resolution of 2560 x 1600, which is the number of pixels in each direction. 1600 pixels is a lot more than an HDTV's 1080 pixels.

Monitors can also come with built-in *card readers* (e.g., to download photos from a digital camera's memory card), USB hubs and speakers. All of these increase cost but the added convenience and reduced clutter on the desktop may be worth it.

Monitor Cable/Connection types: HDMI, DisplayPort, DVI, S-Video, VGA.

HDMI is typically for HDTV's and Blu-ray players. They have a digital video signal which also includes the audio, thus requiring fewer cables. The newest computer to monitor cable is the **DisplayPort** (make sure your graphics card and monitor both support it, or that you have the proper adaptors). **DVI** is a digital cable that has been around for a few years as has **S-Video** (S-Video is found on some laptops and not commonly used). Finally, **VGA** is the age-old analog cable, which is best to avoid as it is desirable to have the best picture possible due to the time spent looking at the screen.

Computer: **Speakers**

Speakers are not necessary for CAD software directly. However, many training videos and webcasts over the internet make speakers a highly recommended option.

Computer: **Mouse**

The main thing to know about a mouse is that it should have a decent scroll wheel. In AutoCAD, and Revit, the scroll wheel is used to quickly **zoom** in and out as well as **pan** around the current drawing. *FYI: Panning is moving the part of the drawing seen on the screen, not actually moving the drawing.* Try to avoid scroll wheels that tilt left and right to scroll horizontally in MS *Word* and *Excel* as they make the button action of the wheel more difficult to operate accurately.

A wireless mouse is nice but more of a convenience than a necessity.

Computer: **Input/Output**

Printer
Most school and business printers are capable of printing on 8 ½″ x 11″ and 11″ x 17″ paper. Toner based printers are usually faster than ink based (aka, inkjet) printers; they are also less susceptible to smudging than ink.

In workgroup environments, the printer may be built into the copier, which can also have a scanner and fax machine built in. They are connected to a network and located in a central area in the office or class lab.

Plotter
A plotter is only different from a printer in the size of paper on which it prints. A plotter prints on large paper, such as 22″ x 34″ or 36″ x4 8″. The paper is typically on a roll; when the plotter is done printing it cuts the paper off the roll at the required length. An example of a plotter can be seen in the image below.

This image shows a large format plotter (right) and scanner (left). Scans can be sent directly to the plotter as a copy or to a file for use in various software programs such as Photoshop.

Scanner

Most design firms have the ability to scan paper (i.e., hardcopy) documents to a digital file. Many multi-function printers can scan 8 ½″ x 11″ (i.e., letter) and 11″x17″ (i.e., tabloid) sized paper. Scanners often have something called an automatic document feeder on top which allows several pages to be loaded and scanned automatically. The final file can even be a single, multi-page PDF (PDF = Portable Document Format), a highly shareable file format.

Another standard option in most design firms is a large format scanner. Oftentimes the drawings of an original building need to be scanned and saved to a file because the originals must to be returned to the client or building owner. These scanned files can be used to reference dimensions when drawing the existing building on the computer. The digital files can even be linked into the CAD/BIM program and traced over if the quality and accuracy is good enough.

TIP:

Scanned images can be very large files depending on the scanner settings. Factors such as resolution (dpi) and color can make a big difference. When scanned images need to be printed at a large size, the resolution needs to be increased to keep the printout from looking pixilated (i.e., like little boxes). Also, scanning a drawing with redlines would likely require a color scanner, all of which can significantly increase the file size. Finding the right balance takes practice, trial and error.

Finally, linking large scanned images into a CAD/BIM program can seriously slow down the program, e.g., Open, Zoom, Pan, Save, etc. Oftentimes it would be better to redraw a building rather than rely on a scanned image. It might be acceptable to link the image in temporarily to trace over it and then remove it when complete.

Software

Once the computer hardware is in place, it is necessary to have the appropriate software to utilize it. Software is the part of a computing experience that cannot be touched *per se*; it is possible to touch a hard drive, but it does not feel any different if it is empty or totally full of software or data.

Software may come preloaded on a computer, be downloaded from the internet or come on a CD/DVD, or be written by the computer user.

Software: **Operating System**

When the computer is first turned on the *Operating System (OS)*, stored on the hard drive, is loaded into RAM and displayed on the screen.

Most computers are sold with an OS, so the only time someone usually buys an OS apart from a computer is when they are upgrading. For example, if a two year old computer has Microsoft Windows Vista, it may be upgraded to Windows 7 (the newest OS from Microsoft at the time of this printing).

Microsoft Windows 7 is the newest operating system from Microsoft. This is the box provided when purchasing the software apart from a computer.

This image shows the Graphical User Interface (GUI) for a typical PC Operating System; this loads automatically every time the computer is turned on.

Most of the CAD world is standardized on the PC versus the Apple Macintosh (Mac). There are some CAD applications that run on the Mac such as AutoCAD; SketchUp and Photoshop also have Mac versions. Revit and 3DS Max are only designed to run on a PC along with Microsoft's OS. It is possible to run Revit on a Mac using an add-on program for the Mac (e.g., Apple Boot Camp, Parallels Desktop, etc.).

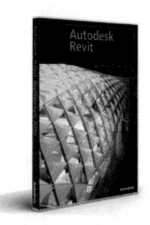

Also, it is possible to install a Microsoft OS on a Mac. When the computer is started you select which OS you want to launch. You have to purchase a full version of the Microsoft OS in addition to the Mac computer (which comes with a proprietary OS). Additionally, if you have a program such as Adobe Photoshop, it would have to be installed twice. Once for each OS, in order to use it in both OS environments.

The student will likely get a better value sticking with a PC and will gain experience and learn workflows that are more likely encountered in the workplace than if a Mac were used.

Software: **Applications**

Once a person has a computer with an *operating system* they can then begin to purchase and install *applications*. The only limit on the number of applications you can have installed on a computer is your budget and available space on your hard drive.

Applications (i.e., software) can cost anywhere from nothing to thousands of dollars. Think of applications as tools, much like your desk chair, lights, stapler, pens, etc., used to get your work done accurately and efficiently. The cost of software often relates to:

1. How sophisticated it is (e.g., it was time consuming and challenging to write the software).
2. The amount of work it can help you to do compared to other programs or doing it manually (i.e., drawing with pencils or using a calculator).
3. Competition. Do other programs exist that help keep the price competitive?

Most professional applications have hundreds of employees that write the software, test it to make sure it works correctly, write user manuals and tutorials, market the product and the list goes on. All this and regular updates cost a lot of money. Autodesk updates their design software yearly.

Application costs (approximately):
- Autodesk Revit Architecture: $5,495
- Autodesk AutoCAD: $3,995
- Adobe Photoshop CS5: $699
- SketchUp Pro 8 $495
- Microsoft Office Home & Student: $149

Each application has its own set of system requirements that should be compared to your computer system before buying any software. Some programs require a lot of horsepower to make the program run smoothly. This information can be found on the packaging, if shopping in a store, or on the manufacturer's website.

NOTE: Some programs such as AutoCAD and Revit cannot be purchased in a store; they must be obtained through authorized resellers.

Applications can come on CD, DVD or be downloaded from the internet.

> *TIP:*
> *Beware of buying "used" software. Some software is pirated, which is illegal, and updates and upgrades are therefore not available. Also, the software license agreement which you accept before you can use the software often forbids resale of the software; this is the case with Autodesk software. Really cheap software online typically IS too good to be true and should be avoided.*

Autodesk provides free software to students. If you are a student with a valid EDU email address, you should be able to register and download Autodesk design software for free. Autodesk allows students to download and install a student version of their design software (e.g., Revit and AutoCAD) for use in the education process. The software is usable for 13 months from the day it is activated. The student version is the same as the full version with few exceptions. The student version cannot be used in any way to make money (i.e., you cannot draw up someone's house plans for a few hundred dollars). Also, a student stamp appears on the four edges of any page that is printed.

Visit the following website to learn more: **students.autodesk.com**.

> **WARNING:**
> *If you are working in a design office while going to school, do not open and edit your employer's CAD files. The student stamp will be permanently added to the file. Even when printed from a full version of AutoCAD, not the student version, the "student version" stamp will appear at the perimeter of the page.*

An application's size on the hard drive can vary greatly. The list below compares five applications (note that 1 GB is equal to 1000 MB).

- AutoCAD: 812 mb
- Autodesk Revit Architecture: 1.56 gb
- Adobe Photoshop: 416 mb (64bit pro version)
- Microsoft Office: 419 mb (professional version)
- SketchUp   131 mb

Software: **32bit versus 64bit**

Virtually all computer CPUs and motherboards (aka, computer architecture) have been 64bit for a number of years now. However, software has mainly been 32bit, thus not taking full advantage of the additional power, bandwidth and memory available. Software needs to be significantly re-written to support 64bit operating systems and hardware.

A lot of 32bit applications will run on a 64bit operating system. This is because the operating system has a "compatibility" mode built into it. This helps sell customers on 64bit OS, knowing that they will not have to immediately buy all new application software.

One of the major benefits of the 64bit OS and applications in the CAD world is the access gained to more RAM. Programs such as Revit can require a significant amount of RAM when working on large multi-million dollar projects. A 32bit OS can only access about 3.5 MB of Ram, whereas a 64bit OS does not have a practical limit. Technically speaking, a 64bit OS could have a little over **17 billion GB of RAM**. However, not too many computer manufacturers are providing this configuration yet! A computer with 8 – 16 GB of RAM is considered pretty high at the moment.

Most of Autodesk's products come in both 32bit and 64bit versions. If you buy AutoCAD, the DVD will have both versions on it. Other than the size of file/project that can be worked on, there is usually no discernable difference to the user when working with the software.

> *TIP:*
> *Some older hardware, such as printers, scanners, palm pilots, digital cameras, etc., may not work at all in a 64bit OS environment. Manufacturers of some of these products may have discontinued support for outdated technology in order to focus on new and future technology.*

Software: **Updates and Upgrades**

Advanced applications, such as AutoCAD, Revit and Photoshop, are always changing to meet the demands of the design industry. Every year or two a software company will come out with an update to their application(s). This provides new features with the goal of creating better designs more efficiently. Updates also help keep the software companies in business! Operating systems are updated less frequent due to their large impact on hardware and applications. However, security patches or bug fixes are done on a monthly basis to keep systems safe and stable.

Upgrades cost a fraction of the original cost of the software.

Application upgrade costs (approximately):
- Autodesk Revit Architecture: $895
- Autodesk AutoCAD: $595
- Adobe Photoshop CS5 $199
- SketchUp Pro 8 $95

With Autodesk software, a subscription option exists which allows you to budget a specific amount each year for the applications you have. Then, when a new version is released you have automatic access to the software and any extras that are only available on the subscription website. Over time, this works out to be the cheapest way to go. It is not less expensive to skip every other release either because the cost goes up when the program you are upgrading from is older. For example, the AutoCAD upgrade price above is for upgrading from release 2010 to 2011. To go from release 2009 to 2011 is $1,995, not $595.

Also, given the complexity of the software and its ability to be customized, the inevitably of "bugs" (i.e., errors in the programs code) are found in the software. When "bugs" are found, software manufacturers release "service packs" (or web updates, hot fixes, patches, etc.). These "fixes" are typically downloaded from the internet for free. You may have to periodically check for these updates as some software manufacturers do not inform you that an update is available.

Some software can automatically check for updates and let you know when they are available. For example, Microsoft's operating systems and the Office suites are able to do this. This can be very important when it comes to the OS as some of the updates deal with viruses and security issues.

Software: **Documents**

Once you have a computer, with an OS, and one or more applications, you can start creating *documents*. Whenever you save your work within an application, you are creating a "document" file on the computer's hard drive.

Here are a few examples of documents and their extensions: MS Word letter (DOCx), MS Excel spreadsheet (XLSx), AutoCAD drawing (DWG), Revit project (RVT), SketchUp (SKP), and Photoshop (PSD).

The OS and application files tend to take up more space on your hard drive than do document files. However, document backups, archives and copies can take up a significant amount of space. Therefore, it is good practice to occasionally check the amount of free space on your hard drive. Running out of disk space while saving can corrupt your document.

Enough cannot be said about backing up your document files. The document files, for the most part, are the only files that need to be backed up. If your computer crashes and you replace it or the hard drive, it is better to reinstall the OS and the applications from the original CD/DVD's than restore them from a backup. Also, backing up the OS and applications would take a lot more time to complete.

Most organizations require that all document files be saved on a server so everyone has access to them and they automatically get backed up every night by the IT department, or in a smaller office where the architect, interior designer or engineer wears multiple hats.

Software: **Viruses and Hackers**

It seems there is always somebody in the world looking to make a dishonest buck or make another person's life more complicated. In the computer world, these come in the form of *viruses* and *hackers*.

A *virus* is a program that somehow becomes installed on your computer and does something you have not authorized. Sometimes the virus causes great harm to your computer's data (i.e., files on the hard drive) and other times they send personal information over the internet without your knowledge.

Several *anti-virus software applications* exist to help protect your computer from viruses and hackers. It is absolutely critical that a high quality anti-virus application be installed on your computer. If you are using a computer in a school lab, it will have likely have an anti-virus program running. Additionally, the entire institution will usually be behind a *Firewall* (which detects viruses and hackers before they even get close to the end user's computers).

Software: **Piracy**

As the saying goes "nothing in life is free"; this is mostly true for software. Unfortunately, it is a challenge to get everyone who uses the software to pay for it. This is not a problem for hardware manufacturers; if someone wants a new hard drive they have to pay for it before one is given to them. With software, things are a little different. It is possible to illegally share software with others and download bootlegged software from the internet. Most software manufacturers develop ways to prevent this by requiring software to be activated online using a unique serial number before the software becomes fully functional.

Most software licenses only allow installation onto one computer. It does not matter if a person owns three computers and would only ever use one at a time. However, some programs have what is called a network license, in which case it can be installed on every computer. This is when a user opens a program (e.g., AutoCAD), a license is "pulled" from the pool of available licenses.

Installing software that has not been paid for is called *piracy*. The software company has intellectual rights to the software and its usage. When it is discovered that a business or person is illegally using software (i.e., pirating), a lawsuit is filed in order to get compensated.

Oftentimes students have access to cheap or free software. Student software usually has a built-in time limit (e.g., Autodesk software is 13 months); at the end of that time period, if still a student, the new version may be downloaded and used for another 13 months.

For more information on software piracy, visit Business Software Alliance:
www.bsa.org

Network

A typical network involves one or more servers and several clients (i.e., your computer). Each client computer, network printer/copier and VoIP phone (Voice over IP – i.e., network cables) has a physical wire that runs to the server room. There the unit connects to a large panel called a switch, which then connects to the server.

A server can be a regular computer or a room with modular computer components installed on racks. A server does the following:

- centralizes hard drives
- performs the scheduled backups
- manages network enabled printers
- runs the email system
- provides a connection to the internet
- controls security (who has access to what)
- ties into the VoIP (voice over IP) telephone system
- allows external access to office recourses

The main things a student needs to know about a network are that it provides access to your files from multiple computers on the system and it is where all documents are backed up.

Wireless Network

A wireless network allows access to the network via radio waves and thus does not require a wire. This technology has advanced in recent years by improving speed and security. However, a wired connection is still faster and more secure, although wireless networks allow computers to be placed where it would be difficult to run wires.

Many places now provide wireless network connectivity to their patrons. For example, coffee shops, hotels, public libraries, schools, etc. This can be handy if you have a laptop and need to access the internet while studying away from home or school. Of course, this can be a distraction as well. Spending too much time browsing the web or checking out social networking sites can burn up valuable study time!

Make sure your internet security suite [which includes firewall, malware, antivirus, and antispyware] is up-to-date prior to using any public/un-secured wireless network. A computer infection can happen within minutes when your internet security suite is out of date; always update your internet security suite prior to surfing the web on a new wireless network.

Section 1-2
Windows User Interface

Introduction:

Every program or software application has a **user interface**(UI). This is the way in which you, the "user", tell the computer what you want it to do. The UI can also be referred to as a *graphical user interface* (GUI) due to the graphical icons and dialog boxes, as compared to the mainly text interface that was once common several years ago.

The image below shows the UI for Microsoft's **Windows 7**operating system (OS). This, or something very similar, is what is seen when the computer first starts. The text following this image and on the next few pages describes each of the main components of the UI.

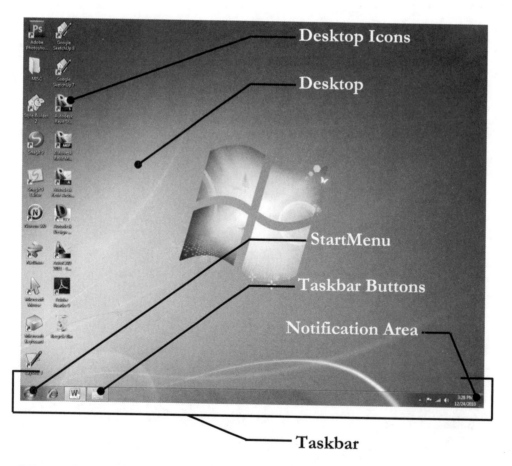

Microsoft's *Windows XP* and *Windows Vista* are very similar to what is shown above for *Windows 7*. You should be able to follow with any of these operating system versions.

Desktop:

The desktop serves two main purposes:

1) To hold *desktop icons*(see next section), and

2) As an area on which one or more *application window(s)* is open

Application windows can be "<u>maximized</u>" (i.e., "full screen") to fill the entire screen or they can be "<u>sized</u>" on the *Desktop* in order to view two or more applications at once. Also, applications can be "<u>minimized</u>" to the *Taskbar* so they are not visible on the *Desktop*, but are still open and quickly accessible.

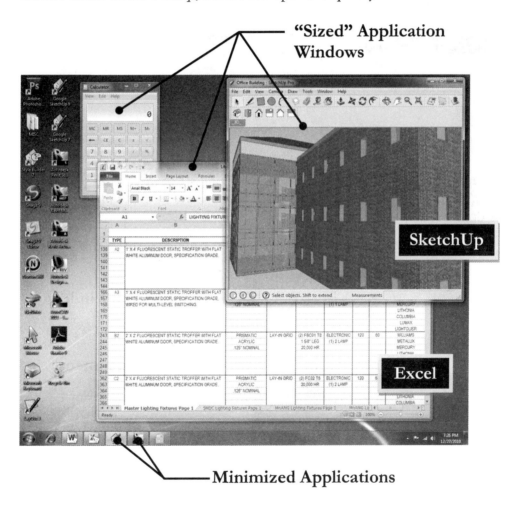

"Sized" Application Windows

SketchUp

Excel

Minimized Applications

This notion of "windows" on the *Desktop* is where the name of the OS comes from; i.e., Microsoft's *Windows 7*.

> **FYI:** Microsoft *is the name of the company that makes the software, and* 7 *is the specific version of Windows OS.*

In the upper right corner of each application window are three buttons. The middle one changes depending on the current state of the window size. When the application window is "<u>maximized</u>", that is, it fills the entire *Desktop*, the middle button shows a graphic in the button that represents "<u>sized</u>" windows. Thus, clicking it changes the window from being "<u>maximized</u>" to being "<u>sized</u>" (see the first image below). Conversely, if the middle button shows a "<u>maximize</u>" icon, then the window is currently "<u>sized</u>" (see second image below).

The far left icon (in both images below) will "<u>minimize</u>" the application down to the *Taskbar* so it is not visible on the *Desktop*. On the far right is the "**Close** application" icon. When clicking the red "x" to close an application, it will prompt you to save any changes that have not already been saved before closing.

Window Icons while maximized   *Window Icons while sized*

Some applications, such as AutoCAD, have a second set of these icons (see image below). The upper set is for the application, and the lower set is for the current *active* document.

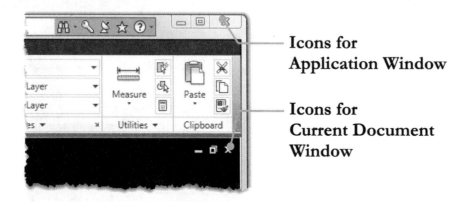

Icons for Application Window

Icons for Current Document Window

When the document windows are "sized", each document window has its own set of icons, as seen in the image below.

One document window is always "active"; the title bar is darker to indicate this.

Title Bar

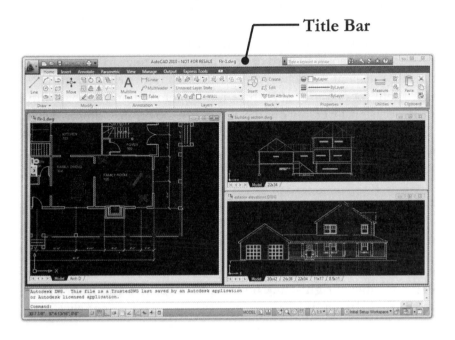

> *TIP:*
> *Double-clicking on the Title Bar for an application or document will "maximize" or "tile" it – the setting will be opposite of whatever the current state is.*

Desktop Icons:

The *Desktop* may contain the following types of files in general:

- Documents
- Folders
- Shortcuts (for folders, documents and programs on your computer).

The image to the right shows a sampling of *Desktop icons* presented in the same order as the list above (i.e., in the top row are documents, next folders and then shortcuts).

02157LIGH... CFB Shed.rvt _02157LIGH...

Misc Kitchen temp

AutoCAD 2010 - E... Autodesk Revit Arch... Adobe Acrobat 9 Standard

Another icon found on the *Desktop* is the **Recycle Bin**.
Anytime a file is deleted from your computer's hard
drive, it is moved into the *Recycle Bin*. This is good
information for the student learning to use computers
and/or CAD. On occasion you may need to double-
click on the *Recycle Bin* icon and retrieve a file or two.
Consequently, a deleted file is not really deleted and still
takes up space on your computer's hard drive. There are settings to control how
space is used. Once this limit is reached, the oldest files in the *Recycle Bin* are
deleted to make room for newer files. If space is at a premium on your hard drive,
you may want to occasionally empty out the *Recycle Bin*. To do this, simply right-
click on the *Recycle Bin* icon and select *Empty Recycle Bin*. If you have plenty of disk
space, it is better to leave the files in the *Recycle Bin* so they are accessible if needed
at a later time.

Recycle Bin   Recycle Bin
  empty   *filled*

> **NOTE:** *Files deleted off of a network drive or flash drive are **not** copied to your*
> *computer's hard drive and placed in the Recycle Bin. The image above shows the empty*
> *versus filled (not necessarily full) icon.*

The *Desktop* icons can be manually dragged around to reposition them on the
Desktop. It is also possible to **right-click on the *Desktop*** and select from a few
options related to *Desktop* icon organization and visibility. Those right-click
options are shown in the two images below:

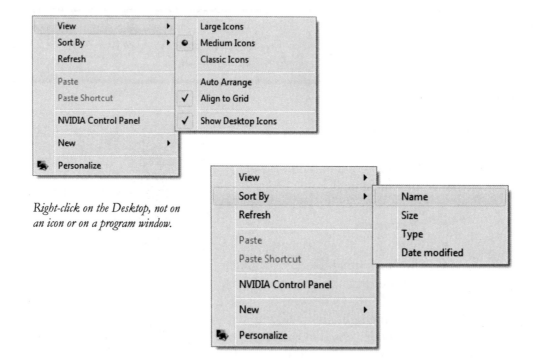

Right-click on the Desktop, not on
an icon or on a program window.

Start Menu:

The *Start Menu* is a pivotal tool in the UI. The *Start Menu* allows quick, convenient access to several tasks. Below is a brief overview followed by a more detailed description:

- Start installed programs
- Access icons for recently used programs
- Search for files, folders, and programs
- Adjust computer settings
- Turn off the computer

Click here to access the Windows *Start Menu*

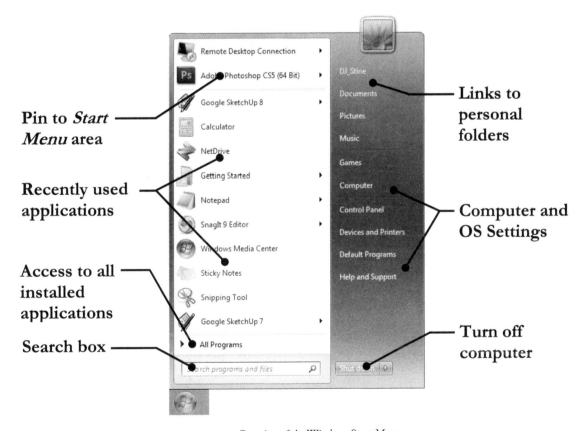

Overview of the Windows Start Menu

Recently used applications

This area shows a list of recently used applications. This is convenient as it takes less time to get to the icons for programs you use frequently (note that the terms *application* and *program* are synonymous). Single-clicking on one of these files starts the program. Right-clicking on one of these files shows a handful of options, including "Remove from this list" and "Pin to Start Menu" so it always shows.

All Programs

When clicking on the *All Programs* link in the image on the previous page, the "recently used applications" list is replaced with the *All Programs* list.

The image to the right shows the *All Programs* list and the number of clicks required to start AutoCAD 2011. Note that the first click is on the *All Programs* list (seen in the image above), which then changes to the "Back" link shown in the image to the right.

> **TIP:** *Dragging an icon from this list to the Desktop, while holding the* **Ctrl** *key, will add a copy of the icon to the Desktop.*

Computer and OS Settings

A computer has many options and settings to control how it operates and looks; the two groups of links in the lower right are for this. The *Computer* link opens a window that allows you to copy, move and delete files and folders.

The *Control Panel* gives you access to hardware settings; for example, you can specify how fast you have to double-click an icon before Windows will run it. You can also add and remove programs via the *Control Panel*.

Search Box

Rather than browsing through the *Start Menu* looking for a specific tool, icon, or *application*, you can just start typing its name in the *Search Box*. As soon as you start typing, Windows begins to search for items; you do <u>not</u> need to press **Enter**.

A sample search for Revit is shown in the image to the right. Notice the search box only has the first three letters entered and the Revit application has already been located. Windows searches for *Programs*, *Favorites and History*, *Files* and *Communications* (i.e., emails).

Start Menu: using the Search Box to locate programs, files and emails.

Clicking the "**X**" to the right of the *Search Box* will restore the *Start Menu*. Closing the *Start Menu* (by clicking off of it somewhere, or pressing the **Esc** key, will also restore the *Start Menu* to its original hidden condition.

Links to personal folders

The links in the upper right of the *Start Menu* are shortcuts to your personal folders, which are tied into the login name used to access the computer; this mainly applies to computers in an office or at school. If multiple people use the same computer, Windows will make a set of folders for each user; each user's icons will be mapped accordingly, based on login name.

> ***WARNING:*** *The files in your "personal" folders are still accessible by others; they are just not "connected" to the links in the Start Menu. This is another reason to back up often!*

Taskbar:

The *Taskbar* can generally be thought of as the entire bar across the bottom of the *Desktop* as shown in the image below.

The *Start Menu*, on the far left, was covered in the previous section. The remaining elements of the Window's *Taskbar* will now be covered.

Quick Launch Toolbar (only for Windows xp and Vista)

The *Quick Launch Toolbar* is shown in the image below. It is the series of icons directly to the right of the *Start Menu*. These icons are always visible, unlike the *Desktop* icons, and only require a single-click. It is typically not turned on by default on most computers. However, it is a very handy feature and easy to enable.

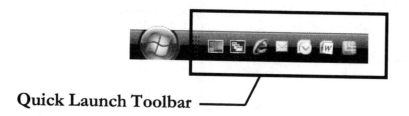

Quick Launch Toolbar

To enable the *Quick Access Toolbar* do the following:
1. Right-click on the *Taskbar*.
2. Select *Properties* (see image below).
3. On the *Taskbar*, check "Show Quick Launch."
4. Uncheck "Lock Taskbar" (see image on next page).

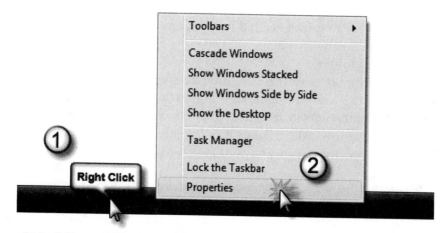

Right-clicking on the Windows Taskbar

TIP:
In Windows 7 you can right click on any button within the Start Menu and select "Pin to Taskbar". This will add a button to the taskbar; it is always there, even when the program is closed. So, the Quick Launch Toolbar is essentially built in to the taskbar in Windows 7.

Taskbar Properties (pre Windows 7)

Application icons may be dragged from the *Desktop* or the *Start Menu* onto the *Quick Launch Toolbar*. It is also possible to right-click on any icon (on the *Start Menu* or *Desktop*) and select "Add to *Quick Launch*" from the pop-up menu. Also, by unlocking the *Taskbar*, it is possible to adjust the width of the space used on the *Taskbar* by the *Quick Launch* bar. Setting the *Taskbar* to *Auto-hide* will provide additional height for your applications.

It is also possible to remove an icon by right-clicking on the icon in the *Quick Launch Toolbar* and selecting *Delete*.

TIP:
Take a few moments to explore the other tabs and options on the Taskbar and Start Menu Properties dialog shown above.

Taskbar Buttons

When an application is opened, a "button" is added to the *Taskbar*. This provides a quick way to switch between each application that is open. Also, when an application is minimized, the "button" is all that is visible; left-clicking it restores the window to its previous state.

Taskbar buttons (Windows XP and Vista)

When several applications are open and the *Taskbar* becomes full, the "buttons" will begin to "stack" for similar items (such as Internet Explorer, email, etc.). Otherwise, the "buttons" get narrower and thus become harder to read because less of the application name is visible.

> **FYI:** *The* Taskbar *can be dragged to any edge of the* Desktop. *It is also possible to drag the inside edge of the* Taskbar *to make it taller, displaying more application "buttons". It is not usually necessary to enlarge the* Taskbar *because the number of open applications should be kept to a minimum to avoid slowing the computer down.*

In Windows 7, notice the graphic preview one receives when hovering their cursor over the "stack" of *Internet Explorer* buttons (image below). Moving your cursor over the previews presents a larger preview (the application window temporarily restored) and an "x" to close the window with the need to restore it first.

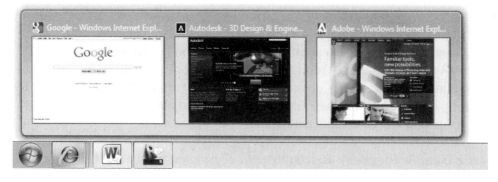

Taskbar buttons (Windows 7)

Notification Area

The most obvious aspect everyone notices about the *Notification Area* is that it displays the current time (and date in Windows 7).

Hovering your cursor over the "clock" will display the date as shown in the image to the right.

Notification Area (Windows Vista)

Notification Area (Windows 7)

The various icons to the left (of the clock) show various "background" tools and features that are running. These icons are automatically added by Windows or when applications are installed on your computer. When printing, for example, a small printer icon will appear until the print job has completely left your computer. Hovering over the icon will display additional information via a tooltip.

Double-clicking and right-clicking on these icons will open a program, a dialog box or a pop-up menu.

Some icons are hidden, which is good because the number of icons that appear here can get quite large at times. Clicking the "arrow" icon at the far left will temporarily expand this area to show all icons. It will automatically reset itself after a few moments.

If the time or date is incorrect, simply right-click on the "clock" and select "Adjust Date/Time" in the pop-up menu.

Self-Exam:

The following questions can be used as a way to check your knowledge of this lesson. The answers can be found at the bottom of this page.

1. RAM is a type of software. (T/F)

2. A printer can make larger printouts than a plotter. (T/F)

3. Software is updated every year or two. (T/F)

4. The _____ _____ holds deleted files.

5. It is a good idea to keep track of the amount a space available on your hard drive. (T/F)

Review Questions:

The following questions may be assigned by your instructor as a way to assess your knowledge of this section. Your instructor has the answers to the review questions.

1. The *CPU* is the "heart" of the computer. (T/F)

2. Most computers can read Blu-ray discs. (T/F)

3. The latest software takes advantage of the new 32bit technology. (T/F)

4. When an application is only visible on the *Taskbar* it is considered "minimized". (T/F)

5. The *Quick Launch Toolbar* shows the current time. (T/F)

6. An application window is _____ when not *Maximized* or *Minimized*.

7. The file extension *SKP* is for a Photoshop document. (T/F)

8. Backing up your files regularly is vital to ensure data is not lost. (T/F)

9. A *graphics card* is not that important to CAD/BIM applications. (T/F)

10. Autodesk makes much of its software available free to students. (T/F)

Introduction to Computers Part II

Although many SketchUp/CAD/BIM students have some experience using computers, many do not have a good working knowledge of how to manage files. The goal of this chapter is to provide a solid foundation in computer data management. With this knowledge you will be less likely to lose important files. The information in this chapter builds upon what was covered in the previous chapter.

Section 2-1
File Management Introduction

It is primarily important to keep track of document files created using an application. This starts from the very first time you save; where you specify the name and location of the file. Then you need to know where the file is located and what it is called the next time you want to work in it. It is also important to back up your document files to help prevent losing files.

It is not necessary to know where the program files are or files related to the operating system. In fact it is better that you don't until you become more proficient using the software and come across a need to delve deeper into the computers file structure.

In AutoCAD (an application), each drawing (e.g., floors plans, elevations, sections, details, etc.) is an individual file that ends with the file extension (.DWG). With Revit and SketchUp (also applications), each project (.RVT or .SKP) is a single file which can become quite large: 100-300mb or more.

It is important to understand where these files are on your computer and how to back them up. This is what you will begin to study now.

Windows Explorer (aka, *My Computer*, or simply *Computer*) allows you to manage the files on your computer's hard drive as well as on a network, flash drive, digital camera and CD/DVD drives. This is a feature that is built into the Microsoft Windows operating system (OS). There are a number of different ways in which to open *Windows Explorer*:

- Click the **Start** icon and then **Computer** (see Figure 2-1.1).

- Right-click on the **Start** icon and select **Explore** (see Figure 2-1.2).

- Press the "**Windows key**" and then the letter "**E**", the quickest and most efficient method.

Windows key, as found in the lower left corner of most PC-based keyboards.

FIGURE **2-1.1** Accessing Windows Explorer via the Start Menu

FIGURE 2-1.2 Accessing Windows Explorer via the Start Menu

The image below shows an example of the interface (Windows 7 shown):

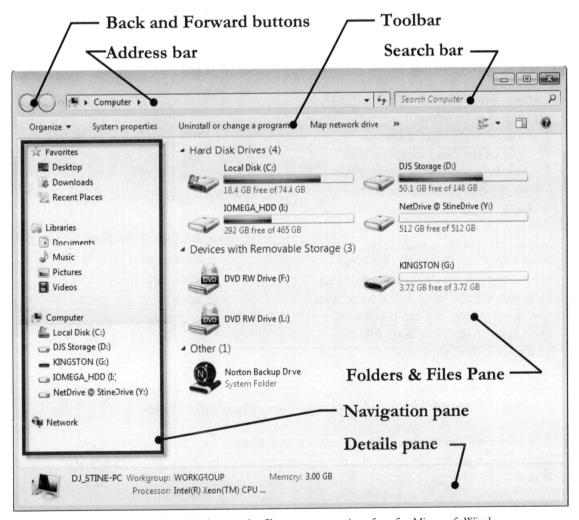

FIGURE 2-1.3 Windows Explorer – the file management interface for Microsoft Windows

The following provides details about each area identified in Figure 2-1.3:

Navigation Pane

The *Navigation Pane* is typically where you start when using *Windows Explorer*. This interface provides access to all **drives** and **folders** on your computer. You cannot see any **files** in this pane.

NOTE: A drive could be:

- **Hard drive** (in the computer)
- **External hard drive**
- **Network drives** (when on a network)
- **Cloud Drive** (storage on the internet – see Y drive in Figure 2-1.3)
- **Flash drive** (via USB connection)
- **Floppy drive** (obsolete)
- **CD/DVD/BD Drive**
- **Memory card reader**
- **Camera** (via cable connection)

Figure 2-1.3 shows how *Windows Explorer* looks when first opened (by pressing the "Windows" key + "E" key). The image to the right shows an example of the *Navigation Pane* with a few folders opened. The *Address Bar* shows the exact path to the current location.

When your cursor is within the *Navigation Pane* you can see little icons appear next to *drives* and *folders* that may be expanded, meaning they have at least one sub-folder which can be viewed. Solid right-triangles indicate folders which have been expanded.

Clicking an open triangle icon will expand the adjacent folder, and clicking a solid icon will collapse a folder to hide its content and "clean up" the pane.

Any folder within another folder is called a ***sub-folder***. Any *file* or *folder* at the highest level, or directly under the drive letter, is said to be at the "root" level of that drive.

Folders and Files Pane

Once you have expanded and selected a folder in the *Navigation Pane*, you can then see the selected folder's contents directly to the right in the *Folders and Files Pane*.

In Figure 2-1.4 below, the **sub-folder** "Adobe Photoshop CS5 (64 Bit)" is selected in the *Navigation Bar*, and its contents are shown in the pane to the right, which includes several **folders** and **files**.

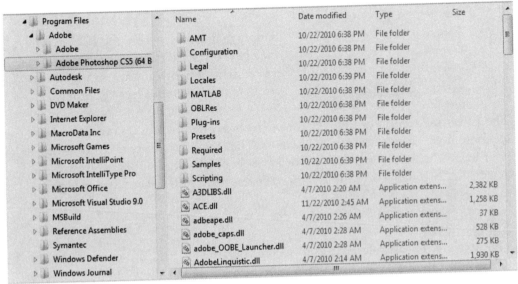

FIGURE 2-1.4 Windows Explorer – "Folders and Files pane" on the right

So, where the *Navigation Pane* only shows **drives** and **folders**, the *Folders and Files Pane* only shows **folders** and **files** – no drives. Notice that both areas show folders.

The format in which this information is displayed can vary. This will be covered in the "toolbar" section below.

> *TIP:*
> Folders *and* sub-folders *always have a small yellow "folder" icon next to them. Files usually have an icon provided by the software manufacturer which helps describe, graphically, the various types of files.*
>
> *Notice a* **File Name** *has descriptive text indicating what the file is and is then followed by a* **dot** *(i.e., a period) and then three to four characters. The portion after the dot is called the file's* **Extension***. Like the icon, this too helps to identify the file type.*
>
> *The file extension may not be visible by default but can be turned on if desired.*

Navigation Pane: *Favorites* and *Libraries*

If you find yourself browsing to the same folder often, that folder should be added to your **Favorites** section to save time. A single click on a link here will instantly update the *Navigation Pane* and the *Folders and Files Pane* to show the contents of the "favorite" folder.

Simply drag a folder from the *Folders and Files Pane* onto the *Favorites Link* area to add a new item. When you want an item to go away, right-click and select "Remove".

The **Libraries** section of the *Navigation Pane* provides quick access to the default location in which to save your documents. The location you are taken to is tied to your login if working on a network or in a school lab. Most applications will automatically bring you to the *Documents* folder when you select **Save** or **Open**.

Address Bar

This area gives you a reference as to where you are in the file structure. The information shown is mostly a duplication of information shown in the *Navigation Pane*.

Clicking on a folder listed here will redirect the *Panes* to the selected folder's location.

If you click within the *Address Bar*, the more formal **path** is displayed (see image below). Notice the path always starts with the drive letter and then the folders separated by a backslash.

This path can be copied to the *Windows Clipboard* by highlighting it and pressing **Ctrl+C** on the keyboard. This information could then be pasted (**Ctrl+V**) into an email to inform someone of a specific file's location.

Folders and Files Panel: *File List Headings*

Each column in the *Folders and Files Pane* has a **file list heading** (as shown in the image below); the example below is set to the "Details" view type.

Name	Date modified	Type	Size	Tags
DJS55803AD...wg	2/22/2008 1:36 PM	AutoCAD Drawing	79 KB	
DJS55803ADE03.dwg	2/22/2008 1:37 PM	AutoCAD Drawing	68 KB	
DJS55803ADE04.dwg	2/22/2008 1:37 PM	AutoCAD Drawing	68 KB	
DJS55803ADE05.dwg	2/22/2008 1:38 PM	AutoCAD Drawing	95 KB	
DJS55803ADE06.dwg	2/22/2008 1:39 PM	AutoCAD Drawing	104 KB	

Each header/column can have its width adjusted by dragging the vertical line between two header labels. A small icon, pointed out in the image above, indicates how the files are being sorted. In the example above, the files are being sorted by the filename in **ascending order**. If you click on the *Name* header, the files will be sorted in descending order. Also, notice the icon in the header changes direction for ascending versus descending (see image below).

Name	Date modified	Type	Size	Tags
DJS55803AIE05.dwg	2/22/2008 1:42 PM	AutoCAD Drawing	163 KB	
DJS55803AIE04.dwg	2/22/2008 1:41 PM	AutoCAD Drawing	151 KB	
DJS55803AIE03.dwg	2/22/2008 1:41 PM	AutoCAD Drawing	148 KB	
DJS55803AIE02.dwg	2/22/2008 1:40 PM	AutoCAD Drawing	142 KB	
DJS55803AIE01.dwg	2/22/2008 2:59 PM	AutoCAD Drawing	175 KB	
DJS55803AGD01.dwg			84 KB	

Clicking on another header, such as *Size*, will then sort the files by size.

Name	Date modified	Type	Size	Tags
DJS55803AIE05.dwg	2/22/2008 1:42 PM	AutoCAD Drawing	163 KB	
DJS55803AIE04.dwg	2/22/2008 1:41 PM	AutoCAD Drawing	151 KB	
DJS55803AIE03.dwg	2/22/2008 1:41 PM	AutoCAD Drawing	148 KB	
DJS55803AIE02.dwg	2/22/2008 1:40 PM	AutoCAD Drawing	142 KB	
Room Finish Schedule....	2/22/2008 1:43 PM	AutoCAD Drawing	116 KB	
DJS55803ADE06.dwg	2/22/2008 1:39 PM	AutoCAD Drawing	104 KB	

Be careful not to click and drag on the headers as it is possible to rearrange them. If you right-click on the headers, you may also turn on additional columns of information. This information is called *Meta Data*, which is data about the file and not really part of the primary use of the file.

Search Bar

Windows7 (and Vista) has a very efficient search feature in *Windows Explorer*. Simply click in the *search box* and begin typing a word and before you finish typing, Windows will start searching for any files with that name.

In the example below, "autocad" was entered into the search box. The results are then listed below. Now you can select a file listed to copy it or open it. Right-clicking on a file, listed in the search results, provides an option to "open file location" which makes that location current in the *Navigation Pane*. Or, you can click the **Back** button to return to where you were.

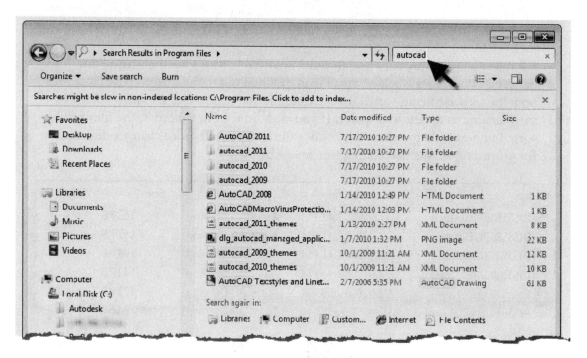

For best results and the most thorough search, click the **C:** drive in the *Navigation Pane* first (as shown in the image to the right). If you know the file is in a general location on your hard drive, you should select that folder before typing the search. Windows will begin looking in the selected folder and any of its sub-folders. This could save a lot of time on a large drive which is close to capacity.

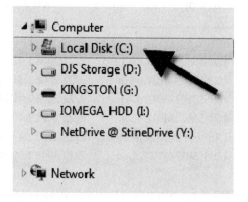

Details Pane

The *Details Pane* shows information about the selected file. In some cases, as in the example below, a preview image is shown (on the left).

Toolbar

The *toolbar* changes depending on what is selected. The first example below shows the options available when a **folder** is selected. The options may vary depending on programs installed on your computer.

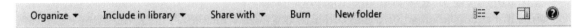

The next example, below, shows the options when a **file** is selected. Here you can quickly print or email the selected file(s).

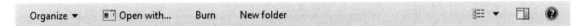

The ***Views*** option changes the format of the *Folders and Files Pane*. When you click the down arrow next to the *Views* icon, on the *toolbar*, you see the pop-up menu shown in the image below. The first image shows the "Details" mode, while the next image (on the left) shows "Large Icons." You should try each and decide which one you prefer.

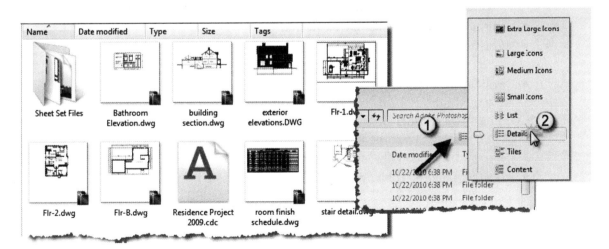

This concludes the overview of the *Windows Explorer* user interface.

Now that you are generally familiar with the *Windows Explorer* user interface, you will be given instruction on a few specific and important tasks. Namely:

- Creating new folders and sub-folders
- Creating new files
- Copying files
- Moving Files
- Deleting files and folders
- Copying files to a flash drive
- Recovering files from the *Recycle Bin*

Creating new folders and sub-folders

It is important to create *folders* in order to organize your files. This is the same concept as putting printed pages in folders within a file cabinet; if all files were placed in a single folder, it would be hard to find specific files.

This example will show how to create a folder and a few *sub-folders* in the *Documents* folder (aka, *My Documents* folder in Windows XP). These files will be located on your computer's hard drive. Any files saved here should be backed up in another location other than the same hard drive. If the hard drive crashes, all files could be lost.

The following steps describe how to create a folder (Figure 2-1.5):

- Open *Windows Explorer* per the methods previously mentioned (e.g., "Windows" key + "E" key).
- In the *Favorites* list, click **Documents**.
- For Windows 7
  - Select **New Folder** on the *Toolbar*.
- For Windows XP and Vista:
  - In the *Folders and Files Pane*, **right-click in the white space** (not on a folder or file).
  - Hover over the **New** fly-out menu.
  - In the *New* fly-out, select **Folder**.
- Begin typing the folder name: **CAD Class**; press **Enter** when done.

The following steps describe how to create a sub-folder (Figure 2-1.6):

1. Double-click on the **CAD Class** folder within the *Folders and Files Pane* (or expand *Documents* and select *CAD Class* within the *Navigation Pane*).

2. Right-click in the white space of the *Folders and Files Pane*.

3. Create a new folder as outlined above named **Exercise 1**.

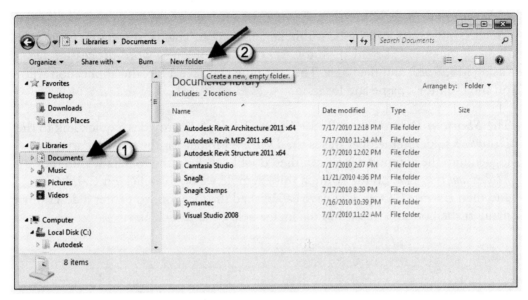

FIGURE 2-1.5 Creating a folder

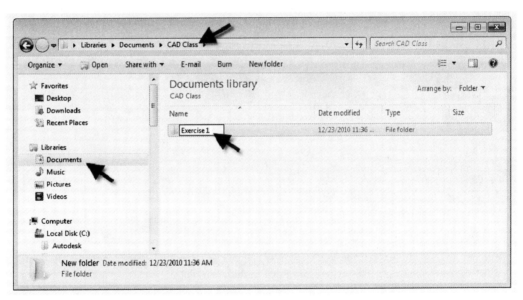

FIGURE 2-1.6 Creating a Sub-folder

Creating folders and sub-folders on other drives and locations is the same. Just navigate to the desired location. When you click the **New Folder** button on the *Toolbar*, a new folder will be created in the location listed in the Address Bar.

If you don't provide a name, the folder will be called "New Folder". At any time you can right-click on a folder and select "rename" to change the folder name. You should never change the name of a folder in the *Program Files* or *Windows* folders as this could seriously mess up your computer.

Creating new files

Creating a file is typically done within an application. That is, you start a new drawing file (using SketchUp, AutoCAD or Revit) or a new word-processing file (using MS Word) and then *Save*. The first time you save a file, the application will prompt you for a name and location.

The ***Shortcut Pane*** on the left (See Figure 2-1.7 – #1) provides a quick link to the *Documents* folder; remember this is the *Documents* folder for the person currently logged into the computer. You can then double-click on the folders within the *Folders and Files Pane* on the right; in this example we double-click on *CAD Class* and then *Exercise 1*. Once you have established the location, you enter a descriptive name at the bottom (Step #3 in the image below), and click *Save*.

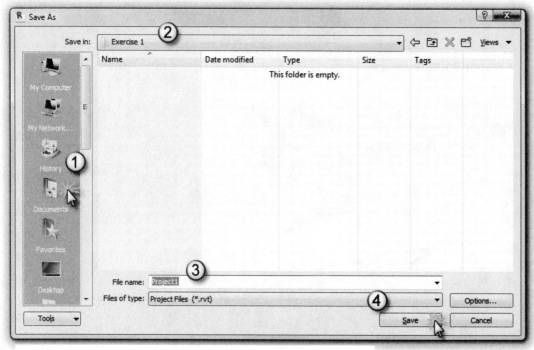

FIGURE 2-1.7 Creating a file (saving from Revit in this example)

It is important to pay close attention to the locations and names of your files so you can find them in the future when necessary.

In addition to creating files within an application, you can create an empty "place holder" file for a few file types. In *Windows Explorer,* simply right-click in the white space within the *Files and Folders Pane* (see image to the right).

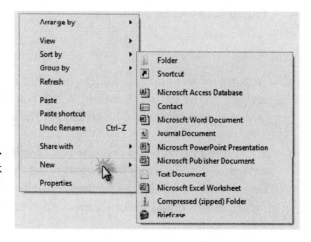

Copying files

Knowing how to copy a file is important. You mainly do this when backing up files. However, whenever you are experimenting with a drawing or document, it is a good idea to make a copy first and then edit that file.

There are two main ways in which to copy a file:

1. Right-click method:

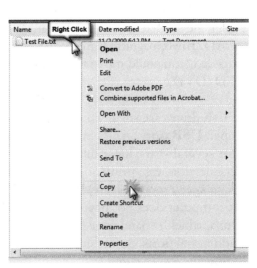

    a. Select a file (or files) to be copied.

    b. Right-click on the file (cursor must be over one of the selected files when right-clicking).

    c. Select **Copy**.

    d. Browse to another folder.

    e. Right-click in the white space and select **Paste**.

2. Keyboard shortcuts method:

    a. Select a file (or files) to be copied.

    b. Press **Ctrl+C** on the keyboard (for **Copy**).

    c. Browse to another folder.

    d. Press **Ctrl+V** on the keyboard (for **Paste**).

SELECTING MULTIPLE FILES

Here are a few tips for selecting multiple files:

***Drag a window** –*
Start clicking in "white space" and then move the cursor, while holding down the left mouse button, over the desired files.

***Use the Shift key to select blocks of files** –*
Click the first file and then, while pressing the Shift key, click the last file. All files in between are selected.

***Use the Ctrl key** –*
Select individual files in any order while pressing the Ctrl key. Clicking on an already selected file unselects it.

Any combination of the above options also works. For example, you have a large group of files you want to select with the exception of two random ones in the middle. Use the Shift key to select the block of files and then use the Ctrl key to remove two from the current selection.

Copying files to a flash drive

This section will walk you through the steps required to copy files to and from a *USB flash drive* (aka, *jump drive*). A flash drive is one of the most convenient ways to back up files and transport them between work, school and home. A 2 to 4gigabyteflash drive will likely be sufficient for a student in a CAD/BIM program; if more space is needed, you could move the older files to a CD/DVD.

Flash Drive connected to a laptop computer

Flash drives are small which makes them easy to carry around. They plug into any open **USB port** on a computer.USB ports have now been standard on computers for several years; most things that plug into a computer do so via a USB connection, e.g., printers, digital cameras, mice, keyboards, external hard drives, high speed modems, etc. Because everything uses the USB port, you may find that a computer does not have a port available. In this case you can purchase a **USB hub**, which expands one port into several more; a hub usually has three to six additional ports. Some higher end monitors have a USB port built into them allowing you to connect flash drives and the like to ports on its side.

Connecting a flash drive to a computer:

1. Turn computer on.

2. Insert the flash drive into an open USB port.

   a. Do not force it; the flash drive only goes in one way. You may have to flip it over and try again.

3. The first time your flash drive is connected to a computer, the computer will automatically install software which allows the computer to work with the specific type of flash drive. You will see a "balloon" message similar to the one shown in the image below.

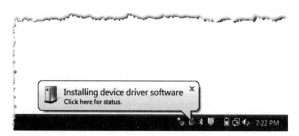

Flash Drive installing automatically

4. Finally, a message will appear, depending on how your computer is configured, asking you what you want to do (see image to the right). Select **Open folder to view files**.

At this point you are in *Windows Explorer* which has been covered in the last several pages. The steps are identical, with the exception that you are using a different *drive letter* (i.e., other than **C:**, the computer's primary hard drive).

The drive letter can vary from computer to computer depending on the number of things installed or connected to the computer that require a drive letter; such as:

- Hard drive
- Second hard drive
- CD/DVD
- Second CD/DVD (maybe a burner)
- Floppy drive (rare)
- Memory card drive (for digital cameras and cell phones)

Copying a file(s) to the flash drive:

1. Select a file (or files) to be copied.

2. Press **Ctrl+C** on the keyboard (for **Copy**).

3. Locate the newly added drive letter (see image on next page).

   a. Click on the drive in the *Navigation Pane* to make it active.

4. *Optional:* Browse to a sub-folder (or create one).

5. Press **Ctrl+V** on the keyboard (for **Paste**).

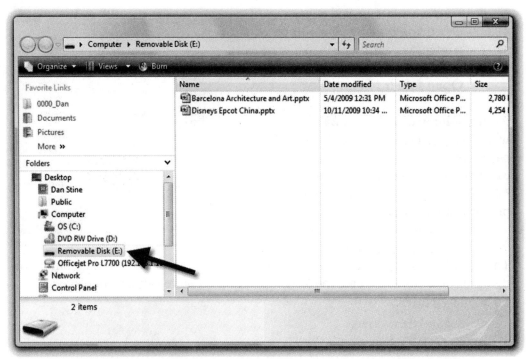

Copying a file(s) from the flash drive

The steps are simply reversed from the ones outlined on the previous page.

Verifying free space:
It is a good idea to keep track of the amount of space available on your flash drive. You should know the selected files will fit on the flash drive before trying to copy them so you minimize the chance for problems. You may need to free up space on a flash drive before trying to backup several files in an office or classroom setting. It is easy to verify free space.

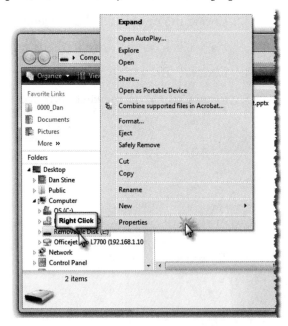

1. Open *Windows Explorer.*

2. Right-click on the flash drive letter in the *Navigation Pane* (see arrow added to image above).

3. Select *Properties* (see image to right).

The image to the right shows the status of the selected drive; note this technique can be used on the C: drive as well.

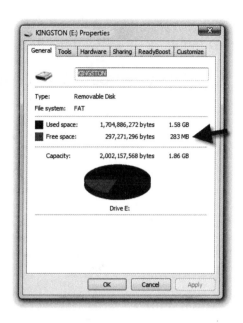

The flash drive in this example only has 283 MB free of 2 GB (nominal). This is not considered very much free space, especially if working with Revit files or large CAD files.

"Safely removing" the flash drive:
It is important to follow the proper procedure when removing a flash drive from a computer. Files sometimes continue to copy in the background, so removing a flash drive suddenly may cause files to be incomplete and thus corrupt.

1. Click on the **Safely Remove Hardware** icon in the *Notification Area.*

    a. You may have to fully expand the *Notification Area* to see all the icons located there.

2. Select **Safely remove USB Mass Storage Device – Drive(E:)**; see image below.

    NOTE: The drive letter may vary.

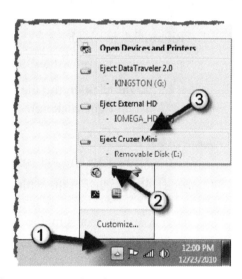

3. Click **OK** to the prompt that it is safe to remove the device.

4. Remove the flash drive.

A couple of warnings:

Don't work directly off the flash drive! Although it is possible, you can run into problems if the flash drive becomes full or is suddenly removed from the computer. Work off the **C:** drive and then copy the files to your flash drive via *Windows Explorer.*

Don't use *Save As* to copy the file to the flash drive! When finished working on a file, close the application (e.g., Revit, AutoCAD, Excel, Word, etc.).Then use *Windows Explorer* to copy the file. New students often get the current file mixed up between the flash drive and the C: drive.

> ***FYI:*** *If you open a file, do some work in it and then just do a Save-As, the original file is unchanged and only the new file will have the current changes. This works well in some cases, but not when you think you are making a duplicate backup.*

Moving Files

The steps to move a file are similar to copying a file:

1. Right-click method:

    a. Select a file (or files) to be moved.

    b. Right-click on the file (cursor must be over one of the selected files when right-clicking).

    c. Select **Cut**.

    d. Browse to another folder.

    e. Right-click in the white space and select **Paste**.

2. Keyboard shortcuts method:

    a. Select a file (or files) to be copied.

    b. Press **Ctrl+X** on the keyboard (for **Cut**).

    c. Browse to another folder.

    d. Press **Ctrl+V** on the keyboard (for **Paste**).

A file will not be deleted from its original location until it has been pasted somewhere else. So, if you select **Cut** and then never **Paste** the file(s) anywhere, you will not lose the files.

Deleting files and folders

It is important to remove unnecessary files to keep your hard drive clean and get rid of incorrect data. However, you should never delete files unless you know for sure what they are for. **Deleting certain files from your computer could render it inoperable!**

To delete a file simply:

1. Right-click:

    a. Select a file(s).

    b. Right-click (directly on the file).

    c. Select **Delete** from the pop-up menu.

2. Keyboard shortcuts:

    a. Select a file(s).

    b. Press the **Delete** key on the keyboard.

Recovering files from the *Recycle Bin*

One last important item to cover concerning file management is the *Recycle Bin*. This feature can really save you at times. Whenever you delete a file from your computer it is actually moved to the *Recycle Bin* rather than being totally deleted. The file will remain in the *Recycle Bin* until the space is needed, then the oldest files are permanently deleted. Simply select the *Recycle Bin* icon in the *Navigation Pane* to see its contents; and then copy any needed files to another location.

Self-Exam:

The following questions can be used as a way to check your knowledge of this lesson. The answers can be found at the bottom of this page.

1. Cutting a file is the same as copying a file. (T/F)

2. It is safe to remove a flash drive at any time. (T/F)

3. A folder within another folder is considered a sub-folder. (T/F)

4. The _____ _____ only shows *Drives* and *Folders* in *Windows Explorer*.

5. Holding *Shift* selects a block of files in *Windows Explorer*. (T/F)

Review Questions:

The following questions may be assigned by your instructor as a way to assess your knowledge of this section. Your instructor has the answers to the review questions.

1. Add your main folders to the *Favorites* list to save time. (T/F)

2. You should verify available space on your flash drive before copying new files to it. (T/F)

3. In *Windows Explorer*, the _____ _____ shows information about the selected file.

4. Pressing the *Windows* key plus the *E* key quickly opens *Windows Explorer*. (T/F)

5. Clicking the "size" heading sorts the files by file size. (T/F)

6. Name the *Windows* file management utility: _____ _____.

7. This book recommends working off your flash drive rather than the computer's (or server's) hard drive. (T/F)

8. Deleting certain files can make your computer stop working. (T/F)

9. A file extension is the characters after the "dot" in the file name. (T/F)

SketchUp Introduction Part I

This chapter will introduce you to SketchUp. You will study the User Interface and learn how to open and exit a project and adjust the view of the model on the screen. It is recommended that the student spend an ample amount of time learning this material, as it will greatly enhance your ability to progress smoothly through subsequent chapters.

Section 3-1
What is Google SketchUp used for?

It might be easier to answer what SketchUp is not used for. SketchUp is an all-purpose 3D modeling tool. The program is primarily developed around architectural design but it can be used to model just about anything. The program's relative ease of use and low cost (the basic package being free) makes it a very popular tool within the AEC design community.

SketchUp models are also used to populate Google earth with real buildings which have been modeled to scale. Check out this website for more info: http://sketchup.google.com/yourworldin3d/index.html.

Why use SketchUp?

As just mentioned, it is easy to use and free! It is an easy way to quickly communicate your design ideas to clients or prospective employers. Not only can you create great still images, SketchUp also is able to produce fly-by videos!

SketchUp is owned by Google. Some of you may have heard of them before you heard of SketchUp! With a solid company such as Google behind SketchUp, you can be fairly confident the program will be well supported and updated.

When creating interior designs using SketchUp, you have access to a massive amount of content with Google's 3D Warehouse. You can take a peek now if you want: http://sketchup.google.com/3dwarehouse/

SketchUp versus other Applications?

There are several other 3D modeling applications (aka programs) on the market which compete with SketchUp to varying degrees. Every program has its strengths and weaknesses when compared to another. SketchUp is mainly geared towards concept designs rather than construction documentation. Its ability to quickly develop and present the designer's ideas makes it very popular. However, it is not very good at adding notes and dimensions. So, at some point the SketchUp design needs to be exported to a CAD format, such as Autodesk's DWG format and finished in AutoCAD or a similar program.

Another popular modeling approach is Building Information Modeling (BIM). SketchUp is not a BIM application. However, SketchUp can still have a place in the BIM workflow. An application such as Autodesk's Revit Architecture does have many SketchUp-like features, but many designers prefer the simplicity and limited scope (i.e., SketchUp is designed to do one thing, and it does that one thing very well – similar to Five Guys burgers!).

SketchUp is a face-based modeling program, as opposed to a solid modeling program. This has its pluses and minuses. It is great for concept modeling as it keeps the size and complexity of the model down to a minimum. This allows the designer to quickly spin around the model and zoom in and out, whereas a solids-based model could take nearly a minute to spin around where SketchUp could do it in seconds. This is all relative to the project size – a small simple project would not be a problem in either program, but a 200,000 square foot school or hospital likely would be.

One of the drawbacks to face-based modeling is the designer cannot get information from the model such as cubic foot of material for a concrete wall. Luckily nobody really cares about that in the early stages of design! A similar problem is things in section look hollow in SketchUp whereas in a solids-based program they would not. This can be seen in the SketchUp model example on the next page.

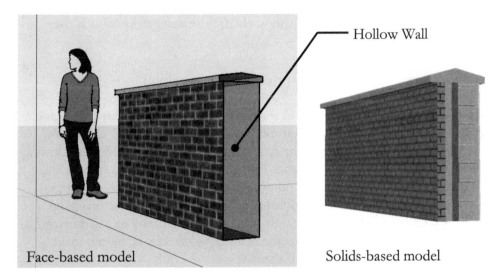

FIGURE 3-1.1 SketchUp is a face-based program, not solids-based. The left image shows a masonry wall cut using the section tool. Notice the wall appears hollow. SketchUp does not know this is a masonry wall, or even a wall for that matter. The right image is a BIM model – notice the solid core.

As already mentioned, it is possible to export a SketchUp model to a CAD program. This format does not work too well in a BIM program – but it can be used to varying degrees. It is also possible to export a BIM model to a format that can be imported into SketchUp – thus allowing some of SketchUp's tools to be used: hand sketch effect, easy navigation and simple animation setup and creation.

SketchUp Pro versus the Free version?

The free version of SketchUp is very powerful and can model just about anything. The Pro version, which costs $495 at the time of this printing, has several advanced features such as:

- Technical support
- Solid modeling
- Import and Export AutoCAD DWG files
- Layout 3
    - o a separate program used to compose multiple views of the same model on a page
    - o More printing options
- Style Builder
    - o a separate program used to transform your model into a unique hand drawing.

You can see a more detailed comparison of the free versus pro version at the following web address:

- http://sketchup.google.com/product/whygopro.html

For most design firms, the pro version is a must, if just for the ability to use and export AutoCAD DWG files. For example, you might import a 2D DWG file provided by the client and use that line work to quickly start modeling the existing conditions. SketchUp also has a network license. This allows a firm to have the software installed on everyone's computers but the number of people who can access the program is limited to the number of network licenses the company owns. So, if your firm has six licenses, the seventh person gets a denial message. That person can keep trying until a license becomes available or, better, make a few calls or send out an email to see if someone can get out!

Given the introductory nature of this textbook, only the tools and techniques found in the free version of SketchUp will be covered. Once you understand the concepts covered in this book, you most likely will be able to figure out the other tools on your own.

Mac versus PC?

SketchUp has been designed to work on either the Apple Macintosh or Microsoft Windows based computer system. Most Architectural and Interior Design offices tend to favor the PC due to cost and general availability of other programs geared towards the industry. However, there is not much that cannot be done on a Mac, especially with its ability to run Windows when using Mac's *Boot Camp* or a virtual environment.

All screen shots in this book are from a PC running Windows 7 64bit. If the reader is using a Mac or another version of Windows, there might be slight differences in some screen shots. However, the main SkechUp *User Interface* should be the same; the User Interface is covered next.

Section 3-2
Overview of the SketchUp User Interface

The first step in learning any new computer program is figuring out the **User Interface** (UI). SketchUp is organized very much like other programs. It has menus across the top, toolbars that can float or be docked to a side, a status bar across the bottom and a large area in the middle to do your work. SketchUp has chosen not to implement the *Ribbon* as a number of other software makers have (e.g., Microsoft and Autodesk). Which UI style is better is a hotly debated subject.

The image below highlights the primary components of the *User Interface*. A few of the items identified are not really considered a part of the UI, but help paint a better overall picture for the new user.

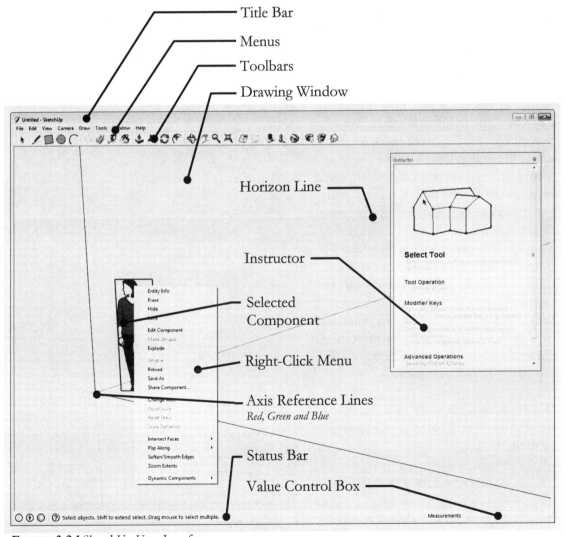

FIGURE 3-2.1 SketchUp User Interface

Title Bar:

The program title bar displays the name of the file currently being worked on, *TFDM Office Expansion.skp* in this case. And just in case you forgot, the name of the program you are using is listed to the right of the file name: *SketchUp*, right? On the far right are the typical controls for the application's window:minimize, maximize/restore down, close.

FIGURE 3-2.2 Title Bar

Menus:

Below the title bar are several pull-down menus. When clicked on, these menus reveal a list of commands. The menus are a way to break the list of commands down into smaller, task specific lists. A *Menu* is closed when a command is selected or the **Esc** key is pressed.

Notice in the image provided (Figure 3-2.3), the Camera menu is expanded. Some items have a check mark on the left to show that item is active (projection type in this case). Also, some items in the list are fly-out menus. A fly-out menu can be identified by the black arrow pointing to the right (Standard Views in this case). Hovering over a fly-out menu item reveals another sub-set of menu options. Whenever a command or toggle has a keyboard shortcut, it is listed on the right. Finally, any command or toggles which are not relevant to the current tool or drawing will be grayed out to avoid any confusion.

When reference is made to a command within the menu system, it will be shown as such:

Camera → Parallel Projection

This means: click the **Camera** menu and then click the **Parallel Projection** command in the list.

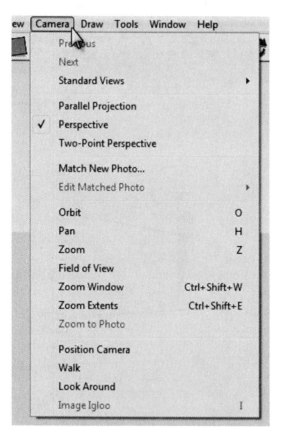

FIGURE 3-2.3 Menus

Toolbars:

Toolbars are a favorite for most SketchUp users as they provide small graphical images and are only a single click away. When SketchUp is first started (after being installed) only the *Getting Started* toolbar is showing (Figure 3-2.4). Additional toolbars can be toggled on and off via **View → Toolbars**. Whenever a toolbar is visible on the screen it can be dragged so it is "docked" along the perimeter of the drawing window, or it can "float" anywhere on the screen.

The book will give specific instructions when certain toolbars are required. It is recommended that toolbars be only turned on when instructed to minimize any possible confusion and so the reader's screen matches the images in the book.

FIGURE 3-2.4 Menus

Drawing Window:

The drawing window is, of course, where all the modeling is done! Using various tools from the menus, toolbars and keyboard shortcuts, you create and interact with your model in the drawing window.

Status Bar (and Value Control Box):

The *Status Bar* is found across the bottom of the application (Figure 3-2.5). On the far left are three small round icons; hover your cursor over them to see what they are. Next you have a circle with a question mark which toggles the *Instructor* visibility on and off (see the next topic for more on this feature). The next section provides prompts for any command you are currently using. The example shown is letting you know SketchUp expects you to pick a point in the model to define one of the corners while using the *Rectangle* tool. Finally, on the right hand side of the status bar is the *Value Control Box*. This box shows the length or size of an object being drawn. It is not necessary to spend a lot of time moving the mouse into just the right location, so the dimension reads correctly, as you can more quickly (and accurately) type this information in (either before or after picking your last point).

FIGURE 3-2.5 Status Bar

Instructor:

The *Instructor* is not necessarily part of the *User Interface*, but it automatically appears on the screen when SketchUp is opened. This feature is intended to help new users understand how to use various tools. For example, when you select the *Rectangle* tool, the *Instructor* provides an animated graphic and steps on how to sketch a rectangle (Figure 3-2.6). This feature compliments this book in that it will remind you how various tools are used. This book works through many of SketchUp's commands in a systematic way, and once a command is covered it is not typically covered again in as much detail.

Once you become familiar with SketchUp you will want to turn off the *Instructor* in order to free up more screen space. This can be done via **Window → Instructor**; clicking this toggles the *Instructor* on and off. Also, as mentioned in the previous section, the question mark icon on the status bar will turn the *Instructor* on, if off – and it will also minimize it if already on.

FIGURE 3-2.6 Instructor window

If you have a dual monitor computer system, the *Instructor* can be moved to the second monitor to increase the usable portion of the *Drawing Window*.

Right-Click Menu:

SketchUp allows you to right-click on something to both select it and present a contextual pop-up menu which provides quick access to tools used to manipulate the selected component, line/edge or face. Notice, in the Figure 3-2.7a, that there are fewer options to choose from when an edge is selected than for a component (Figure 3-2.7b). Also, some options in the right-click menus have a black triangle pointing to the right. Hovering over these reveals a sub-menu with additional tools, similar to the pull-down menus.

Clicking a tool from the right-click menu or pressing the **Esc** key closes the right-click menu.

FIGURE 3-2.7A
Right-click menu:
Edge Selected

FIGURE 3-2.7B
Right-click menu:
Component Selected

Section 3-3
Open, Save and Close

Opening **SketchUp** is just like opening most any other program. You can either locate the file using *Windows Explorer* (aka, *My Computer* or just *Computer*) and then double-click on the file, or you can open SketchUp and then create a new file or open one previously created.

If SketchUp is properly installed on your computer, you can launch the program from the Window's Start menu. To do this, make the following clicks within the Start menu (Figure 3-3.1):

Start → All Programs → Google SketchUp 8 → Google SketchUp

Or double-click the **Google SketchUp 8** icon from your desktop.

Google
SketchUp 8

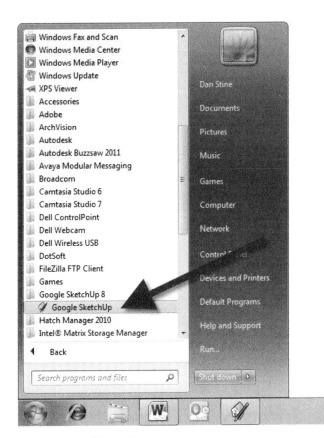

This may vary slightly on your computer depending on the version of Windows you are using (or if you are using a Mac); see your instructor or system administrator if you need help. It is possible to have more than one version of SketchUp installed on a computer. Make sure you are using version 8 to gain access to all the new features and to ensure your screen matches the images in this book!

FIGURE 3-3.1 Start Menu

Open a New SketchUp Model:

By default, SketchUp will open in the *Welcome to SketchUp* dialog as shown (Figure 3-3.2). Here you have access to more ways to help yourself learn SketchUp and the various templates provided. Make sure you select the correct template before clicking the **Start Using SketchUp** button.

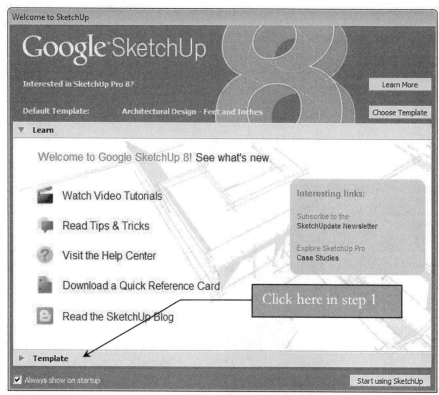

FIGURE 3-3.2 Welcome to SketchUp Interface

TIP:
Experienced SketchUp users will uncheck the "Always show on startup" option in the lower left so they can get right to work. You should NOT *uncheck this option until you consider yourself somewhat proficient in the program.*

Here you will learn how to open a new SketchUp model.

1. Click the arrow next to the word *Template* (pointed out in the image above).

SketchUp provides several templates. You will be selecting the one setup with the architect and interior designer in mind: *Architectural Design – Feet and Inches.*

2. Click to select **Architectural Design – Feet and Inches** from the list of available templates (as shown in the image below).

> ***FYI:*** *This will be the default template selected the next time SketchUp is opened.*

3. Click the **Start using SketchUp** button in the lower right (Figure 3-3.3).

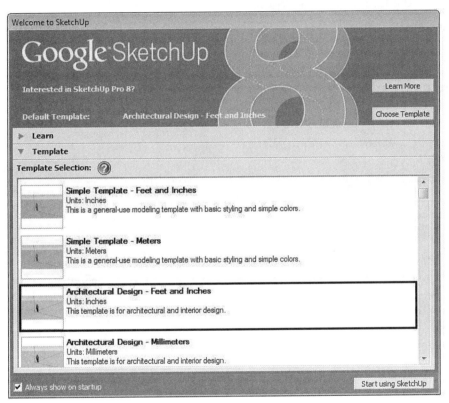

FIGURE 3-3.3 Welcome to SketchUp – Templates

You are now in a new SketchUp file! Notice the red, green and blue axis lines, the person pre-loaded (which is a great scale reference), and the implied ground which extends to the horizon. At this point you are in an unnamed file. The first time you click **Save** you will be prompted to select a location and provide a file name; make sure you pay close attention to where you save the file and what you call it!

Open an Existing SketchUp Model:

Now that you know how to open SketchUp and create a new file in which to model, you will open an existing SketchUp file. You will select a sample file provided on the CD that came with this book.

1. Open SketchUp per the previous steps (opening a new model).

2. From the **File** menu click **Open**.

> *TIP: Pressing **Ctrl + O** will also get you to the Open dialog.*

3. In the *Open* dialog, browse to your CD/DVD drive and select **Office Building.SKP**.

> *TIP: If you cannot locate the CD that came with this textbook, you can substitute any SketchUp file.*

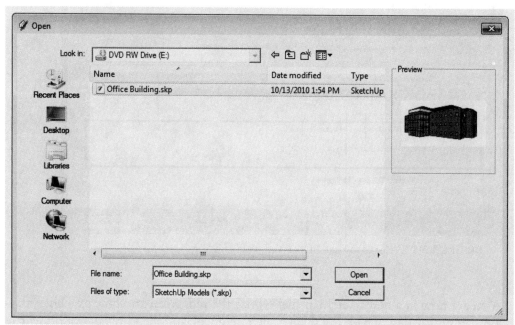

FIGURE 3-3.4 Open Dialog

4. Click **Open**; if you are prompted to save the current model, choose **No**.

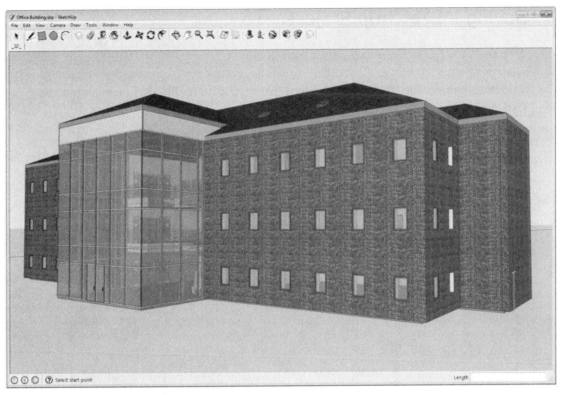

FIGURE 3-3.5 File opened

You are now in the *Office Building* file (Figure 3-3.5). Because you did not do any work in the new file you had just created, SketchUp discards that file in favor of the file you are opening. However, if you made any changes, SketchUp would have prompted you to save before closing the file. In SketchUp you can only have one file open at a time, but it is possible to have multiple sessions of SketchUp open – each with a different file.

> *TIP: To open multiple copies of SketchUp, simply double-click on the desktop icon or the SketchUp icon via Start menu.*

Closing a SketchUp File:

Because you can only have one file open at a time, and one file must be open, the only way to "close" a file is to open another file or exit SketchUp.

The previous section discusses opening a file, and exiting SketchUp will be coming up.

If you have not saved your file yet, you will be prompted to do so before SketchUp closes. **Do not save at this time**.

Saving a SketchUp Project:

NOTE: At this time we will not actually save a project.

To save a project file, simply select **Save** from the **File** menu. You can also press **Ctrl +S** on the keyboard.

When the *Standard* toolbar is open you can also click the **Save** icon.

You should get in the habit of saving often to avoid losing work due to a power outage or program crash. The program automatically creates a backup file every time you save; that is, the current SKP file is renamed to SKB. So the SKP file will have the most current model and the SKB will be the state of the model the last time you saved. The backup and auto-save options can be set via Window (menu) → Preferences (Figure 3-3.6).

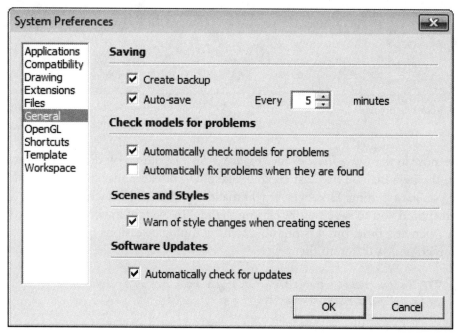

FIGURE 3-3.6 System Preferences Dialog

Auto-save files are saved in the same folder as the file. If SketchUp crashes, the file can be used to recover what would otherwise be lost work. When SketchUp closes properly, the auto-save file is deleted and thus cannot be accessed.

Closing the SketchUp Program:

Finally, from the **File** menu select **Exit**. This will close the current file and shut down SketchUp. Again, you will be prompted to save, if needed, before SketchUp closes. **Do not save at this time.**

You can also click the red "X" in the upper right corner of the SketchUp Application window.

Section 3-4
Viewing SketchUp Models

Learning to get around in a SketchUp model is essential to accurate and efficient design and visualization. We will review a few tools and techniques now so you are ready to use them with the first design exercise.

You will select a sample file from the CD that came with this textbook.

1. Open SketchUp and then select **File→Open**.

2. Browse to the **CD** (usually the D drive, but this can vary).

3. Select the file **Office Building.skp** and click **Open** (Figure 3-4.1).

    TIP: If you cannot locate the CD that came with this textbook, substitute any other SketchUp file.

You should see a view of the SketchUp model similar to that shown in Figure 3-4.1.

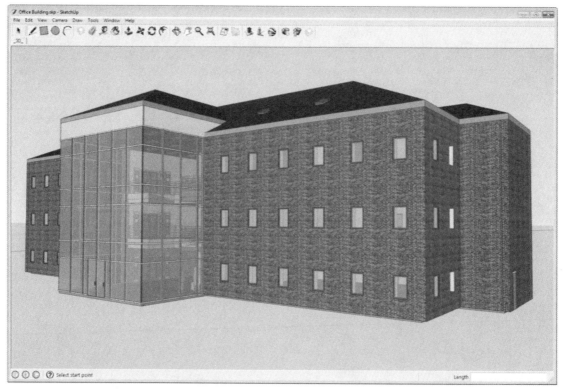

FIGURE 3-4.1 OfficeBuilding.skp model

Using Zoom and Pan Tools:

You can access the navigation tools from the *Getting Started* toolbar – shown in the image below. The tools are, from left to right: *Orbit, Pan, Zoom* and *Zoom Extents*.

These tools do the following:
- Orbit: Fly the camera view about the model
- Pan: Pan the camera view vertically and/or horizontally
- Zoom: Zooms in or out – centered on current view
- Zoom Extents: Zooms view so everything in the model is visible

You will now have an opportunity to try each of these tools.

 Orbit

4. Select the **Orbit** icon from the *Getting Started* toolbar. *Keyboard Shortcut:* **O**

5. Drag your cursor across the screen from right to left – holding down the left mouse button. Stop when your view of the building looks similar to Figure 3-4.2.

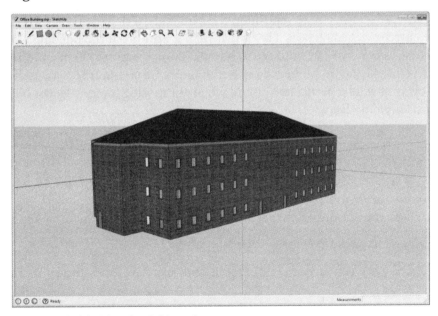

FIGURE 3-4.2 Using the Orbit tool

Spend a little time using the **Orbit** tool, looking at the model from the top, bottom and each side.

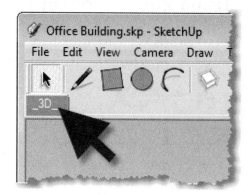

FIGURE 3-4.3 Scene tab

6.   Click the **Select** icon to cancel the current tool and get back into the default mode of being able to select things in the model (Figure 3-4.3).

7.   Once you are done experimenting with the *Orbit* tool, you can quickly get back to your original view by clicking the "_3D_"**scene tab** (Figure 3-4.3).

Additional *scene tabs* can be added, saving views of different parts of the building – both interior and exterior. The scene tabs can also be used to define the outline of an animation, where SketchUp smoothly transitions from location to location. This animation can also be exported and shared with others or used in a presentation.

 Pan

The **Pan** tool allows you to reposition the camera left/right or up/down relative to the current view direction. This is helpful if a portion of the building extends off the screen and you want to see it, but you do not want to change the angle of the view (i.e., see more of the side rather than the front) – as the *Orbit* tool would do. This tool will be particularly useful when composing interior views. Next, you will test-drive the *Pan* tool.

8.   If your view is not reset, do so now per the previous step.

9.   Click the **Pan** icon from the *Getting Started* toolbar. *Keyboard Shortcut:* **H**

Notice how the cursor has changed to a hand symbol to let you know the *Pan* tool is active.

10. Drag the cursor from right to left, until the view looks similar to Figure 3-4.4).

As you can see, the camera moved, which is similar to you walking by a building. As you walk by, you see a little more of what is around the corner than when you were right next to the front. Later you will learn how to toggle between **Perspective** and **Parallel Projection**, the first being more realistic with vanishing lines, the latter is like a flat 2D drawing. When the view is in projection mode, you do not see more or less of anything – the view stays the same, it is just being moved around on the screen.

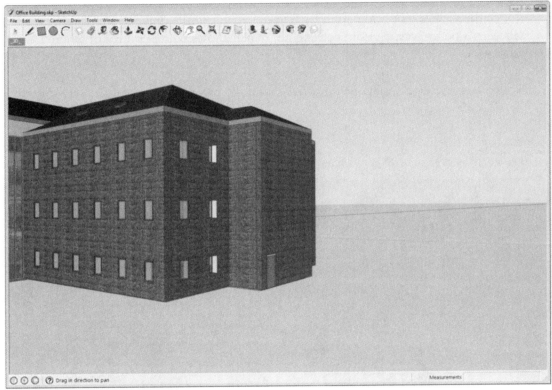

FIGURE 3-4.4 Using the Pan tool

 Zoom

The **Zoom** tool basically does what the name implies… it zooms in and out of your model. Keep in mind it is not changing the size of anything. This feature is not the same as zooming in and out on your camcorder. With the camcorder analogy, you would actually be walking closer to the building when zooming rather than simply magnifying an area. In fact, you can zoom in so far you actually enter the building. Don't forget, you can click the *scene tab* to quickly restore your view if things get messed up.

11. Select the **Zoom** icon from the *Getting Started* toolbar. *Keyboard Shortcut:* **Z**

Notice the cursor changes to a magnifying glass symbol to let you know you are in the *Zoom* command. This will be active until you press the **Esc** key, click to start another command, or click the **Select** icon.

12. Drag your cursor from the bottom of the screen to the top, until the view looks similar to Figure 3-4.5.

Notice the view is only zoomed relative to the center of the drawing window. You will learn a better way to zoom coming up, which allows better control of where you zoom.

Notice how the high quality textures (i.e., building materials) appear more realistic the closer you get.

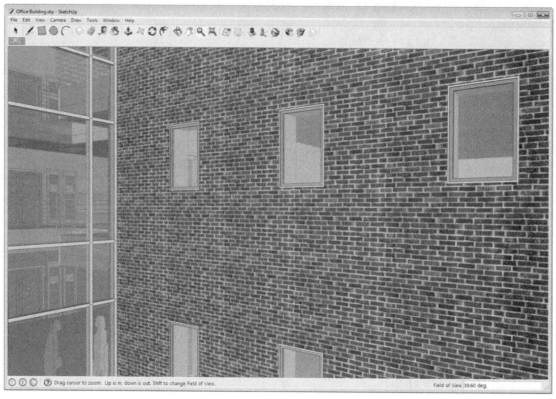

FIGURE 3-4.5 Using the zoom tool

Sometimes you need to make several dragging motions with your mouse to zoom in far enough (because there is not enough room on the desk or your arm simply will not reach). To do this, click and drag as far as you can, and then release the mouse button, move your mouse back, and then repeat the process (i.e., click and drag).

Dragging the mouse in the opposite direction zooms out.

13. Try zooming out, using the **Zoom** tool, dragging from top to bottom.

14. When finished testing the *Zoom* tool, click the **scene tab** to reset the view.

> *FYI:* Holding down the Shift *key while zooming changes the field of view degrees. This is similar to changing the lens on a camera. A larger angle gives you a wide-angle view, allowing you to see more in a smaller space. However, the view can be more distorted as the angle is increased.*

Zoom Extents

The **Zoom Extents** tool is a quick way to make sure you are seeing everything in the model from your current vantage point. You simply click the icon and SketchUp does the rest. This can be tricky if something is floating way out in space because using *Zoom Extents* will show the line and the rest of your model on the same screen – which means your model might be a tiny dot on the screen somewhere.

15. Try the **Zoom Extents** tool:

   a. Zoom in on the building (similar to Figure 3-4.5).

   b. Click the **Zoom Extents** icon. *Keyboard Shortcut:* **Shift+ Z**.

In this example this would not be any faster than clicking the *scene tab*. However, there will not always be a corresponding *scene tab* for every angle from which you will be looking at your model. So the *Zoom Extents* tool is very useful.

Using the Scroll Wheel on the Mouse

The scroll wheel on the mouse is a must for those using SketchUp. In SketchUp you can *Zoom* and *Orbit* without even clicking the *Zoom* or *Orbit* icons. You simply **scroll the wheel to zoom** and **hold the wheel button down to orbit**. This can be done while in another command (e.g., while sketching lines). Another nice feature is that the drawing zooms into the area near your cursor, rather than zooming only at the center of the drawing window. Give this a try before moving on. Once you get the hang of it you will not want to use the icons. The only thing you cannot do is Zoom Extents so everything is visible on the screen.

To use the ***Pan*** feature (aka, *hand* tool), simply hold down the **Shift** key while pressing the center wheel button.

Section 3-5
Help System

Using the *Help* system is often required when you are having problems or trying to do something advanced. This section will present a basic overview of the *Help* system so you can find your way around when needed. It is important that you don't skip this section as it can help reduce your stress level when/if you run into problems.

1. Open SketchUp if not already open.It does not matter if you are in a blank file or a sample file.

2. Select **Help → Help Center**.

Your default internet browser opens and you are in SketchUp's *Help* system (Figure 3-5.1). The entire *Help* system is internet based, thus allowing Google the ability to make revisions and additions as needed.

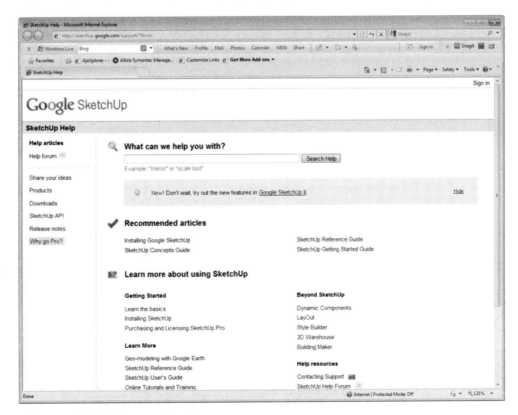

FIGURE 3-5.1 Help system interface

Searching for answers

The various links found on the *Help* page speak for themselves. However, most of the time you can just type a command name and press **Enter** to get a refined list of options from which to choose. You will try that now.

3. Click within the search box and type **ORBIT**.

4. Press **Enter** or click the **Search Help** button to the right.

FIGURE 3-5.2 Entering a word to search for within Help

It should be no surprise that Google SketchUp uses the Google search engine to return help topics related to your search parameters. The image below shows the results (Figure 3-5.3). Since this is a web based search, the results can change over time. Of course, you also need internet access for the search to work.

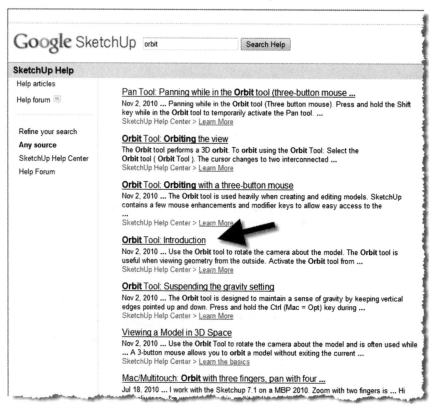

FIGURE 3-5.3 Search results for "orbit"

The most relevant item may not always be first. The example's first item relates more to the *Pan* tool rather than *Orbit*. The first place to start might be the introduction link, which is fourth in the list (Figure 3-5.3). Also notice the word(s) you typed is bold in the title and description.

5.   Click on the link titled **Orbit Tool: Introduction**.

Your result should look similar to Figure 3-5.4. Notice the various options: Basic description, keyboard shortcut, tabs to display additional information on this topic, a convenient print link and a quality control type survey at the bottom.

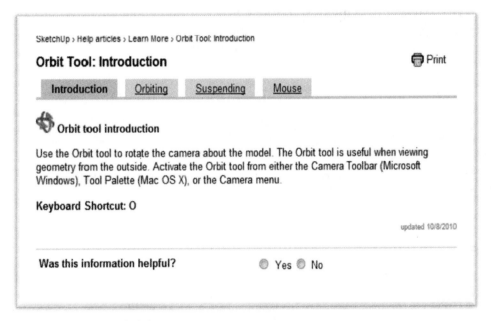

FIGURE 3-5.4 Sample help item

6.   Try clicking on the tabs (i.e., *Orbiting*, *Suspending* and *Mouse*) to see the information that is shown.

Most of the results come from the formal SketchUp *Help* system. However, some of the help results point to the SketchUp user-to-user forum (Figure 3-5.5). The green text below the description indicates where the information is coming from (see previous image and the one below). The forums can be a great source of information, but you do need to understand that this is not official SketchUp advice – so users beware.

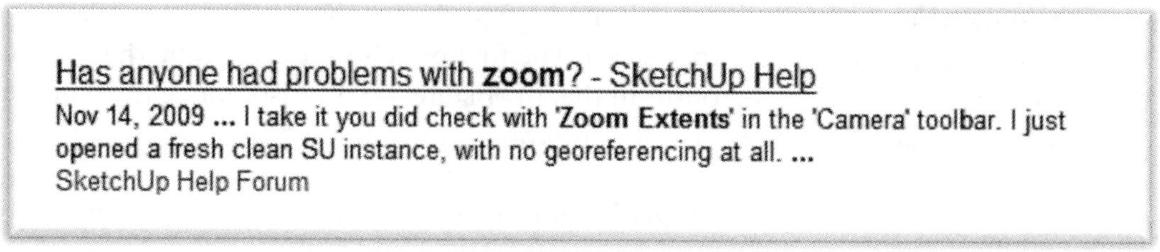

> **Has anyone had problems with zoom? - SketchUp Help**
> Nov 14, 2009 ... I take it you did check with 'Zoom Extents' in the 'Camera' toolbar. I just
> opened a fresh clean SU instance, with no georeferencing at all. ...
> SketchUp Help Forum

FIGURE 3-5.5 Search result pointing to user forum

If you are searching for a multi-word tool it is best to add quotation marks around the entire search text to narrow the search. For example, if you want to search for information on the *Zoom Extents* tool, you should enter:

- "zoom extents" rather than: zoom extents

Google will show results with both words, but if quotation marks are not used, it will also show results with just one of the words.

Anytime you want to return to the initial help screen you can click the "Help Articles" link in the upper left.

SketchUp User's Guide

Another way to learn and do research on SketchUp is via the user's guide. This is an indexed list which makes it easy to find information on a specific topic (e.g., placing a camera). You might not even know the name of the command you want to use. In the user's guide you can look for it by process of elimination. This is a great way to stumble across information you were not even looking for – similar to randomly opening a book to a page and something catches your eye, so you start reading about it.

The user's guide can be found via a link on the initial help page. The highest level of the index tree is shown to the right (Figure 3-5.6).

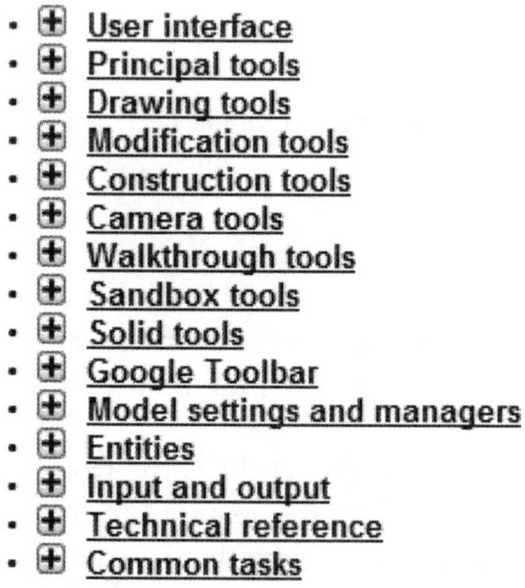

- ⊞ **User interface**
- ⊞ **Principal tools**
- ⊞ **Drawing tools**
- ⊞ **Modification tools**
- ⊞ **Construction tools**
- ⊞ **Camera tools**
- ⊞ **Walkthrough tools**
- ⊞ **Sandbox tools**
- ⊞ **Solid tools**
- ⊞ **Google Toolbar**
- ⊞ **Model settings and managers**
- ⊞ **Entities**
- ⊞ **Input and output**
- ⊞ **Technical reference**
- ⊞ **Common tasks**

FIGURE 3-5.6
User's guide index

Be sure to refer to the *Help* system anytime you get stuck to see if it can help you find the answer to your problem.

Self-Exam:

The following questions can be used as a way to check your knowledge of this lesson. The answers can be found at the bottom of this page.

1. The basic version of SketchUp is free. (T/F)

2. SketchUp is the only 3D modeling software used by architects. (T/F)

3. SketchUp is a "solids" modeling program. (T/F)

4. Press and hold down the _____ _____ on the mouse to quickly begin orbiting the model.

5. Use the _____ _____ tool to see the entire model.

Review Questions:

The following questions may be assigned by your instructor as a way to assess your knowledge of this section. Your instructor has the answers to the review questions.

1. SketchUp is a face-based 3D modeling program. (T/F)

2. SketchUp is strictly a 2D drafting program. (T/F)

3. SketchUp can have more than one model open during the same session. (T/F)

4. The right-click menu is always the same list of options. (T/F)

5. SketchUp was not primarily created for architecture. (T/F)

6. The icon with the hand picture (/⁒) allows you to _____ within a model.

7. The toolbar that you see when SketchUp is first started is the only toolbar available within the program.(T/F)

8. The *Help* system requires a connection to the internet. (T/F)

Notes:

Chapter

4

SketchUp Introduction Part II

This chapter will build upon what was covered in the previous chapter. You will begin to learn how to create geometry and modify it. A very basic introduction will be presented, with additional information provided later in the book as the need arises.

Section 4-1
The Basic Entities

Given the amazing images one can create using SketchUp, it is somewhat surprising that there are mainly just eight types of entities that can be added to a model.

They are:

- Edges
- Surfaces
- Annotation
    - Dimensions
    - Test
    - 3D Text
- Components
- Groups
- Guide (reference line)

The next few pages will provide a brief overview of each of these entity types.

Edges

SketchUp is a face-based program, and all surfaces (i.e., faces) must be defined by an edge. This is the fundamental building block of a SketchUp model.

Edges are created with one of thedraw tools:

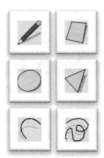

- Line
- Circle
- Arc
- Rectangle
- Polygon
- Freehand

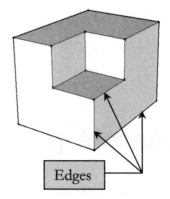

FIGURE 4-1.1 Edges pointed out

Edges can be created with very specific length (or radius) or arbitrarily by clicking anywhere within the drawing window. It is easy to snap to one of the three planes (axes) while drawing lines. This makes it possible to draw 3D shapes from a single 3D view (more on this later).

A basic cube has twelve edges. Figure 4-1.1 has 21 edges and Figure 4-1.2 has two edges.

Even circles are made up of small edges. When one is being created, the *Value Control Box* (on the Status Bar) lists the number of sides that will be used to approximate the circle. This number can be increased to make larger circles smooth, or decreased to make smaller circles less complex (which can be a burden on model performance).

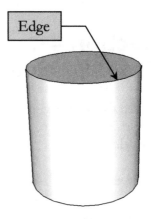

FIGURE 4-1.2 Edge pointed out

Later in this chapter you will get some practice drawing edges and editing them.

Edges can be modified with a number of tools. For example, an edge can be scaled, rotated, divided, copied, offset and erased. These tools are accessible from the *Tools* menu, toolbars (which may not be visible yet), right-click menus (when the edge is selected) and keyboard shortcuts.

Edges can also be placed on *Layers* in order to control visibility. A *Layer* can be turned off, making everything assigned to that *Layer* invisible.

Surfaces

A surface is the second most significant type of entity in SketchUp. You might be surprised to learn that no tool exists to create a surface! They are created automatically when the conditions are right.

What are the conditions in which a surface is automatically created? The simple answer is **when a series of edges form an enclosed area**. When the last edge is drawn which defines an enclosed area, a surface is created. This can be as few as three edges – forming a triangle.

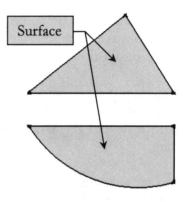

The image to the right (Figure 4-1.3) shows two examples of three connected edges defining a *surface*. Note the edges can be a combination of straight and curved lines.

If an *edge* is erased, the *surface* is also erased, seeing as it no longer has a boundary.

FIGURE 4-1.3
Surfaces defined by at least three edges

In addition to *edges* forming a closed perimeter, there is another important requirement a new modeler needs to be aware of, That is, **all the lines forming the enclosure must be coplanar**.

If you don't already know, the easiest way to describe coplanar is to think of all the edges as lines drawn on a flat piece of paper. As long as all the lines are in the same plane (i.e., on that flat piece of paper) a *surface* will be created.

Surfaces may have materials painted on them. They can also be placed on *Layers* in order to control visibility.

FIGURE 4-1.4
Coplanar on left; not on right

A surface can be deleted; simply select it and press the **Delete** key on the keyboard. The only way to get another surface is to draw a line directly on top of one of the existing *edges*. SketchUp will then create a surface and delete the extra line, as it does not allow two lines to exist directly on top of each other.

FIGURE 4-1.5 Another angle of Figure 4-1.4

Dimensions

Dimensions can be added to your SketchUp model. These are smart entities; they are not sketched lines and manually entered text. A *dimension* entity becomes a permanent part of the model, unlike the *Tape Measure* tool (which is used to list distances without drawing anything).

To place a dimension you simply pick three points; the first two are what you want to dimension and the third is the location of the dimension line and text. SketchUp automatically displays the correct length.

The dimensions are associative, relative to the first two points picked. The dimension will grow or shrink if the geometry is modified. However, if the geometry is deleted, the dimension will remain (but is no longer associated to anything).

Dimensions can be tricky in that they may appear correctly and legible from one angle (Figure 4-1.6a) but not another (Figure 4-1.6b). But the visibility of a *dimension* can be controlled by *Layers* or by *Scene* (more on what scenes are later).

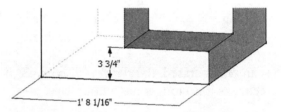

FIGURE 4-1.6A Dimensions added while viewing
the model from this angle

To adjust various settings related to how dimensions are created, go to **Window → Model info** and then click *Dimensions* in the list on the left.

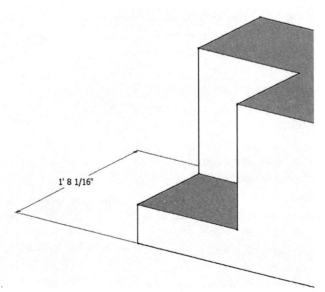

FIGURE 4-1.6B One dimension still visible when
view angle is changed using orbit

Text

SketchUp has a tool which allows you to add notes with leaders (i.e., pointing at something). To place a *Text* entity you make two clicks and then type (or accept the default value). Default value? If you point to a *surface*, SketchUp will automatically list the area of that surface. If an *edge* is pointed to, SketchUp will list its length. An example of each can be seen in the image below (Figure 4-1.7).

If you don't want a leader, simply click in empty space and you can just type text. The text "Option A" is an example of text without a leader (Figure 4-1.7).

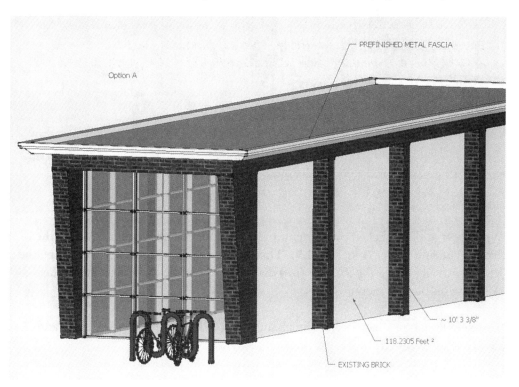

FIGURE 4-1.7 Notes added using the Text tool

Similar to dimensions, text entities remain visible when the vantage point is changed, using *Orbit* for example. As you can see in the Figure 4-1.8, this can get a bit messy. *Text* visibility can also be controlled with *Layers* and *Scenes* like *dimensions*.

For the most part, notes and dimensions are left until the end of the modeling or added outside of SketchUp – in LayOut or a CAD program such as AutoCAD or Revit.

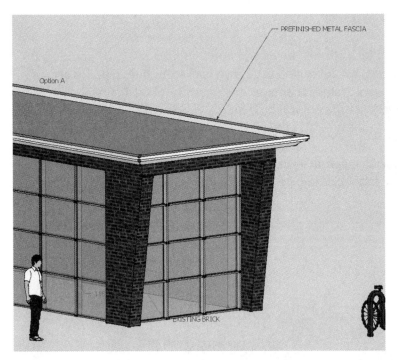

FIGURE 4-1.8 Notes still visible when model rotated using orbit

When text is right-clicked on, a menu pops up which allows you to change the arrow type and leader (Figure 4-1.9). These options, plus the ability to change the font, are available via the ***Entity Info*** dialog. This can be turned on from the Window pull-down menu.

The default settings for text can be changed via **Window → Model Info**, and then selecting *Text* from the list on the left.

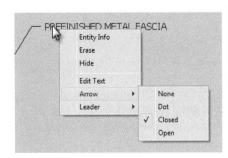

FIGURE 4-1.9
Right-click options for text

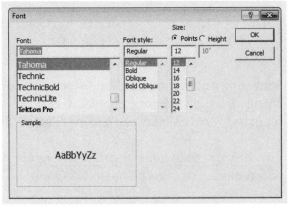

FIGURE 4-1.10 Changing font for text entity

3D Text

The *Text* tool, just covered, is meant for notes and comments about the model. *3D Text* is meant to be part of the model. This tool is used to model text on signs or letters on the face of a building. Unlike notes created with the *Text* tool, *3D Text* stays right where you put it.

Placing 3D Text is easy. Select the tool, and the *Place 3D Text* dialog appears (Figure 4-1.11). Enter your text and select the options desired for font style, height and thickness (i.e., extruded). Click **OK** and then pick a location on a face to place it.

Once the 3D Text is placed, the *Paint Bucket* tool can be used to apply a material.

FIGURE 4-1.11 Adding 3D Text

FIGURE 4-1.12 3D Text placed

Once the text is created, it becomes a component that cannot be easily edited (in terms of typing new words).

It is possible to see the properties for 3D Text, or anything else selected, using the ***Entity Info*** dialog (Fig. 4-1.13). This can be turned on from the Window pull-down menu. The information presented varies depending on what is selected. This dialog can remain open while modeling.

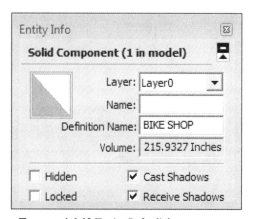

FIGURE 4-1.13 Entity Info dialog

Components

In SketchUp one can think of *Components* being something like clipart in a word processing program – but clipart on steroids! They are pre-built models which can be reused in your SketchUp model. Some components are flat 2D models while others are complex 3D models. The simple, flat components reduce the resources required of your computer, making it easier to smoothly orbit and inspect your model. For example, many of the trees designers use in SketchUp are 2D due to the number typically needed. If 3D trees were used, the file would be large and unmanageable. The 2D components can be setup so that they always face you – plus they cast shadows (see Figures4-1.14 and 4-1.15).

FIGURE 4-1.14 2D vs. 3D components; two items are 2D and two are 3D.

FIGURE 4-1.15 Rotated view of previous image

Right-clicking on a *component* allows you to edit it, explode it (reduce it down to individual entities) and add parameters and parametrics using the advanced **Dynamic Components** functionality.

Editing a *component* causes all instances of that component, in your model, to instantly update. You will see an example of this in the next section.

One of the truly great things about using SketchUp is the amount of content the designer has access to. Google hosts a site called ***Google 3D Warehouse*** which has thousands of components ready for the taking.

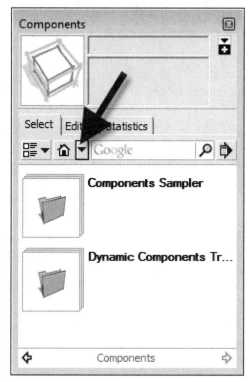

FIGURE 4-1.16 Components dialog

Some of the content found on *Google 3D Warehouse* is provided directly by Google, while other content comes from manufacturers of products (who hope you will ultimately buy or specify their products) or from end users like you.

Of course, *users beware* on anything one downloads and uses in their design. As a design professional (or would-be, someday, design professional) you are responsible for code and performance compliance. So you cannot just assume the toilet or the door you downloaded is the correct size. You need to double check it with the manufacturer's data sheets. Now, if the content was created by the manufacturers, it is highly probable that it is the correct size.

The *Components* dialog (Figure 4-1.16) is the easiest way to add components to your model. This can be accessed from the Window menu. The down arrow highlighted reveals a menu which provides shortcuts to groups of content, such as Architecture, People, Playground, etc.

It is also possible to search for components. You may be surprised at what you can find. Figure 4-1.17 shows some of the results when searching for "**pizza**"! Notice the author of the component is listed directly under the name.

Try a few searches to see what you can find – maybe try goat, newspaper, or snowboard.

See the next section for more on *components*.

FIGURE 4-1.17 Components search

Groups

A *Group* is similar to a *Component* in that you can select one part of it and the entire representation is selected (selecting potentially hundreds of entities with a single pick). However, that is about all that is the same between them.

Groups are meant for one-off type items. That is, a unique reception desk, a built-in entertainment center, etc. A *Component* is used when your model will contain many instances of an object.

Both *Groups* and *Components* are easy to create. You simply model something, select it and then right-click (on it). At this point you can select either **Make Group** or **Make Component** (Figure 4-1.18).

Both *Groups* and *Components* can be copied around the model (using the *Move* tool and holding down Ctrl). They both can also be edited by right-clicking and selecting "edit" from the pop-up menu.

FIGURE 4-1.18
Right-click menu

It is important to note that editing a *Group* only changes the specific *Group* you are editing. But editing a *Component* instantly causes all instances of that *Component* to update (see Figures 4-1.20 and 4-1.21). This means SketchUp duplicates all information required to define each copy of a *Group*. A single definition is all that is needed for multiple instances of a *Component*. Of course, this means a file with many copies of a *Group* will be larger than one with many copies of a *Component*.

The main thing to keep in mind is that *Groups* are quick and require minimal decisions. *Components* can be much more sophisticated and take a lot of time setting up (creating parameters and parametric relationships, and adding formulas).

When you right-click and select *Make Group*, SketchUp just makes it without asking any questions. It can be selected and named via the *Entity Info* dialog if you wish.

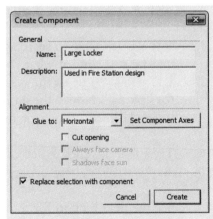

When creating a *Component*, the *Create Component* dialog appears (Figure 4-1.19). Notice the various options:

- Glue to – does the tree stick to the ground or float in the air?
- Always face the camera – this is ideal for flat two-dimensional items.
- Replace selection – turn the current selection into one of the *Components* you are creating.

FIGURE 4-1.19 Right-click menu

The images below compare what happens when a *Component* is edited versus a *Group*. Notice all instances of the *Component* are updated, whereas only the selected *Group* being edited is updated (even though the other *Groups* are copies of the one being edited).

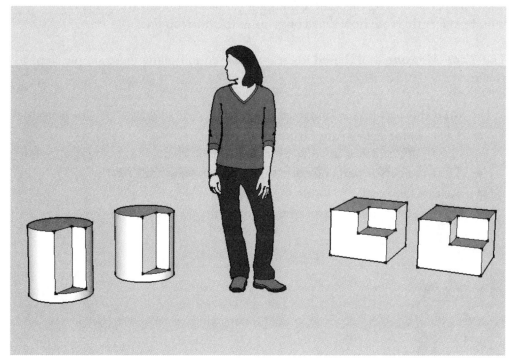

FIGURE 4-1.20 Components vs. groups – components on the left, groups on the right

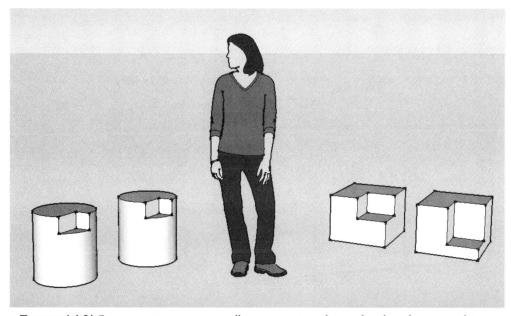

FIGURE 4-1.21 Components vs. groups – all components update, only selected group updates

Guide

Guide lines (or construction lines) are useful for new users and for a general design reference grid. The image below (Figure 4-1.22) shows the main *Axes* and a few *Guides* at 5'-0" intervals. These lines are parallel to the main *Axes* and are infinite in length. Note how they converge at the horizon line.

The ***Tape Measure*** tool is used to create *Guide* lines. Follow these simple steps to create one:

- Start the *Tape Measure* tool.
- Click on the *Edge* of any shape or *Axes*
  FYI: Clicking on an endpoint creates a Guide Point.
- Drag the cursor perpendicular to where you want the *Guide*.
- Release the mouse to locate the *Guide*.
- Type in a length to (retroactively) adjust the *Guide* location.

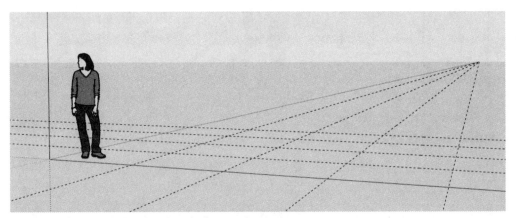

FIGURE 4-1.22 Guides added at 5'-0" intervals

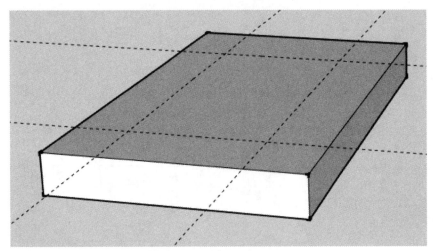

FIGURE 4-1.23 Guides added on top of a surface

Guides can be selected and deleted. They can also be relocated with the *Move* tool. They can be rotated with the *Rotate* tool as well.

You can quickly hide the *Guides* via the *View* menu (Figure 4-1.24). Notice the *Axes* can also be toggled off/on here as well.

Guides can also be placed on a *Layer* and hidden. This would allow you to hide some *Guides* while leaving others visible. Simply create a *Layer* using the *Layer* dialog (*Window* → *Layers*). Then select the Guide(s) and switch them to another *Layer* via the *Entity Info* dialog (see page 4-7).

If you can see *Guides* on the screen, they will print. You need to hide them before printing if you do not want them to print.

FIGURE 4-1.24
Guides visibility

Section 4-2
Beginning with the Basics

In this section you will practice sketching basic 2D lines and shapes to get the hang of using a few of the draw and modify tools, as well as specifying specific dimensions. In the next section you will circle back and see how easy it is to turn these 2D sketches into 3D drawings.

Setting up the model

The first thing you need to do is start a new model and make a few adjustments. You will complete these steps for each drawing in this section, unless noted otherwise (UNO).

1. Start a new SketchUp model using the **Architectural Design – Feet and Inches** template.

2. Select the person *Component*, and press the **Delete** key on the keyboard.

To break things down into the simplest terms, you will change to a non-perspective plan (or top) view.

3. From the *Camera* menu, select **Parallel Projection** (Figure 4-2.1).

4. Also from the *Camera* menu, select: **Standard Views → Top**.

You can also go to *View → Toolbar → Views* to turn on a toolbar which provides quick access to the standard views (top, front, iso, etc.).

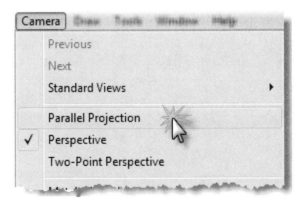

FIGURE 4-2.1 Parallel Projection mode

You are now looking at a plan view (Figure 4-2.2). This view is similar to what you would see on a printed out floor plan (aka, blueprints or construction documents). Use caution not to press and drag your center wheel button, as this action will activate the *Orbit* tool and throw you out of *Top* view; you would still be in "parallel" mode however. If you accidentally do this, simply select "top" again from the *Camera* menu. Selecting *Undo* does not help.

Notice how the axes are centered on the screen.

You can adjust which part of the model you are looking at using the *Pan* tool. When finished panning, click the *Select* icon. Do not pan at this time.

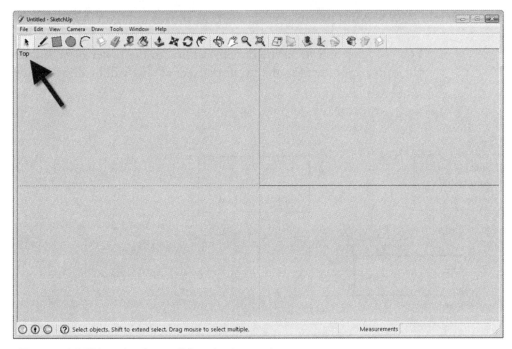

FIGURE 4-2.2 Top view in parallel projection mode

file name: **Bookcase**

This is a simple rectangle that represents the size of a bookcase. The black dot represents the starting point, which should align with the intersection of the axes. **Do not draw the black dot.**

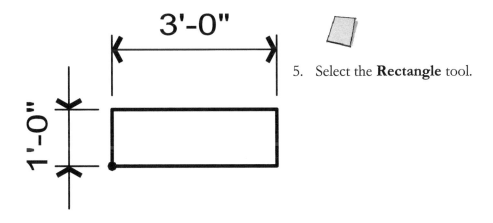

5. Select the **Rectangle** tool.

6. **For your first point**, click the intersection of the axes (Figure 4-2.3).

    a. Be sure your cursor snaps to the *Origin*; you will see a yellow circle and a tooltip appear.

7. **Select your second point** approximately as shown in Figure 4-2.3).

    a. You can keep an eye on the dimension box in the lower right, but do not worry about getting the number exact as that will be done in the next step.

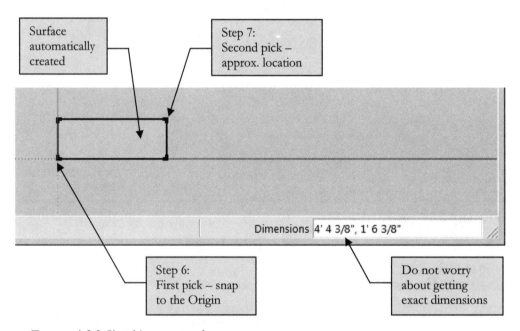

FIGURE 4-2.3 Sketching a rectangle

8. After clicking the second point (step 7) and before doing anything else, simply type **3′,1′** and then press **Enter**.

    a. You do not need to click in the *Dimensions* box; just start typing.

9. Save your file as **Bookcase.skp**.

Notice the surface which was automatically created once an enclosed area was created. You are done with this file for now. You will come back to it later and turn it into a 3D bookcase.

file name: **Coffee Table**

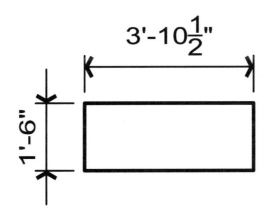

Next you will start a new file, using the steps previously covered (Setting up the Model; steps 1-4). The previously created file can be closed and set aside for use in the next section.

The *Coffee Table* drawing will introduce you to entering fractional values.

10. Start a new model, following steps 1-4.

It would be fairly easy to use the *Rectangle* tool again to draw this item, however you will use the basic *Line* tool so you can see how it works and get practice entering specific lengths.

11. Select the **Line** tool from the toolbar.

12. Snap to the *Origin* (the intersection of the red and green axes).

13. Begin moving your cursor to the right (Figure 4-2.4):

   a. Ensure your cursor is "snapped" to the horizontal.
   b. When horizontal, you should see the "**On Red Axis**" tooltip.
   c. Once you are pointing in the correct direction and snapped to the horizontal, you may type in a length (see the next step for this).

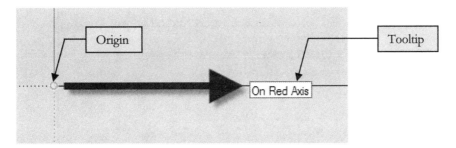

FIGURE 4-2.4 Sketching a line

14. Without moving the mouse, type **3'10.5** and then press **Enter**.

You always have to enter a foot symbol if feet are needed, however the inch symbol never needs to be typed as it is assumed when nothing is specified.

The *Line* tool will remain active until you pick the *Select* icon or another tool. Next, you will draw one of the vertical lines.

15. While the **Line** tool is still active (Figure 4-2.5):
    a. Start moving your cursor straight up.
    b. Ensure the "**On Green Axis**" tooltip is showing; meaning vertical.
    c. Type **1′6** and then press **Enter**.

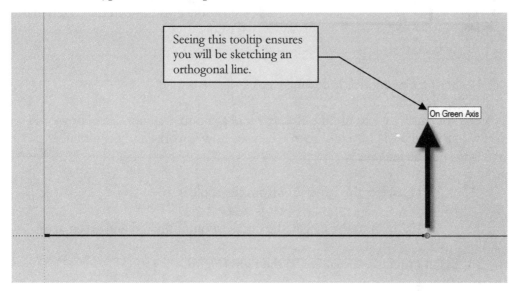

Seeing this tooltip ensures you will be sketching an orthogonal line.

On Green Axis

FIGURE 4-2.5 Sketching another line

16. Using one of the alternative methods of entering 3′ 10 ½″ (see below), sketch the top horizontal line from right to left.

Entering fractions: the 3′-10½″ can be entered several ways.

o	3′ 10.5	*Notice there is a space between the feet and inches.*
o	3′10.5	*Notice space can also be left out.*
o	3′ 10 1/2	*Note the two spaces separating feet, inches and fractions.*
o	3′10 1/2	*The second space is always required.*
o	0′ 46.5	*This is all in inches; that is, 3′-10½″ = 46.5″.*
o	46.5	*SketchUp assumes inches if nothing is specified.*

---

*TIP: Even when you are in a model using imperial units you can type a metric value and SketchUp will automatically convert it. For example; typing **150mm** draws a **57/8″** line.*

To draw the last line you could type in the value but you can more quickly snap to the endpoint of the first line drawn. This will complete the rectangular shape.

17. Snap to the **Endpoint** of the first line drawn (Figure 4-2.6).

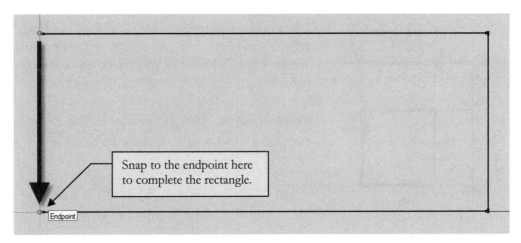

Snap to the endpoint here
to complete the rectangle.

Endpoint

FIGURE 4-2.6 Completing the rectangle

Once a closed perimeter is defined, as your rectangle, a surface is automatically created. You should use the *Tape Measure* tool too occasionally to double check your lengths. Simply select the *Tape Measure* tool from the toolbar and then pick two points in the model. The *Value Control Box* in the lower right of the application lists the measurement. Give it a try!

18. Save your file as **Coffee Table.skp**.

file name: **SmallDesk**

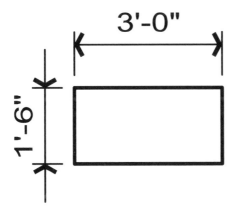

3'-0"

1'-6"

Next, you will start another new file and create this rectangular shape.

19. Create a new model (per steps 1-4) and create this small desk using either of the methods just covered.

20. Save your file as **Small Desk.skp**.

Don't worry, things will get more challenging. These steps are laying the groundwork for all of the 3D modeling you will be doing! So make sure you take the time to understand this material.

file name: **Night Table**

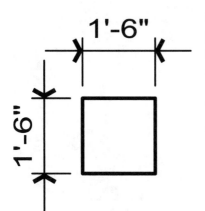

Obviously, you could draw this quickly per the previous examples. However, you will take a look at copying a *file* and then modifying an existing model.

You will use the *Move* tool to stretch the 3'-0" wide desk down to a 1'-6" wide night table.

21. With the *Small Desk* SketchUp model still open, select **File → Save As**.

22. Type **Night Table** for the *File name* and click **Save** (Figure 4-2.7).

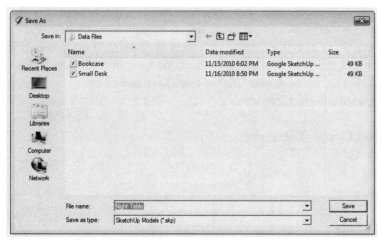

FIGURE 4-2.7 SaveAs dialog

You are now in a new file named *Night Table.skp*, and are ready to manipulate the file. The original "small desk" file is now closed and will not be affected.

You will use the *Move* tool to change the location of one of the vertical lines, which will cause the two horizontal lines to stretch with it. SketchUp's *Lines* automatically have a parametric relationship to adjacent lines when their endpoints touch each other.

23. Click the vertical line on the <u>right</u> and then select the **Move** icon on the toolbar.

24. Pick the mid-point of the selected line; move the mouse towards the left – while locked to the vertical (Figure 4-2.8). **Do not click yet.**

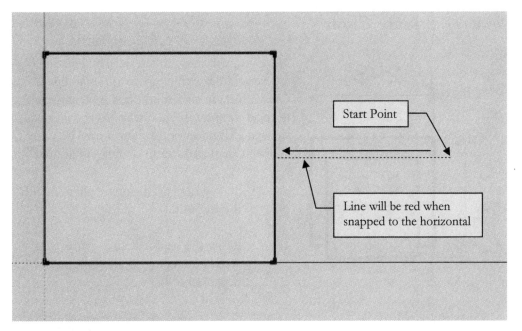

FIGURE 4-2.8 Moving an edge

25. While in the *Move* command and snapped to the horizontal (i.e., red axis), type **1′6** and then press **Enter**.

That is it! You essentially just stretched the rectangle. The two horizontal lines automatically shrunk in length and the surface resized itself as well.

26. **Save** your *Night Table.skp* file.

file name: **Small Dresser**   *file name:* **File Cabinet**

27. Draw the *Small Dresser* and the *File Cabinet* per the previous instructions.

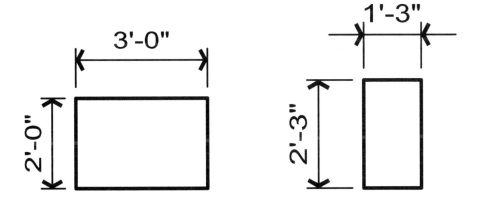

file name: **Square Chair**

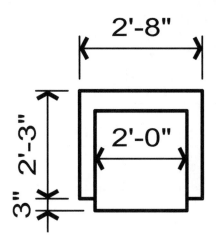

Next you will draw this squarish-styled chair. You could draw this by setting up a few *Guides*, but another method will be shown. It is good to know several ways to accomplish the same thing as one solution may be more efficient than another in certain situations.

28. Start with a 2′x2′ square aligned with the origin.

29. Draw the backrest and armrests as separate rectangles, near the square (Figure 4-2.9).

30. Use the **Move** tool to move the rectangles into position (Figure 4-2.10).

SketchUp does not allow overlapping lines. Therefore, when you moved the rectangles into place the lines were merged, with any endpoints remaining. This will allow you to delete the extra lines identified in Figure 4-2.10.

31. **Delete** the extra lines identified in Figure 4-2.10; select it and press the **Delete** key on the keyboard.

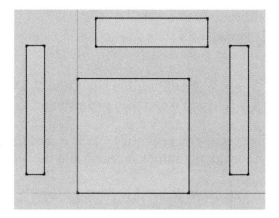

FIGURE 4-2.9 Creating the chair

When the two lines were removed, the surfaces automatically joined together within the newly enclosed area (Figure 4-2.11). At this point you only have two surfaces defined, each of which can be extruded into separate shapes, which you will do later in the next chapter.

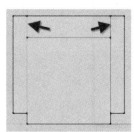

FIGURE 4-2.10

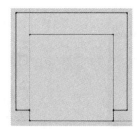

FIGURE 4-2.11

You have completed the square chair – for now anyway. You can save your file and move on to the next one.

Selecting Objects:

At this time we will digress and take a quick look at the various techniques for selecting entities in SketchUp. Most tools work the same when it comes to selecting elements.

When selecting entities, you have two primary ways to select them:
o   Individually select entities one at a time
o   Select several entities at a time with a window

You can use one or a combination of both methods to select elements when using the *Select* tool.

Individual Selections:
When using the *Select* tool, for example, you simply move the cursor over the element and click; holding the **Ctrl** key you can select multiple objects. Then you typically click the tool you wish to use on the selected items. Press **Shift** and click on an item to subtract it from the current selection set.

Window Selections:
Similarly, you can pick a *window* around several elements to select them all at once. To select a *window*, rather than selecting an individual element as previously described, you select one corner of the *window* you wish to define. That is, you pick a point in "space" and hold the mouse button down. Now, as you move the mouse you will see a rectangle on the screen that represents the windowed area you are selecting; when the *window* encompasses the elements you wish to select, release the mouse.

You actually have two types of windows you can use to select. One is called a **window** and the other is called a **crossing window**.

Window:
This option allows you to select only the objects that are completely within the *window*. Any lines that extend out of the *window* are not selected.

Crossing Window:
This option allows you to select all the entities that are completely within the *window* and any that extend outside the *window*.

Using Window versus Crossing Window:
To select a *window* you simply pick and drag from *left to right* to form a rectangle.

Conversely, to select a *crossing window*, you pick and drag from *right to left* to define the two diagonal points of the window.

file name: **Square Sofa**

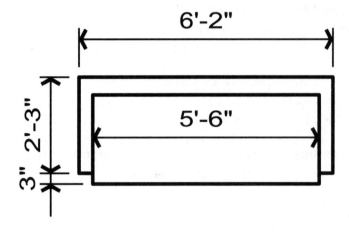

Similar to how you turned the *Small Desk* into a *Night Table*, you will turn the *Square Chair* into this *Square Sofa*.

This is a little trickier as you have to select multiple lines as part of the *Move* command.

32. Once you are sure you saved the *Square Chair* file, do a **Save As** to create the **Square Sofa** file.

33. Select the three lines shown in Figure 4-2.12.

Moving these lines will cause the horizontal lines to follow – or stretch, thus growing the chair into a sofa!

34. Select **Move** from the toolbar.

35. Pick anywhere in the drawing area and begin moving the cursor to the right, snapped to the horizontal (i.e., on red axis).

36. Without clicking a second point, type the desired length you wish to move the lines (i.e., stretch the sofa); this is the difference between the chair and the sofa.

Notice how the horizontal lines extended because they have a parametric relationship to them. The surface has also updated.

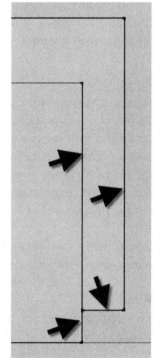

FIGURE 4-2.12

37. Use the ***Tape Measure*** tool to double check your dimensions. Make any corrections needed before moving on.

Keep in mind that all these basic steps will be directly applicable to the more advanced 3D modeling coming up.

file name: **Range**

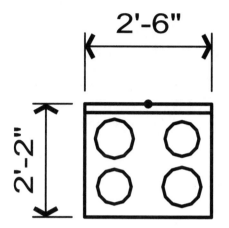

Now you will draw a kitchen range with four circles that represent the burners.

In this exercise you will have to draw temporary lines, called *Guides*, to create reference points needed to accurately locate the circles. Once the circles have been drawn, the *Guides* can be erased.

38. In a new file, **Draw** the range with a 2″ deep control panel at the back; refer to the steps previously covered if necessary.

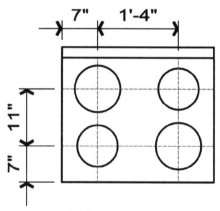

FIGURE 4-2.13 Adding guides

39. Use the ***Tape Measure*** tool to create the four guides dimensioned in Figure 4-2.13.

   a. With the *Tape Measure* tool active, click and drag on an edge to create a *Guide* parallel to that edge.

   b. Once you let go of the mouse the *Guide* is created.

   c. Once placed, type the distance and then press **Enter** to position it.

40. Using the ***Circle*** tool, draw two 9½″ Dia. circles and two 7½″ Dia. circles using the intersections of the *Guides* to locate the centers of the circles (Figure 4-2.13).

41. Using the ***Select*** tool, select each of the *Guides* and press the **Delete** key on the keyboard to remove them from the model.

Circles are made up of several straight line segments. The default number is 24. If your circle is large, the number of edges needs to be increased to maintain the look of a circle. This can be done just before clicking to locate the circle's center, by just typing a number and **Enter**. This number, the radius and *Layer* can all be changed at any time using the *Entity Info* dialog.

file name: **Rounded Chair**

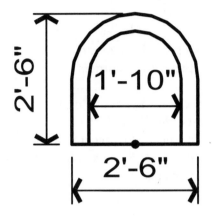

These last two drawings will involve using the *Arc* tool. The *Offset* command will also be utilized.

You will start this chair drawing by sketching the perimeter and then offsetting it inward.

42. Draw the three orthogonal lines shown in Figure 4-2.14.

    a. The horizontal line is centered on the green axis and aligned with the red axis.

    b. The two vertical lines are 1'-3" long.

43. Use the **Arc** tool to add the rounded backrest.

    a. Pick the three points shown in Figure 4-2.14.

    b. When picking the third point, you should see a "half circle" tooltip before clicking the mouse button.

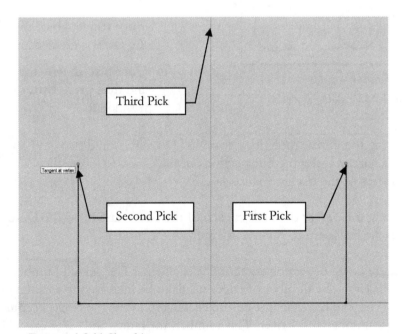

FIGURE 4-2.14 Sketching an arc

You now have the perimeter of the chair defined. Next, you will use the *Offset* command to create the backrest.

44. Select the **Offset** tool from the toolbar.

45. Select the arc – just the line, not the surface.

46. Start moving your cursor towards the middle of the chair and then type **4** and press **Enter**.

47. Draw the two remaining vertical lines.

    a. For the first end of the line, snap to the end of the arc.

    b. For the second end of the line, snap to a perpendicular point on the horizontal line.

The 2D version of the chair is now complete. The drawing now has two surfaces, because two enclosed areas exist: the backrest and the seat area. This will make the 3D extrusion process go smoothly.

file name: **Love Seat**

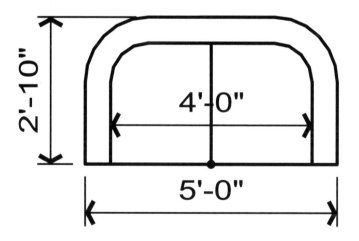

This last 2D exercise will round things off by making quarter round arcs.

One thing that is a little tricky here is setting up points to pick before sketching the arc. When adding an arc it is easiest if the two endpoints are defined by other line work. Thus, you just have to snap to endpoints for your first two picks and the third defines the radius. In this example you will need to add two temporary lines to define the start and end points of the arc.

The radius of the two arcs is 1′-3″.

48. Add the orthogonal lines shown in Figure 4-2.15.

    a. All dimensions can be deduced from the information given.

The two 1'-3" lines are temporary and have only been added to aid in sketching the arcs (which is done in an upcoming step).

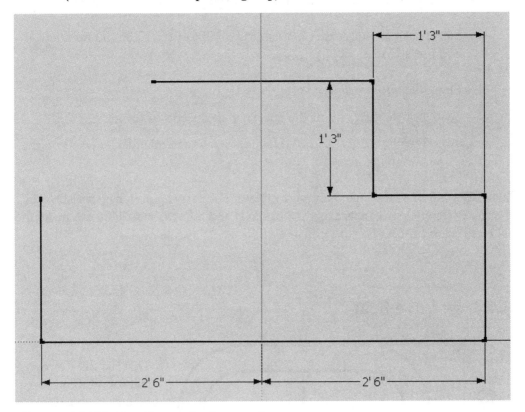

FIGURE 4-2.15 Setting things up for the arc tool

49. **Delete** the two 1'-3" lines.

50. Add one of the perimeter arcs.

    a. Pick the two endpoints provided by the orthogonal lines.

    b. Move the cursor until the arc is purple and the tooltip reads "Tangent at vertex" – this will produce a quarter round arc.

51. Add the other arc per the previous step.

Notice that you did not have to specify the radius of the arc because of the preparation done.

52. Offset the two arcs inward **4"** – similar to the rounded chair (Figure4-2.16).

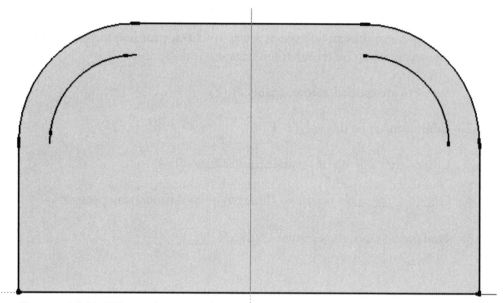

FIGURE 4-2.16 Offset perimeter arcs inward 4 inches

53. Complete the backrest and armrests by "connecting the dots" via the *Line* tool.

54. Draw the vertical line down the middle, representing the cushions.

Sometimes it is better to extrude a shape into the third dimension before adding extra line work such as the cushion line. This issue will be explored more in a later lesson.

Your drawing should be complete (Figure 4-2.17). Note that the drawing has three surfaces based on the line work you sketched. Don't forget to save your file.

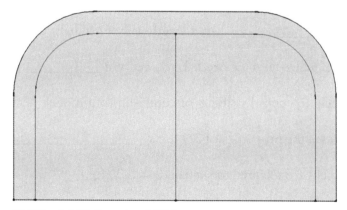

FIGURE 4-2.17 Completed 2D love seat

Self-Exam:

The following questions can be used as a way to check your knowledge of this lesson. The answers can be found at the bottom of this page.

1.   Surfaces are created automatically. (T/F)

2.   Edges cannot be deleted. (T/F)

3.   Circles are made up of several straight lines. (T/F)

4.   A _____ is similar to clipart in a word processing program.

5.   One of the ways you can type 2'-6 ¼": _____.

Review Questions:

The following questions may be assigned by your instructor as a way to assess your knowledge of this section. Your instructor has the answers to the review questions.

1.   Surfaces cannot be deleted. (T/F)

2.   A model can only be viewed in perspective. (T/F)

3.   If the "foot" or "inch" symbol is not entered, inches are assumed. (T/F)

4.   For repetitive items it is better to use a *Group* rather than a *Component*. (T/F)

5.   Text and dimensions can be a little tricky to maintain in a 3D model. (T/F)

6.   _____ _____ lists a length without actually drawing anything.

7.   When reference lines are needed, you can add _____.

8.   *Layers* help to control visibility of entities in your model. (T/F)

9.   Used to see the properties of 3D text: _____ _____.

10. Three picks are required to sketch an arc. (T/F)

SketchUp Introduction Part III

Finally, you will begin to create 3D geometry in this chapter! The previous chapter built the foundation of knowledge needed to start modeling in three dimensions. Hopefully you spent an adequate amount of time learning the 2D concepts in the previous chapter as you will use those skills every time you use SketchUp.

Section 5-1
3D Modeling

In this chapter you will transform the objects created in the previous chapter into three dimensional models. Once the 3D objects have been developed, you will learn how to apply materials to make them look more realistic.

file name: **Bookcase – 3D**

You will open the files from the previous chapter and *Save As* to a new file name so the original files remain intact (just in case you need to start over).

1.   **Open** the **Bookcase.skp** file created in the previous chapter.

2.   Select **File → Save As**.

3.   **Save** the file as **Bookcase – 3D**. (You may save it into another folder if you wish.)

Next, you will turn on the *Views* toolbar to make it easier to switch between 3D and elevation/plan views.

4.   Select **View → Toolbars → Views**.

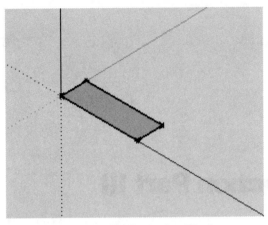

FIGURE 5-1.1 Parallel Projection 3D view

5. Click on the **3D** icon on the *Views* toolbar.

You should now be viewing a 3D view of your bookcase drawing (Figure 5-5.1). Of course it is still just a 2D drawing being viewed from a 3D vantage point. Also recall that the view mode of the model is currently set to *Parallel Projection* rather than the default *Perspective* mode. You will leave it this way for now.

Using the Push/Pull Tool

Now you will use the **Push/Pull** tool to quickly turn the 2D outline into a 3D (face based) object. This tool requires you to select a surface, which means an enclosed perimeter is required. The tool takes the previously defined 2D shape and extrudes it into a 3D shape. So the end result is several additional edges and surfaces which give the appearance of a 3D object.

6. From the *Getting Started* toolbar, select the **Push/Pull** tool.

Next you will simply click and drag on the surface portion of your bookcase (i.e., rectangle) and start moving the mouse straight upwards. You will not worry about an exact height as the precise value will be typed in immediately after using the *Push/Pull* tool.

7. Move your cursor over the surface until it pre-highlights and then click and **drag the mouse up**.

You can only drag in a direction perpendicular to the surface – in this case, straight up or down.

8. **Release the mouse** button at any time, once the 3D geometry appears in the correct direction (i.e., up versus down below the ground).

9. Immediately after releasing the mouse button, type **4'** and then press **Enter**.

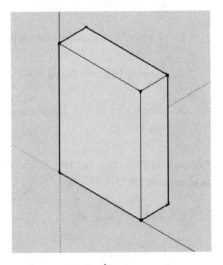

FIGURE 5-1.2 4' high extrusion

You now have a 4'-0" high extrusion which will be further refined to look like a bookcase (Figure 5-1.2).

In addition to the *Push/Pull* tool making solid (or additive) geometry, it can also be used to make voids (or subtractive) geometry. That is, if you sketch rectangles on the face of the bookcase and then use *Push/Pull* you can create a void by "pushing" into the larger 3D object. Conversely, if you "pull" the rectangular shape, you would create a bump-out on the face of the bookshelf.

The following steps can be done in the current 3D view, and are easier once you get used to working in a 3D view. You can try following the next few steps in the current 3D view, or you can switch to the front view (per the very next step) to follow along exactly with the book.

10. Click the **Front** icon on the *Views* toolbar.

You are now looking at the equivalent of a 2D elevation. This is only true if you are still in *Parallel Projection* mode; if not, you see more of a 3D view of the front.

11. Select the **Offset** tool from the toolbar.

Before you click and drag on the edge you want to offset, you need to see the surface highlight first. This lets you know the edge will offset on the correct plane/direction.

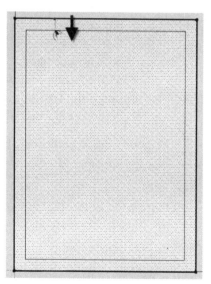

12. Move your cursor over the surface; once you see it highlight, click on the top edge, drag your cursor downward and let go of the mouse button (Figure 5-1.3).

13. Type **1"** and then press **Enter** to make the newly created line work one inch away from the perimeter.

14. Click the **Select** tool, and then select the bottom edge of the newly created rectangle.

15. Use the *Move* tool and reposition the line **3"** up (Figure 5-1.4).

FIGURE 5-1.3
Offset on front face

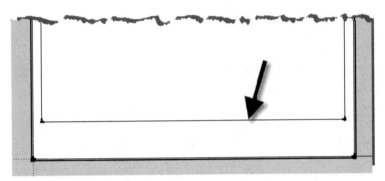

FIGURE 5-1.4 Line moved, 4″ from bottom edge

Now you will sketch the line work for the shelves.

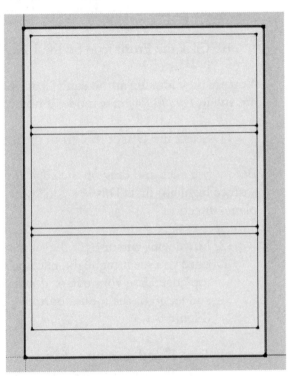

16. Sketch the two shelves (Figure 5-1.5):
    a. Each shelf is **1″** thick.
    b. The shelves are **equally spaced**.
    c. Make the shelves equally spaced. Use the *Tape Measure* tool to list the overall distance within the inner rectangle.
    d. Copy the top or bottom line using **Move** (while holding down the **Ctrl** key to get into *Copy* mode).

FIGURE 5-1.5 Lines added for shelves

As you copied the horizontal line up, a new perimeter was defined on the front surface. So SketchUp created a new surface, and modified the previous surface smaller.

Now it is time to switch back to the 3D view and use the *Push/Pull* tool to carve out the shelf areas. The large rectangular surfaces you are about to push will become the inside face of the back panel for the bookshelf. If that did not make sense, it will in a moment.

17. Switch back to the 3D view.

18. Select **Push/Pull** and then click and drag on the larger top rectangle (Figure 5-1.6).

19. Drag the mouse about halfway into the bookcase and let go of the mouse.

20. Type **11″** and then press **Enter**.

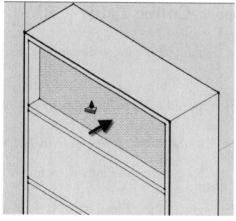

FIGURE 5-1.6 Push/Pull void

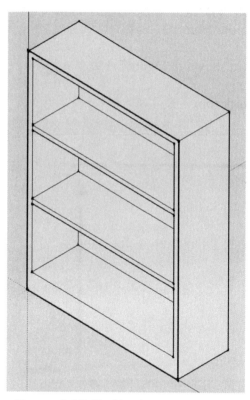

The book case is 12″ deep, so pulling the surface back 11″ gave us a 1″ thick back panel.

21. Repeat this process for the other two larger rectangles (Figure 5-1.7).

The final bookcase should look like Figure 5-1.7. You can press and hold down your center wheel button and *Orbit* around the bookcase to see it from various angles. When finished just click the *3D* icon again.

22. **Save**.

FIGURE 5-1.7 Final bookcase

One last comment on the bookcase (Figure 5-1.8): If you want the face of the shelf to appear flush with the edge panel, you can zoom in and erase the small vertical line (top example). Or, if you want the shelf to appear separate or be recessed slightly you can leave the line in place and use the *Push/Pull* tool (bottom example).

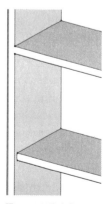

FIGURE 5-1.8 Shelf options

file name: **Coffee Table – 3D**

Using similar techniques to developing the bookcase, you will now create a coffee table.

23. **Open** the 2D coffee table model and do a **Save As** to **Coffee Table – 3D**.

24. Use the ***Push/Pull*** tool to make the 2D rectangle **2′-0″** high.

    a. See the previous steps for more information on how to do this.

25. Switch to the **Front** view.

This will be a heavy mass looking coffee table. The next steps start to define the thickness of the top and legs as viewed from the front.

26. Using the ***Line*** tool, sketch the 5 lines shown in Figure 5-1.9.

    a. Create 3″ wide legs and a 3″ thick top.

FIGURE 5-1.9 Coffee table front view with lines sketched

SketchUp does not allow two lines to overlap. So when you sketched lines 1 and 3 the original line across the bottom split into smaller lines segments based on where your new line stopped. This is good as it keeps the file less cluttered and it ultimately creates a large surface in the middle we will use the *Push/Pull* tool on to carve out that area.

Keep in mind this could have been done from a 3D view. Once you are more experienced, it will be more efficient to do this in a 3D view. The main trick is making sure you stay on the correct axes.

Next you will define the two side views in the same way the front view was developed. You have to do this for both sides, but not the back view. You will see why in a moment.

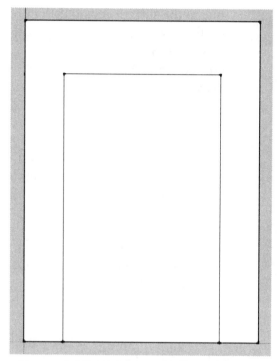

FIGURE 5-1.10 Right view with lines added

27. Switch to the **Right** view and add the 3″ wide legs and a 3″ thick top, per the previous steps (Figure 5-1.10).

28. Repeat the previous step for the **Left** side.

You are now ready to switch back to a 3D view and use the *Push/Pull* tool to remove the large mass below the table.

29. Switch to the **3D view**.

30. Use the ***Push/Pull*** tool to select the large rectangular area on the front of the coffee table.

31. Push the surface back into the model until it "snaps" into alignment with the back face of the model. Release the mouse button.

The model should look like Figure 5-1.11. If not, you can either *Undo* and try again, or grab the surface again using the *Push/Pull* tool. You may need to *Orbit* a little to get a better view (but this should not be necessary). Notice, when the two faces (front and back) come together, SketchUp deleted both and the end result is a void.

If you would have done one of the sides first, you would get the same result. However, now the sides will be a little different due to the top edge now being defined on the back side of the legs. In this case, you will end up needing to manually delete one surface and a line.

32. Use ***Push/Pull*** on one of the side of the table, pushing the surface in to align with the back side of the legs (Figure 5-1.11).

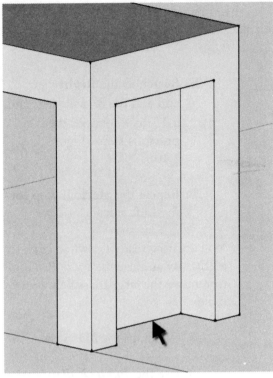

FIGURE 5-1.11 Right side adjusted

Notice the surface and bottom edge did not automatically get deleted when modifying the side view (Figure 5-1.11). Again, this is due to the surface ending directly on the edge of the underside of the 3″ thick top (the top edge was created when the front was extruded back).

This is an easy fix.

33. Use the **Select** tool to pick the bottom edge (i.e., line) and press the **Delete** key.

Once the perimeter is gone, the surface must go as well. You could have deleted the surface and then the line, but that would be more work!

That concludes the coffee table exercise. Be sure to save as a new file name per the first step for this model. Use *Orbit* and *Tape Measure* to inspect your work!

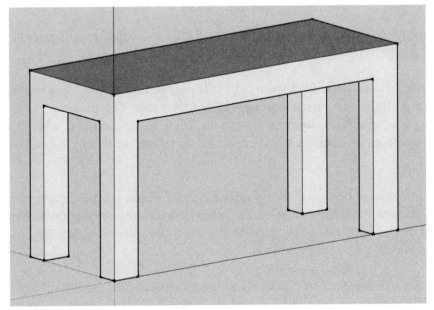

FIGURE 5-1.12 Completed coffee table

file name: Small Desk – 3D

Here you will continue to build on the concepts covered thus far.

34. **Open** the *Small Desk* file and **Save As** to **Small Desk – 3D**.

35. Extrude the rectangle to be **30" high** using *Push/Pull*.

36. Switch to the front elevation view and add the line work shown in Figure 5-1.13. Use the *Line* tool and **Move + Alt** to *Copy* lines rather than *Offset*.

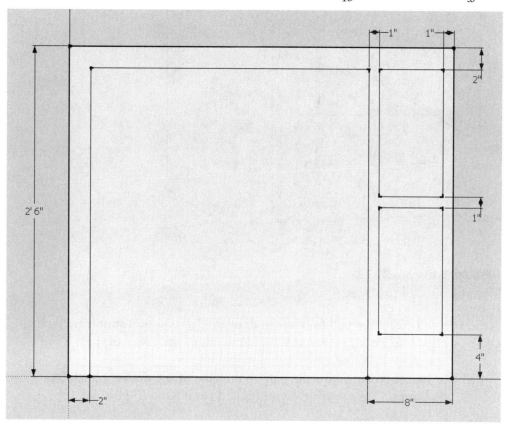

FIGURE 5-1.13 Front elevation of small desk

Next you will carve out the leg space and bump out the drawer panels. Notice you will not sketch in the pulls (i.e., handles) for the drawers yet. If the handles were sketched now you would have another face that would not *Push* or *Pull* with the rest of the drawer panel. Instead, you will get the drawer panel extruded and then sketch the pull outline on the face of the new panel surface.

37. Use *Push/Pull* to modify the desk (Figure 5-1.14):

    a. Knee space should be 1'-4" deep.
    b. Drawer panels should be ½" thick.

Your model should look like this (Figure 5-1.14).

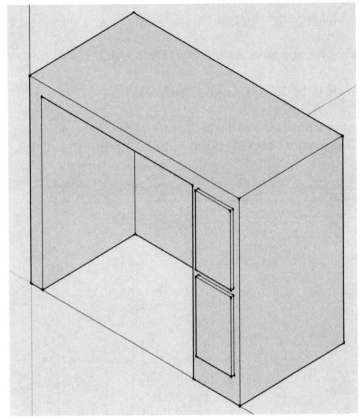

FIGURE 5-1.14 Modified desk

Next, you will create the pull for the top drawer. This will be a simple pull which will be turned into a component and copied down to the lower drawer.

38. Create the rectangle for the pull on the face of the drawer panel. Exact size and location are not critical; just try and get it close (Figure 5-1.15).

39. Use **Push/Pull** to extrude the pull out from the drawer panel (Figure 5-1.16).

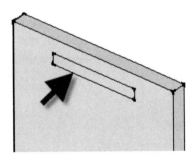

FIGURE 5-1.15 Pull outline

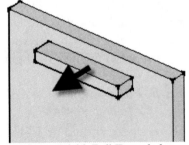

FIGURE 5-1.16 Pull Extruded

40. Sketch the profile of the pull on top of the extruded shape. This is in the 3D view; wait until you see the tooltip which says "on face" for drawing (Figure 5-1.17).

41. Use **Push/Pull** to carve out the back side of the pull (Figure 5-1.18).

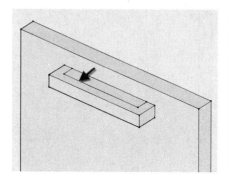
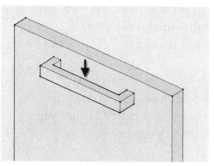

FIGURE 5-1.17 Pull profile   **FIGURE 5-1.18** Pull completed

Next, you will group all the lines and surfaces that make up the pull into a single entity called a *Component*. As mentioned previously in this book, using *Components* is more efficient and makes the file smaller when the item will be used many times.

42. In the 3D view, *Zoom* in on the pull and select a window picking from left to right.

    a. Be sure to pick from left to right and adjust the view so you are only selecting the pull and nothing else behind it.

43. With the pull selected, click the **Make Component** icon.

44. Fill out the dialog as shown in Figure 5-1.19.

45. Click **Create**.

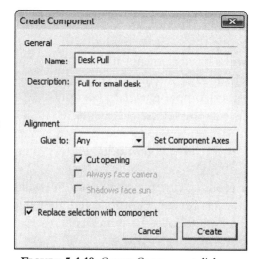

You now have a *Component* created in the model of your pull. Because the "Replace selection with component" was selected, the original lines and surfaces have been replaced with a copy of the new component.

Next, you will copy the *Component* down to the other drawer.

FIGURE 5-1.19 Create Component dialog

46. Select the *Component* and use the **Move + Ctrl** key to copy the pull down to the other drawer. Use the pick points shown in Figure 5-1.20.

Now that the pull is a *Component* you can edit one and the other will instantly update. You will try editing a component next.

47. **Right-click** on one of the pulls and then select **Edit Component** from the pop-up menu.

48. Make a change to the pull, something simple such as using **Push/Pull** to make the extrusion taller (i.e., thicker) or something more detailed like making the pull curved (Figure 5-1.21).

49. When finished editing the component, click away from it and the edit mode is finished.

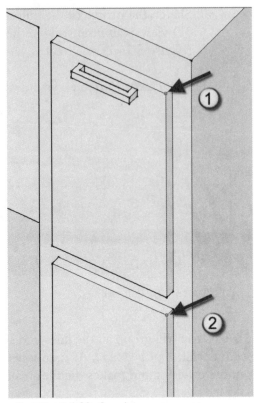

FIGURE 5-1.20 Copying component

Notice both pulls have been updated. This can save a lot of time!

Another right-click option is *Explode*. This allows you to reduce a *Component* back down to its basic elements and be changed differently from the other components. *Explode* only affects the selected elements.

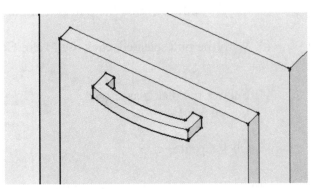

FIGURE 5-1.21 Editing a component

50. **Save** your model.

Before leaving the small desk you will take a look at one more thing. As SketchUp models get more complicated, they become harder to modify. However, the process follows the same general steps as with the 2D shapes.

Next, you will make the desk 8″ wider because the drawers are too narrow.

51. Switch to the front view.

52. Drag a selection window, going from left to right (Figure 5-1.22).

    a. This will not work properly if you pick in the opposite direction.

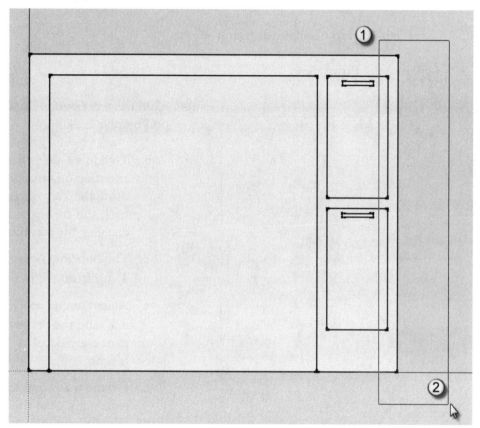

FIGURE 5-1.22 Selection window

53. **Move** the selected entities **8″** to the right.

54. Select the two pulls and move them **4″** to the right.

55. Switch to the **3D view**.

The model is now modified (Figure 5-1.23)!

56. **Save.**

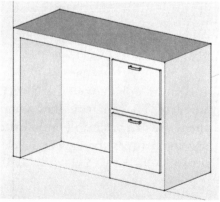

FIGURE 5-1.23 Complete

file name: **Small Dresser – 3D**

Often, it is ideal to add *Guides* to define an area rather than starting with lines. This is because lines can divide other lines and surfaces. You will use *Guides* to define the location of the drawer panels before sketching them.

57. **Open** the small dresser file and **Save As** to **Small Dresser – 3D**.

58. Use *Push/Pull* to make the dresser **4'-6"** tall.

59. Switch to the **Front** view.

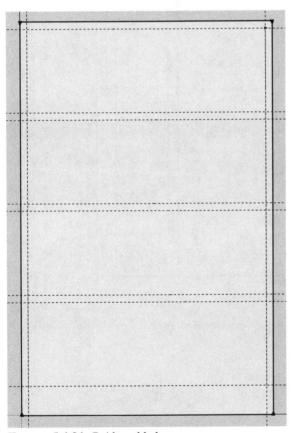

60. Add the ten *Guides* shown in Figure 5-1.24.

    a. To add a *Guide*: click and drag on an edge using the *Tape Measure* tool, and then type a distance for accuracy.

    b. The bottom *Guide* is **4"** up from the floor.

    c. All remaining spacing is **1"** and the drawer panels are equal in height.

    d. Do the math first to determine what the panel height should be.

FIGURE 5-1.24 Guides added

It is worth pointing out that SketchUp has a *Divide* tool, but it will not work in this case. To use it, you draw a line and then right-click on it, select **Divide** and then type in a value and press **Enter**, but this does not take into account the spacing between the drawer panels

With the guides in place you can quickly sketch the rectangles to define the edges of the drawer panels.

61. Use the **Rectangle** tool to define the perimeter of the drawer panels; simply snap to the intersection of the *Guides*.

62. Switch to the **3D view**.

Your model should look like Figure 5-1.25. Note that the *Guides* were created on the plane related to the edge used to define it. Thus, picking the grid intersections cause the rectangles to be created on the correct plane – which subsequently divides the surface. You are now ready to *Pull* the panels.

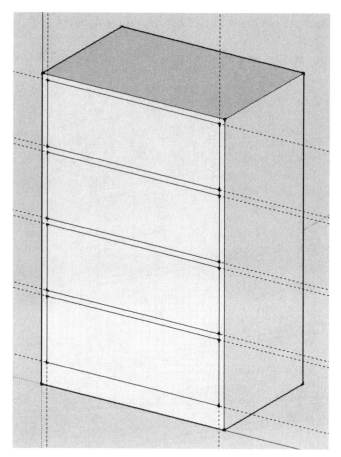

FIGURE 5-1.25 Rectangles added

63. Use **Push/Pull** to extrude the panels ½″ out from the surface.

You could leave the *Guides*, and even turn them off so they are not in the way. However, you will just delete them as they are no longer needed.

64. Select the **Eraser** tool and erase each of the *Guides* (by picking them).

The last step in completing the dresser is to add the pulls. You could recreate them from scratch, following the previous steps covered. However, it would be much faster to open the Small Desk – 3D file and copy one of the pulls to the *Clipboard*, and then *Paste* it into the dresser model. You will see that the pull will want to automatically "snap" to a surface due to the "glue to" setting when the *Component* was created.

65. Open the **Small Desk – 3D** file.

   a. If you browse to the file, using *Windows Explorer*, and then double-click the file, it will open another session of SketchUp. This will allow you to keep the dresser file open.

66. Select one of the pulls and press **Ctrl + C** to *Copy* it to the *Clipboard*.

67. Switch back to the dresser model and press **Ctrl + V** to *Paste* the pull into the current model.

Notice as you move your cursor around the screen, the pull follows the surface below your cursor. It wants to stick to a surface due to the "glue to" option setting when it was first created.

68. Place the pulls approximately as shown in Figure 5-1.26.

You may want to switch to a "front" view and then add *Guides* to get the first drawer set up. Once you have one drawer set, you can copy it from one drawer to the next until they all have pulls.

69. **Save** your model.

The dresser is done for now.

FIGURE 5-1.26 Pulls added

file name: **File Cabinet – 3D**

It is not always necessary to use the *Push/Pull* tool to create an extruded 3D element to represent something. In the case of this file cabinet, it is easier to simply sketch the lines on the face of the cabinet which nicely defines the two drawers. This model can be developed more quickly and is less of a burden on the overall model due the less complex geometry and fewer faces and surfaces.

Worrying about the complexity of this file cabinet may seem trivial now, but in a large model with several chairs, desks, file cabinets, etc., you can see how the overall number of faces and edges could really start to bog down even the fastest computer.

70. **Open** the *File Cabinet* file and **Save** it as **File Cabinet – 3D.skp**.

71. Develop the cabinet:

    a. **27″** high

    b. Pulls ***Copy/Pasted*** from previous file

    c. Use the ***Line*** tool to sketch the drawers:
        i. 1″ space on sides and top
        ii. 4″ space from bottom
        iii. Drawers are equal height

Your file cabinet should look like Figure 5-1.27. Even though new surfaces were made within the perimeter of the drawers, they do not need to be extruded into a 3D element.

72. **Save**.

At this point you have learned to use a majority of the tools typically used on a regular basis by the average SketchUp user. There certainly is more to learn, but you are well on your way!

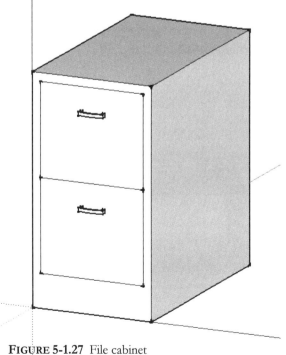

FIGURE 5-1.27 File cabinet

file name: Square Chair – 3D

In this exercise you will learn to modify geometry once it is 3D, making the backrest higher than the armrests.

73. Open the *Square Chair* file and **Save** it as **Square Chair – 3D.rvt**.

74. Use ***Push/Pull*** to make the armrest and backrest **26″** high (Figure 5-1.28).

75. Make the seat area **16″** high (Figure 5-1.29).

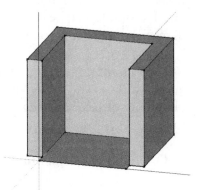

FIGURE 5-1.28 First extrusion

You now have the basic chair defined. However, you decide you would like to have a higher backrest and have the armrests curve down towards the front.

76. *Orbit*, *Pan* and *Zoom* in as needed, and then use the ***Line*** tool to add the two lines shown in Figure 5-1.30.

77. Use ***Push/Pull*** to make the back rest **4″** higher.

78. Select and erase the extraneous lines highlighted in Figure 5-1.31.

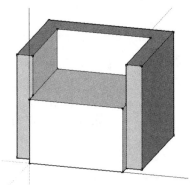

FIGURE 5-1.29 Second extrusion

Notice how the surface automatically heals itself when the lines are deleted.

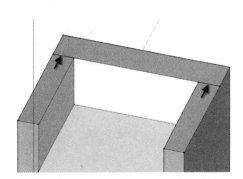

FIGURE 5-1.30 Lines added at backrest

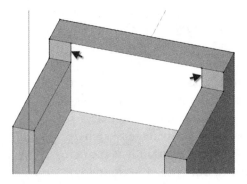

FIGURE 5-1.31 Lines to be erased

Now you will carve out a portion of the arm rests to make them curve down and toward the front of the chair. You will switch to a side view (this can also be done in a 3D view). In the side view you will sketch the profile of the portion you wish to exclude. The *Push/Pull* tool will be used to carve out the portion not needed, just like you did with the coffee table. But, before you use the *Push/Pull* tool, you will want to copy the profile over to the other armrest so you do not have to recreate it.

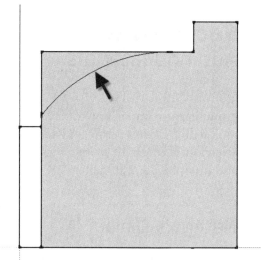

FIGURE 5-1.32 Adding arc to armrest

79. Switch to a side view and sketch an **Arc** similar to that shown in Figure 5-1.32.

80. Switch back to the **3D view** and **Copy** the arc to the other armrest (Figure 5-1.33).

81. Use **Push/Pull** to drag the new surface over to align with the other side of the armrest – this will cause the entire extrusion to be deleted; repeat for other side.

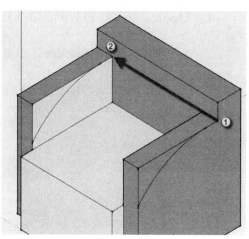

FIGURE 5-1.33 Copy arc to other armrest

As you can imagine, these types of modifications could continue to be made on this chair until it was exactly the way you want it. You may want to do a **Save As** once in a while to make it easy to go back to a previous design state if you get to a point where you are not happy with the design and want to go back.

Keep in mind that edges are required anytime there is a change in direction of adjacent surfaces, but not when surfaces are coplanar. So, the line at the top of the curved armrest is required in Figure 5-1.34, but the lines you deleted in Figure 5-1.31 were not.

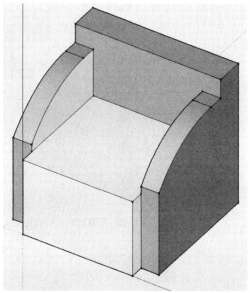

FIGURE 5-1.34 Use Push/Pull on armrest

Section 5-2
Adding Materials

Now that you know how to develop simple geometry, you will make the models look a little more realistic and add materials to them. SketchUp comes with a nice selection of materials from which to choose. It is also possible to scan a material and use it on your model!

Materials Dialog

The *Materials* dialog is used to select and add *Materials* to your model.

1. **Open** your SketchUp model: **Bookcase – 3D.skp**.

2. Select the **Paint Bucket** icon from the toolbar.

You are now in the *Paint Bucket* tool, and if it was not already open, the **Materials** dialog box pops up.

3. Pick **Wood** from the drop-down list in the *Materials* dialog box (Figure 5-2.1b).

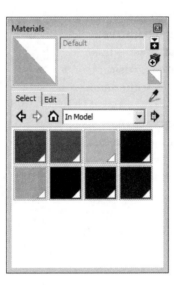

At this point you have ten wood materials from which to choose. Most of these are flooring materials (thus, they have lines in them to represent floor boards) and one material is OSB (Orientated Strand Board) which is not a finish material.

FIGURE 5-2.1A Materials

FIGURE 5-2.1B Materials list

4. Select **Wood_Cherry_Original** from the options listed under *Wood*.

5. Move your cursor into the model area and click on 2 different surfaces to apply the material (only click on two for now).

As you can see, the material is added to each surface as you click on it using the *Paint Bucket* tool. This is handy if you want to have the shelves be a different material than the frame of the unit. Similarly, if you need to add more refined materials, you can sketch additional lines to divide the surfaces into separate areas.

However, clicking each surface would take a bit of time. So the next steps will show you how to quickly add the material to the entire bookcase at once.

6. With the *Paint Bucket* tool still active, right-click on one of the surfaces and pick **Select → All Connected**; the same *Layer* would also work in this case (Figure 5-2.2).

7. Click on one of the surfaces to apply the material to all faces.

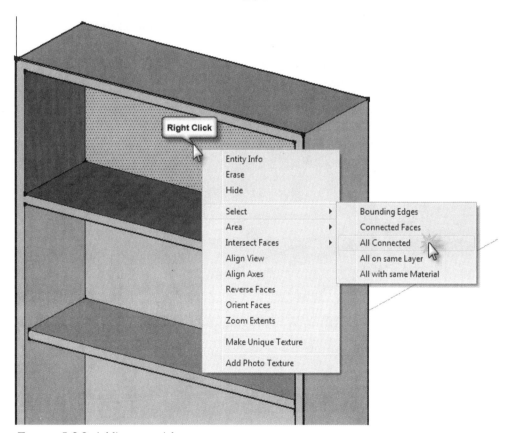

FIGURE 5-2.2 Adding materials

The wood material has now been added to the entire bookcase. The materials are designed to be real-world scale, so you need to model things the same size they would be in the real world. Otherwise, things such as bricks will not look right.

8. **Save** your **Bookcase – 3D** file before moving on.

In the next steps you will add a transparent material to give the appearance of glass. This will be a glass panel in the center of the coffee table.

9. **Open** the **Coffee Table – 3D** file.

The first thing you will do is carve out an area for the glass panel in the center of the table.

10. Switch to the **Top** view and *Offset* the outer edge inward **3″**.

11. Switch back to the **3D** view and use *Push/Pull* to remove the center of the table; click and drag the surface down until it aligns with the bottom edge of the table top.

12. Use the *Select* tool to pick the remaining surface and **Delete** it.

You model should now look like Figure 5-2.3.

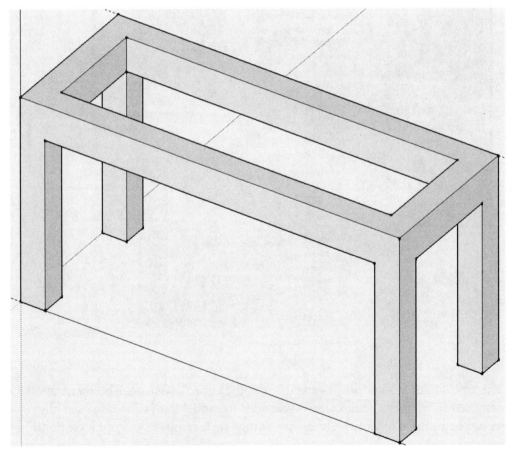

FIGURE 5-2.3 Center of table removed

Before modeling the glass, now is a good time to quickly make everything a wood material.

13. Using the steps recently covered, make all elements material: **Wood_Board_Cork**.

The material may not actually be cork, but the color might be the closest thing to what you are thinking, and that will work for now.

Next, you will create a surface at the top of the new opening to represent the glass. This can easily be done in the 3D view.

14. Select the **Rectangle** tool and then pick two opposite corners of the opening in the center of the table (Figure 5-2.4).

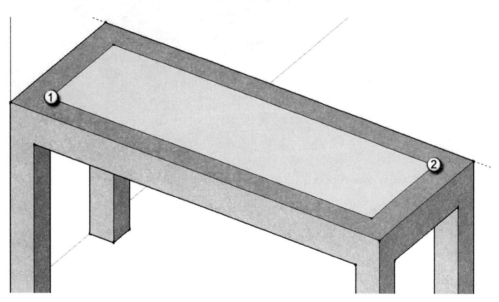

FIGURE 5-2.4 Adding surface at opening

As mentioned earlier, SketchUp does not allow lines to overlap. So the lines for the rectangle were immediately deleted, but they caused SketchUp to check and see if any enclosed areas need a surfaced.

15. Use the *Paint Bucket* tool to set the new surface to **Translucent \ Translucent_Glass_Corrugated**.

The glass material is now added to the coffee table (Figure 5-2.5). There are a number of things you could do at this point. You could select the surface and copy (via **Move + Ctrl**) the surface down ½" inch to give the appearance of thickness.

You can also right-click on the glass surface, and select **Texture → Position**. This gives you the option to rotate and adjust the scale of the material.

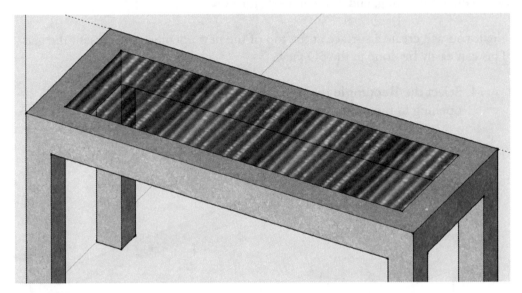

FIGURE 5-2.5 Glass material added to table

Just in case you changed something, the following needs to be set so your screen matches the screen shots in this book.

- View menu
  - Edge Style
    - Edges (checked)
    - Profiles (checked)
    - Extensions (checked)
  - Face Style
    - Shaded with Textures (checked)

Try **X-ray** and **Back Edges** before moving on, and then set things back to the defaults listed above.

As you did with the desk, try adjusting the overall length and width of the table. You have to use very specific selection windows to make this type of modification.

16. **Save** your model.

This concludes the basic introduction to SketchUp. You will learn a few new things later in the book, when you start the design of the interior fit out. However, you are already off to a good start.

Many SketchUp users buy a book just on SketchUp and read a portion of material equivalent to that which has been covered thus far and just learn the rest on their own – using trial and error plus the Help system. Of course, some would benefit from a more advanced book, but what you have learned thus far is almost everything you need to know to do the type of hybrid design that is promoted in this text. That is, use SketchUp to create a framework to establish the existing conditions (if any) and perspective. Then sketch over a printout of the SketchUp model to more quickly come up with design iterations.

Once a more formal design is developed, you could continue to develop the SketchUp model, but you would probably be better off moving to something such as Autodesk Revit Architecture at that point.

The goal should be to develop many rough design options early on and not waste too much time trying to add too much detail or create a masterpiece work of art. The more variations you explore, the more likely you are to find an ideal design solution to the problem at hand.

17. Use the techniques learned here to create the remaining 3D models based on the 2D sketches created in the previous chapter.

18. Apply materials to all remaining models. Try adding multiple materials to one or two of them.

19. **Save** all files before moving on.

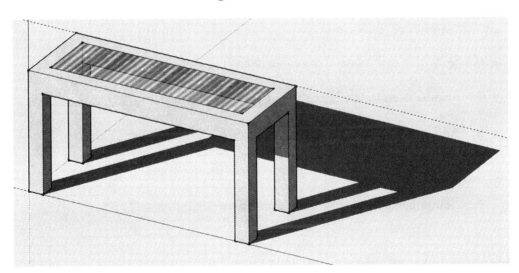

FIGURE 5-2.6 Shadows turned on via the View menu

Self-Exam:

The following questions can be used as a way to check your knowledge of this lesson. The answers can be found at the bottom of this page.

1. The *Offset* tool quickly creates a parallel line. (T/F)

2. Edges are required when adjacent surfaces are not coplanar. (T/F)

3. Lines cannot overlap. (T/F)

4. Tool used to add materials: _____ _____.

5. Tool used to extrude a surface into 3D: _____.

Review Questions:

The following questions may be assigned by your instructor as a way to assess your knowledge of this section. Your instructor has the answers to the review questions.

1. Materials cannot be rotated. (T/F)

2. The "face style" needs to be *Shaded with Textures* to see the materials. (T/F)

3. The only way to add a material is to click on every surface. (T/F)

4. Once a surface has been extruded, it cannot be modified. (T/F)

5. Erasing an edge (i.e., line) between two coplanar surfaces results in the two surfaces becoming one. (T/F)

6. SketchUp can model things accurately. (T/F)

7. Feature used to combine the pull into one element: _____.

8. Adding *Guides* helps define pick points for the *Line* tool. (T/F)

9. The *Push/Pull* tool only works on surfaces, not edges. (T/F)

10. Components cannot be *Copy/Pasted* between models. (T/F)

Adobe Photoshop Introduction

This chapter will introduce you to Adobe Photoshop. You will study the User Interface and learn how to open and exit an image file and adjust the view of the image on the screen. It is recommended that the student spend an ample amount of time learning this material, as it will greatly enhance your ability to progress smoothly through subsequent chapters.

Section 6-1
What is Adobe Photoshop used for?

Adobe Photoshop is a professional image editing application. Although it has a lot of competition, some even being free, Photoshop is still the leading software package among graphic designers, interior designers and architects when it comes to image editing. This dominant market share is partly due to its being around for so long. It was created over 20 years ago by two brothers, Thomas and John Knoll. It being around as long as it has may have helped build momentum in development and loyal customers, but that alone is not why it does so well overall. The program is continually being developed to run faster and offer new features.

Learn more at the Adobe website:
http://www.adobe.com/products/photoshop/photoshop/whatisphotoshop/

Why use Photoshop?

As just mentioned, Photoshop is a feature rich program! It is worth investing your time in learning, as many design firms have this software so this knowledge will allow you to hit the ground running (if you are still in school), or help you to develop your skills in order to better communicate your designs and become more valuable to your employer (if you are currently employed in a design firm).

Photoshop is developed by Adobe. With a solid company such as Adobe behind Photoshop, you can be fairly confident the program will be well supported and updated for years to come.

In addition to Photoshop, Adobe makes many other graphics oriented applications. These include:
- Acrobat
- Dreamweaver
- InDesign
- Illustrator
- Soundbooth
- *Adobe Reader*
- *Adobe Flash Player*

The last two items in the list above are free programs which are installed on virtually every computer in the world. Adobe Reader allows you to view and print PDF files (while Acrobat creates and organizes PDF's) and Adobe Flash Player is a web browser plug in used to animate portions of web sites.

If you have not yet heard of these other Adobe applications, you certainly will as you continue to advance in your design career. Some may be used directly by you, a marketing department or a consultant.

Hopefully this couple of pages will impress upon you the "gold standard" which Adobe has earned in the graphics and architectural design community.

Photoshop versus other Applications?

There are many alternatives to Photoshop, with some even being free. Some of these include (and keep in mind, many others exist):
- Corel PaintShop Photo Pro
- Techsmith's SnagIt
- Gimp *
- Google Picasa *
- Photoscape *   *= free*

These alternative applications, especially the free ones, offer some of the tools and features found in Photoshop. However, you would likely have to use a combination of programs to get close to the full feature set found in Photoshop.

Design firms often shy away from the free applications. These free programs either forbid commercial use, use advertising or are not supported or upgraded often enough.

Photoshop CS5 versus Photoshop Elements version?

While the Photoshop **CS5** version is aimed at professionals, Adobe also provides a "home user" level product called Photoshop **Elements**. This product is meant to compete with the lower cost photo editing products which offer a nice array of tools at a fraction of the price. Photoshop Elements is a very powerful program for the price (approx. $100), as compared to one of the "full" versions of Photoshop; CS5 is approx. $700.00 and CS5 Extended is approx. $1000.00. In fact, some building design firms will provide Photoshop CS5 to the marketing department and a few high level users, but others only get Elements when they just need the ability to do the following

- Crop images
- Adjust brightness and contrast
- Add text
- Apply filters (e.g., watercolor, posterize, etc.)
- Touchup images
    - Using the *Paintbrush* tool
    - Using the *Clone* tool
- Add entourage
    - Snip people and props out of other images and place them in your design.
- Redeye and Whiten teeth!
    - Not really needed for interior design but interesting none the less.

Mac versus PC?

Photoshop, like SketchUp, has been designed to work on either the Apple Macintosh (MAC) or Microsoft Windows based computer system (PC). Most Architectural and Interior Design offices tend to favor the PC due to cost and general availability of other programs geared towards the industry. However, there is not much that cannot be done on a Mac, especially with its ability to run Windows when using *Boot Camp* or a virtual environment.

Occasionally you will see a feature supported only on the Mac or PC. One example relates to a new Mac technology supported called **Multitouch**.

All screen shots in this book are from a PC running Windows 7 64bit – using the 64bit version of Photoshop CS5 Extended. Please note that most everything required to be done by the reader can be done using just about any version of Photoshop (even the Photoshop Elements versions for the most part); the main difference will be where the tool is found and the user interface. If the reader is using a Mac or another version of Windows, there might be slight differences in some screen shots. However, the main Photoshop *User Interface* should be the same; the User Interface is covered next.

Section 6-2
Overview of the Photoshop User Interface

As with SketchUp or any other software, the first step is figuring out the **User Interface** (UI). Photoshop is organized very much like other programs. It has menus across the top, toolbars that can float or be docked to a side, and a large area in the middle to do your work. Photoshop has opted not to implement the *Ribbon* as a number of other software makers have (e.g., Microsoft and Autodesk).

The image below highlights the primary components of the *User Interface*. The following pages provide a brief overview of these components.

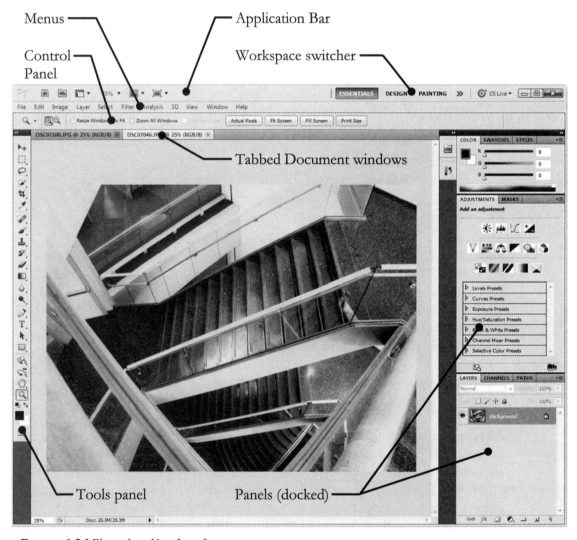

FIGURE 6-2.1 Photoshop User Interface

Application Bar:

The *Application Bar* displays few convenient tools on the left (this is similar to what other programs call the *Quick Access Toolbar*). These tools provide links to the *Bridge* application (for organizing images), extras, zoom level, document arrangement and screen mode (standard, full with menus and full); screen mode allows you to make the working area as large as possible on your monitor. On the far right you have the *Workspace* switcher (see the next item below for more on this) and the typical controls for the applications window: minimize, maximize/ restore down, close.

FIGURE 6-2.2 Application Bar

Workspace Switcher:

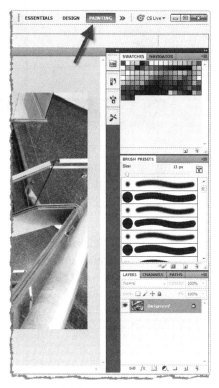

The *Workspace* switcher allows you to quickly change part of the *User Interface* to show tools related to a certain type of task. In Figure 6-2.1 the *Essentials* workspace is selected. Thus the panels are set to common ones (color, adjustments, layers). When you select *Painting*, for example, on the application bar, you see the panels change to show information which is more useful while using the paint tools (Figure 6-2.3).

Clicking the chevron (i.e., the icon to the right of *Painting* with two arrows pointing to the right) shows more *Workspace* options and customization tools.

FIGURE 6-2.3
Workspace & Panels

Panels:

Panels provide options related to modifying your images. These panels are either made visible by toggling the *Workspace* or via the Window menu. Each *Panel* has a pop-up menu option in the upper right corner and icons across the bottom; it can also have multiple tabs across the top to toggle between related information. Panels can be docked (i.e., attached to a side) as shown, or floating. Floating is nice when you have a two monitor system – a working area and a separate tool area.

Menus (Windows OS Only):

Below the *Application Bar* are several pull-down menus. When clicked on, these menus reveal a list of commands. The menus are a way to break the list of commands down into smaller, task specific lists. A *menu* is closed when a command is selected or the **Esc** key is pressed.

FIGURE 6-2.4 Menus

Notice in the image provided (Figure 6-2.4), the *Image* menu is expanded. Some items in the list are fly-out menus. A fly-out menu can be identified by the black arrow pointing to the right (*Mode*, *Adjustments*, etc.). Hovering over a fly-out menu item reveals another sub-set of menu options. Whenever a command or toggle has a keyboard shortcut, it is listed on the right. Finally, any command or toggles which are not relevant to the current tool or image file will be grayed out to avoid any confusion (e.g., *Trap...*).

When reference is made to a command within the menu system, it will be shown as such:

Image → Image Rotation → 90° CW *or* Image → Auto Contrast

This means, click the **Image** menu, then hover on **Image Rotation** and then click the **90° CW** command in the fly-out list.

Control Panel:

Below the *menus* is the *Control Panel*. This is an area you will want to keep your eye on while learning Photoshop as it provides important options and settings related to the current tool, or command, being used. Another way to put it is the *Control Panel* is context sensitive. That is, it changes relative to the current tool. Notice a few examples shown below.

Move tool (shortcut: V)

Select tool (shortcut: M)

Brush tool (shortcut: B)

Erase tool (shortcut: E)

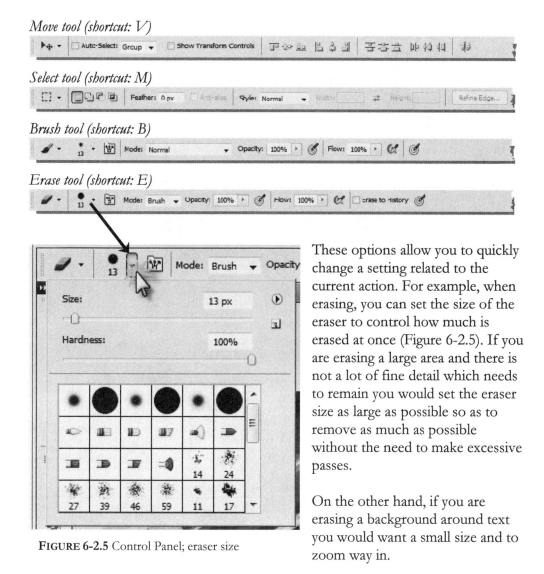

FIGURE 6-2.5 Control Panel; eraser size

These options allow you to quickly change a setting related to the current action. For example, when erasing, you can set the size of the eraser to control how much is erased at once (Figure 6-2.5). If you are erasing a large area and there is not a lot of fine detail which needs to remain you would set the eraser size as large as possible so as to remove as much as possible without the need to make excessive passes.

On the other hand, if you are erasing a background around text you would want a small size and to zoom way in.

Many of the options on the *Control Panel* are straightforward; some will take a little experimenting or a trip to the Help system. You will learn about some of these options as you work through the book.

Tabbed Document windows:

The tabs below the *Control Panel* allow you to quickly toggle between open documents. You can also press **Ctrl + Tab** on the keyboard to cycle through them. As you can see in Figure 6-2.6, right-clicking on a tab reveals a pop-up menu – the options are self-evident.

The tab lists the file name, its current zoom factor and the color mode.

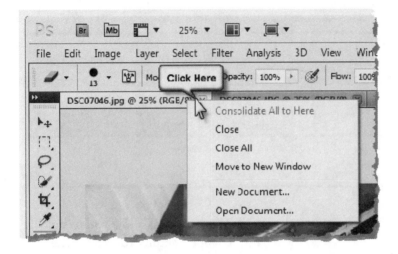

FIGURE 6-2.6 Right clicking on a tab

Tools Panel (toolbar):

The *Tools Panel* provides a small graphical image and is only a single click away as compared to the text only option multiple clicks away in the menu system.

Most tools have multiple related options; these all have a small black right-triangle in the lower right corner of the icon.

Clicking on the icon starts the tool. Clicking, and holding down the mouse button reveals the pop-up menu for the related tool (Figure 6-2.7). When a related tool is selected, it temporarily moves to the top of the "stack" of icons. This makes it easy to use it again. The tool will remain at the top until another tool is selected or the program is closed.

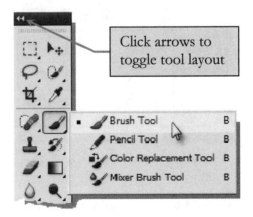

FIGURE 6-2.7 Tool fly out

Panels:

The *Panels* are similar to the *Control Panel* in that they contain settings and options to analyze and manipulate the current image. The difference between the two is that the *Control Panel* changes, while the *Panels* are hard-wired for a specific task. As previously mentioned, the *Workspace* switcher is setup to quickly show the most commonly used *Panels*. Looking at the *Window* pull-down menu, you can see there are a lot of *Panels* available. Try clicking one that is not checked to turn it on; and then click it again to turn it off.

Panels can take up a lot of space, so when they are docked to the side of the application window they can be collapsed to get them out of the way, maximizing screen space, but still only a single click away. When you have a multi-monitor setup, you can have all your *Panels* on the second monitor, leaving the main screen to maximize the working area.

Each *Panel* is slightly different, but they all follow the same general organizational structure. The image below highlights just a few of the many options available on the **Layers** Panel (Figure 6-2.8).

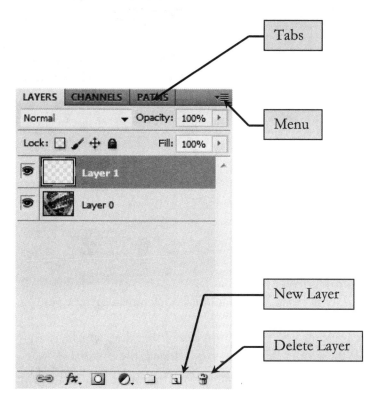

FIGURE 6-2.8 Panel overview

Section 6-3
New, Open, Save and Close

Starting **Photoshop** works like most any other program. You can either:

- Locate an image or Photoshop file using *Windows Explorer* (aka, *My Computer* or just *Computer*) and then double-click on the file. This will cause Photoshop to start and then the selected file will open.

  > ***FYI:*** *This assumes Photoshop was the last graphics editing/viewing program installed. If so, the computer's operating system will have the various graphics files associated with Photoshop and know to use that program when a file is double-clicked on.*

- You can open Photoshop and then create a new file or open one previously created.

Photoshop can open a large number of different graphical file formats. While in the **File → Open** dialog you can see the options at the bottom in the drop down list for *Files of type* (Figure 6-3.1). So if anyone wants to send you a file, or vice versa, you can look at this list and make sure the format is something you can use.

In addition to being able to open many file formats, Photoshop can also convert an image file into many different formats. This is done by opening a file and then using **File → Save As**. Once in the *Save As* dialog, you can specify a new file name and also change the format at the bottom; using the drop-down list next to *Files of type*. This would allow you to, for example, save a TIFF file as a JPG in order to reduce the file size and send it via email.

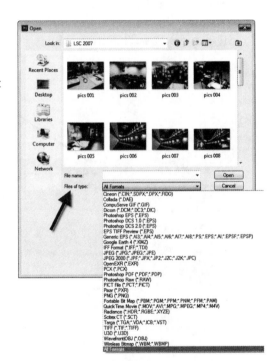

FIGURE 6-3.1 Open dialog; file types

Most raster image files are basically just a collection of colored dots which, together, form an image. If these dots (or pixels) are changed, the original information is lost. For example, if you add text to a raster image, save it and close it, the portion of the image beneath the text is gone. You cannot open the image again later and move the text. The text is not even selectable (at least not easily). This is why Photoshop has its own file format (PSD) which can be used to preserve the original image (in most cases) and maintain functionality of things like text – that is, being able to select the text and even edit it. One of the ways this enhanced functionality is accomplished is by using something called *Layers*. So when txt is added, it goes on a *Layer* rather than being merged with the image and replacing pixels which were part of the image. These *Layers* can be rearranged in the *Layers* list to control which element is in front of another. You will learn more about *Layers* later on.

Photoshop can open a raster image and then save it as a Photoshop file. Later, after the image is finished, you can then save the image back to the original format, or any other supported format, for use in MS Word, on a website or most anywhere else. Not too many programs can use the Photoshop format directly.

Opening Photoshop itself:

Photoshop can be opened from the desktop icon or from the Start menu. If you have a 64 Bit operating system, you may have two icons, one of which says 64 Bit (as seen in the icon to the right). For this book it does not matter which you choose.

Adobe
Photoshop
CS5 (64 Bit)

1. Start Photoshop: **Start → All Programs → Adobe Photoshop CS5**

If you will be using Photoshop a lot, you can pin the icon to the *Start Menu* (Figure 6-3.2) or even to the *Task Bar*. Simply right-click on the icon, from step 1, before clicking on it, and select one of the pin options.

Pinning the Photoshop icon to the *Task Bar* gives you the quickest access to the program as you don't even have to go into the *Start Menu*. When an icon is pinned to the *Task Bar* it appears as shown at the bottom of Figure 6-3.2. When the program is running, the icon looks like it is pressed in, as shown, and when not running it looks like the *Internet Explorer* icon just to the right of the *Start Menu*.

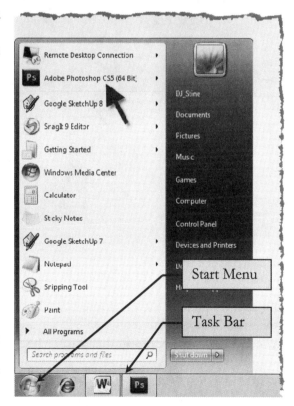

FIGURE 6-3.2 Start menu; pinned icons

Opening Files:

Now that you have Photoshop open you will open a few sample files.

2. From the **File** menu click **Open**.

    TIP: Pressing **Ctrl + O** *will also get you to the Open dialog.*

3. In the *Open* dialog, browse to your CD/DVD drive and select **School Atrium – Looking West.JPG**.

    TIP: If you cannot locate the DVD that came with this textbook, you can substitute any image file.

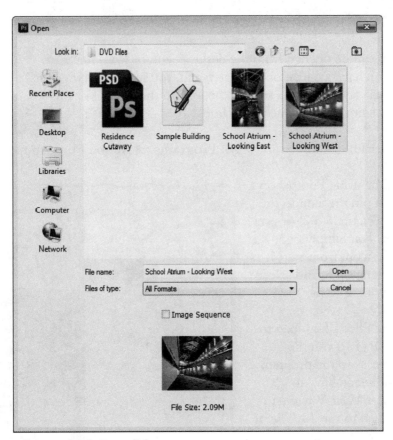

FIGURE 6-3.3 Open dialog

You may have noticed you do not see the file extension listed. If you hover your cursor over the document icon, you can see additional information popup which includes the file type (JPEG in this case).

Because **Files of type** is set to *All Formats* you see all files in the current folder – even files Photoshop cannot open. Notice the SketchUp file is listed here; if you tried to open it you would get an error because Photoshop has not been programmed to understand that type of file.

4. Click the **Open** button.

You are now viewing the image! Your screen should look similar to Figure 6-3.4.

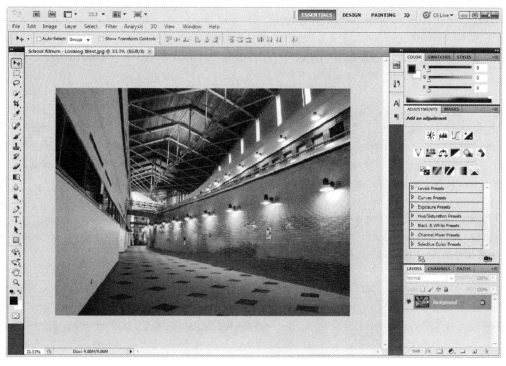

FIGURE 6-3.4 First image file opened

If you want to open a file which was recently opened, you can quickly access it via **File → Open Recent**. This opens a sub-menu which lists the most recent files Photoshop has opened. This can save a lot of time if your files are buried in sub-folders.

When using Windows 7, you can also quickly start the program and open a recent file right from the *Start* menu, as shown in Figure 6-3.5.

FIGURE 6-3.5 Windows 7 option

Opening Multiple Files:

Photoshop allows you to have multiple files open at once. This makes it easy to work on several presentation boards of a project. You can quickly copy elements, such as the project title, between files. Next, you will open another file and see how easy it is to switch between them.

5. Using the previous steps covered, open **School Atrium – Looking East.jpg** from the CD.

Your screen should now look similar to Figure 6-3.6. Notice the *Document Tabs* just above the image (and below the *Control Panel*). These tabs list the file name, the current zoom factor (relative to the actual image size) and the color mode. Notice the current image's tab is highlighted. The next steps will show you how easy it is to switch between the open image files.

The initial zoom factor shown in the tab, and in the lower right corner of the *Application Window*, will vary depending on the size and resolution of your monitor and if the program is maximized or not.

FIGURE 6-3.6 Second image file opened

6. Click the **School Atrium – Looking West** tab to make its contents current.

You should now be viewing the first image file you opened.

The opened files are also listed at the bottom of the *Window* pull-down menu and you can toggle the current document there as well, but this is not as efficient as using the tabs.

Closing Files:

Now that you have some files open, you will learn how to close them. This can be done in a couple of different ways.

7. Click the "**x**" in the *Document Tab* for the **West** image (Figure 6-3.7).

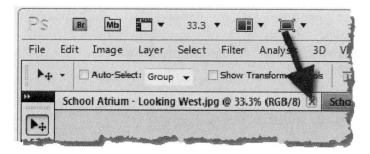

FIGURE 6-3.7 Closing a document

If no changes were made to the file, it will close with no prompts. When changes have been made, and the file has not yet been saved, Photoshop will prompt you to save changes; click *Yes* to save changes, or *No* to discard changes. DO NOT SAVE AT THIS TIME.

The important thing to know about closing a file is you will not accidentally lose any work if you forgot to save before closing. This is because you will always get a prompt to save before the file is closed – if the file contains any unsaved modifications. Of course, if you accidentally click *No* when prompted to save, you will lose work!

Finally, you may also close the current document via **File → Close** (or **Ctrl + W**). However, the document tab method is quicker.

Saving Files:

You will not actually save at this time, but to save the current document you select **File → Save** or press **Ctrl + S** on the keyboard. If the file has not previously been saved, you will be prompted for a name and location.

New Files:

While at times you will simply open an existing image file and add text and adjust colors, there will be situations where you want to start a new file – with a blank slate. Maybe you want to set up a common project title and make copies upon which you will compose images for a presentation. Photoshop supports this with the *New* command.

8. Select **File → New…**

You are now in the *New* dialog box (Figure 6-3.8).

Here you have several options. You can enter a name, the size and resolution of the image and background contents (e.g., white or transparent).

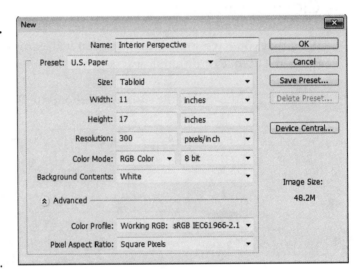

9. For the name, type: **Interior Perspective**.

FIGURE 6-3.8 New dialog

10. Change the *Preset* to **U.S. Paper**.

    a. The *Preset* will default to "clipboard" if there is graphical information in the clipboard.

11. Select **Tabloid** for the Size option (this equals 11″x17″ paper).

You will notice there are only two paper sizes available. However, you can type in any size you want. For example, you might enter 34″ (width) and 22″ (height) to set up a presentation board.

12. Click **OK** to create a new file.

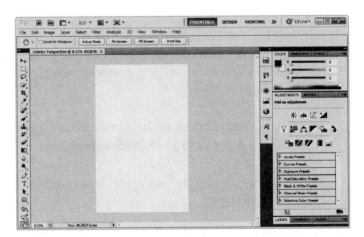

FIGURE 6-3.9 New 11″x17″ document

Section 6-4
Viewing Images in Photoshop

Learning to zoom and pan in a Photoshop document is essential to using the editing tools covered later. We will review a few tools and techniques now so you are ready to use them with the first exercise.

You will select a sample file from the CD that came with this textbook.

1. If Photoshop is not already open, open Photoshop and then select **File → Open**.

2. If the "west" school image is not already open from the last section, browse to **School Atrium – Looking East.jpg**.

Using the Zoom Tool:

First you will use the *Zoom* tool to get a closer look at the library sign in the lower right corner of the image. Although the *Zoom* tools are available from the *View* menu, you will learn to use this feature from the *Tools Panel* and right-clicking the mouse as these are more efficient.

3. From the *Tool Panel* select the **Zoom** tool (or type **Z**).

> *TIP: If your* Tool Panel *has accidentally been turned off, you can turn it back on via the* **Window → Tools** *toggle.*

Now, with the *Zoom* tool active, your cursor has changed to a magnifying glass with a plus in it – the plus means the magnification will be increased when you click or drag a window.

At this point you can click within the image to zoom in on that area, or you can draw a window. Dragging a window is quicker if you know the extent of the area you want to view, as this area will immediately fill the screen. On the other hand, clicking just zooms in a little bit with each click.

FIGURE 6-4.1
Tool panel; Zoom tool

4. With the *Zoom* tool active, click directly on the **Library** sign about four times until the image is magnified approximately as shown in Figure 6-4.2. *Your image does not have to be exactly the same magnification.*

The area where you click is magnified on the screen. Keep in mind the image has not changed at all (e.g., resolution, cropping, DPI, etc.); rather you are just looking a little closer at a portion of the image.

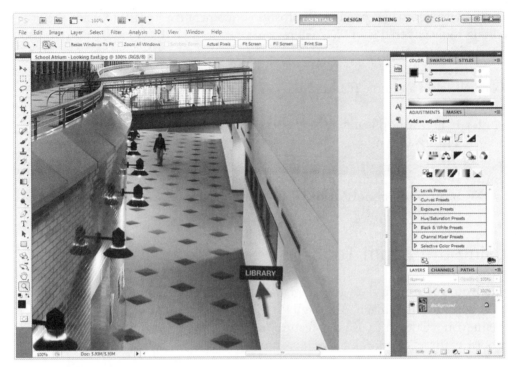

FIGURE 6-4.2 Image zoomed in on the "Library" sign

If you zoomed in a little too far, you can hold down the **Alt** key on the keyboard, while the *Zoom* tool is active, to zoom out.

5. With the *Zoom* tool active, hold down the **Alt** key on the keyboard, and click the mouse twice near the **Library** sign.

Notice the cursor changes to a magnifying glass with a minus sign in it when the **Alt** key is held down.

You should now see more of the image, but not all of it. If you want to quickly see the entire image again, you can right-click and select *Fit on Screen*.

6. While still in the *Zoom* tool, right-click anywhere on the image and select *Fit on Screen* (Figure 6-4.3).

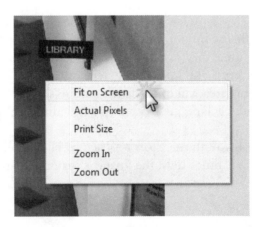

FIGURE 6-4.3 Zoom tool; Right-click options

You should now be viewing the entire image again!

Notice the other *Zoom* options in the right-click menu (Figure 6-4.3). *Actual Pixels* means the zoom factor will be 100%. Remember, these right-click options only appear when the *Zoom* tool is active.

All of these options just covered are also available on the *Control Panel* while the *Zoom* tool is active, plus a few others.

Now you will try the window option for zooming. You will inspect the closest light fixture mounted to the exposed roof framing above.

7. With the *Zoom* tool active, click and drag the cursor to define a rectangle similar to that shown in Figure 6-4.4.

The light fixture now fills the screen (Figure 6-4.5). The proportions might be a little different than the window you selected due to the proportions of your application window and monitor.

FIGURE 6-4.4 Zoom tool; window option

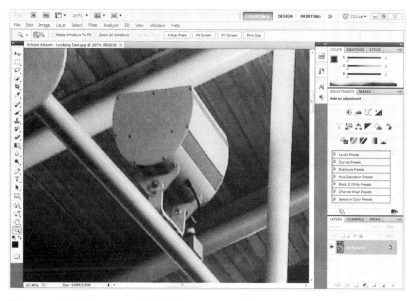

FIGURE 6-4.5 Zoom tool; light fixture magnified

Using the Hand Tool:

Now that you are zoomed in on the light fixture you decide you want to pan over to look at the detail of the structural connection just to the left of the light fixture. Maybe you are considering color or material options for a remodel project. This can easily be done with the *Hand* tool rather than zooming out and then back in again.

8. While still zoomed in on the light fixture, select the **Hand** tool (or type **H**).

Notice the cursor now changes to a hand. The cursor changing is a type of heads-up reminder as to which tool is current.

FIGURE 6-4.6
Tool panel; Hand tool

9. Click towards the left side of the image and drag (i.e., hold down the mouse button) your cursor towards the right. Repeat until you are viewing the portion of the image shown in Figure 6-4.7.

FIGURE 6-4.7 Image repositioned using the hand tool

While using the *Hand* tool you still have access to a few *Zoom* options on the *Control Panel* and via the right-click.

Section 6-5
Help System

Using the Help system is often required when you are having problems or trying to do something advanced. This section will present a basic overview of the Help system so you can find your way around when needed. It is important that you don't skip this section as it can help reduce your stress level when/if you run into problems.

1. Open Photoshop, if not already open; it does not matter if you have a file open or not.

2. Select **Help → Photoshop Help…**

A separate program, called **Adobe Community Help**, is launched (Figure 6-5.1). Unlike some programs, this can remain open even after Photoshop is closed.

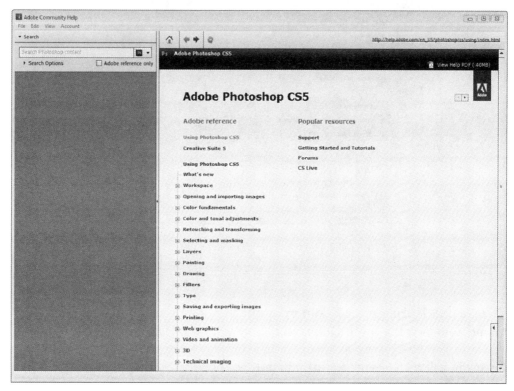

FIGURE 6-5.1 Adobe Community Help screen

The interface is straightforward. You can search or click the links to find information. You have **Home**, **Back** and **Forward** buttons similar to your internet browser.

Notice the internet address in the upper right; this is where the information you are viewing is coming from. This, of course, means you need to have internet access to view this information. The good thing about this is Adobe can correct or enhance the information anytime and you will instantly have access to it.

You will try both the search and link options to view information about the *Zoom* and *Hand* tools you just learned about.

3.   In the main window, click the following links (Figure 6-5.2):
     Workspace → Viewing images → Zoom in or out

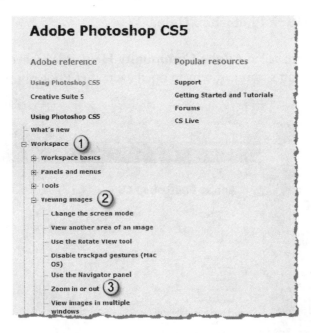

FIGURE 6-5.2 Help system; zoom in or out

You are now looking at the **Zoom in or out** section of the *Help* system. Take a minute to review this information to enhance your knowledge of this feature.

Now you will try to search for information on the *Hand* tool.

4.   In the search box, type **Hand tool** and then press **Enter** (Figure 6-5.3).

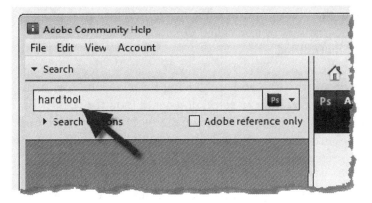

FIGURE 6-5.3 Help system; search option

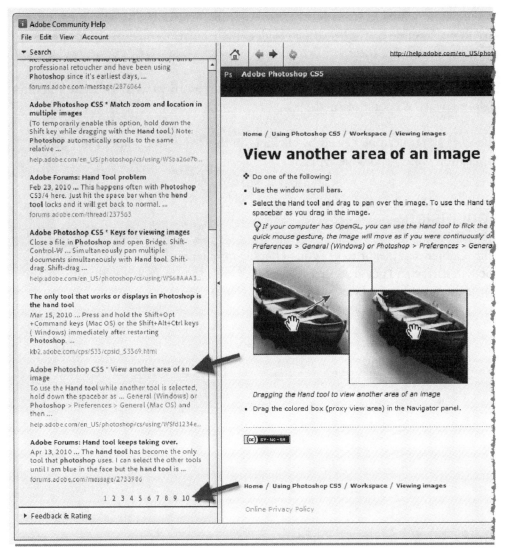

FIGURE 6-5.4 Help system; search results

Take a minute to read about the "flick" option while using the *Hand* tool and when your computer has the graphics option called OpenGL. This is similar to what you experience on a Smartphone.

Sometimes the ideal piece of information you are looking for is not the first item in the search results. In this case you have to scroll down and look for it, possibly opening a few options to see if they relate to what you are looking for. There may be many options depending on what you entered in the search box. In this example, you can see there are several "pages" of search results (Figure 6-5.4).

Notice, below each search result in the list, you see an internet address. Not all the information is coming directly from Adobe unless you check "Adobe reference only" (Figure 6-5.3). However, the non-Adobe information can be very useful. Some of the options are even posts from user forums. This means you might be looking at information from another end user like yourself. This also means you should not assume that information is absolutely correct – just use some caution when accessing user forum information.

If you click the **Home** icon, the main screen will return to what you saw when the Help interface was first opened.

The *Help* system can be closed by clicking on the "X" in the upper right of the application window, or File → Exit.

Conclusion:

This chapter was meant to get you generally familiar with Photoshop and how to open an image and get around it using the *Zoom* and *Hand* tools. This information is just the tip of the iceberg.

Self-Exam:

The following questions can be used as a way to check your knowledge of this lesson. The answers can be found at the bottom of this page.

1. The Photoshop Elements is free. (T/F)

2. The *Application Bar* changes depending on which tool is active. (T/F)

3. The easiest way to switch between open images is via the document tabs just below the *Control Panel*. (T/F)

4. The _____ on _____ option quickly makes the entire image visible on the screen.

5. Use the _____ tool to change which part of the image you are viewing; without changing the size on screen

Review Questions:

The following questions may be assigned by your instructor as a way to assess your knowledge of this section. Your instructor has the answers to the review questions.

1. Photoshop is the leading image editing software. (T/F)

2. The *Help* system may not be up to date. (T/F)

3. Photoshop only works on a PC, not a Mac. (T/F)

4. Several *Panels* can be turned on via the *Window* menu. (T/F)

5. Many tools have a keyboard shortcut. (T/F)

6. The icon with the hand picture (🖐) allows you to _____ within a model.

7. The extension for the Photoshop format: _____.

8. Click the _____ on the document tab to close the file.

9. Using the *Zoom* tool changes the file. (T/F)

10. The *Zoom* tool must be active to see the **Fit on Screen** option. (T/F)

Notes:

Adobe Photoshop Introduction – Part II

This chapter will build upon what you learned in the previous chapter on Adobe Photoshop. Here you will learn to edit images, including adding text, changing colors, cropping, rotating, selecting, and more. These tools will aid you in developing the presentation materials in the design project at the end of the book.

Section 7-1
Selection Tools and Color

Photoshop has several ways in which you can select portions of an image. You will learn a few of these ways in this chapter. You use selection tools to define areas to be removed or modified – for example, erase or change the color.

The first thing you will do is open an image and adjust the wall color. Maybe a client wants you to present a few options; they need to update the interiors and do not like the white walls anymore (Figure 7-1.1). Here you will use Photoshop's selection tools to select the wall and then adjust the selected area's color.

You will also look at the image size and resolution, the *Rotate* tool and more!

FIGURE 7-1.1 Image to be used in this exercise

1. Open the image file **College Library – Wall Detail.jpg**, found on the CD, using Photoshop (Figure 7-1.2).

FIGURE 7-1.2 Wall Detail image opened

Rotating an image

The first thing you need to do is rotate the image. This is a simple task in Photoshop. Keep in mind everything you do in Photoshop only exists in your computer's RAM (random access memory) until you select *Save* (this was discussed in more detail in Chapter 1). So, if you want this modification (i.e., rotated image) to be permanent, you need to save at some point.

2. Select **Image → Image Rotation → 90° CCW** (Figure 7-1.3).

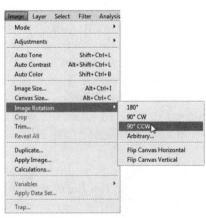

The image is now right-side-up. You do not need to save just yet.

If you clicked the wrong option, you can press **Ctrl + Z** on the keyboard to **Undo** the last command and try again. If your file ever gets really messed up, you can close it without saving and start over.

FIGURE 7-1.3 Image Rotation

Image Quality

It is important to have a basic understanding of image quality. This will help you to achieve acceptable results in a reasonable amount of time. Notice we did not say the "best" results in the "least" amount of time.

Ideally, the file will be adjusted to match the desired output. If you are developing an image to go in a small booklet or be projected on a screen you want to reduce the size and resolution (pixels per inch). This will make the file smaller plus viewing and editing will be much more efficient – especially if you do not have a cutting-edge computer.

3.   Select **Image** → **Image Size** from the menu.

Notice the *Document Size* is 32″ wide and 42″ high. Also, notice the *Resolution* is 72 pixels per inch. If you browse to this file on the CD you will see it is 3.95MB in size. This is a fairly large file for a JPG format.

For our exercise the *Document Size* is too large for the small booklet we plan on putting this image in and the *Resolution* is too low; 72 is good for PowerPoint but not printing.

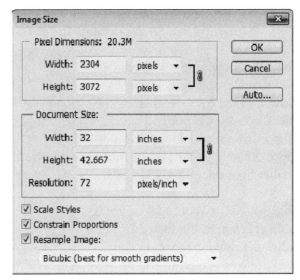

FIGURE 7-1.4 Image Size dialog

It is better to start with a file that is too large, as it can more easily be reduced without losing quality. However, it is difficult to take an image that is too small and increase the quality. Low quality / small file size is often the problem with imagery saved from websites as they have been optimized for download speed and computer screen viewing.

In the next steps you will adjust the image size so it will fit on an 8 ½″ x 11″ page and increase the resolution to 150. Many printers can print 300-600 dots per inch, but 150 will keep the file size down and still look pretty good.

An important part of resizing an image is Photoshop's ability to resample the image. This will help to maintain the images overall quality. If you are reducing an image you should use **Bicubic Sharper** and for enlargements you can use **Bicubic Smoother**. It is best to only resize the image once, so you may need to experiment with a copy of the image and do some test printing first.

Changing Image Size

Now you will reduce the size of the file.

4. Adjust only the following settings (the others will automatically change):
    a. *Document Size* – Width: **8**
    b. *Document Size* – Resolution: **150**
    c. Resample Image: **Bicubic Shaper (best for reduction)**
    d. See Figure 7-1.5

5. Click **OK** to apply the changes to your image.

6. Select **File → Save As**.

7. **Save** the file to your hard drive as **College Library - Wall Detail - Color Study.jpg**; accept the defaults for quality when saving the JPG file.

The file is now properly sized for the intended page size. If you browse to the folder you saved the file in, you should notice a large drop in size; it should now be approximately 1.6MB; this is much smaller than the original 3.95MB.

This exercise is about making things more efficient in the final document rather than saving space on your hard drive or server. In fact, it would be best to save the original file in case you need a larger file later on.

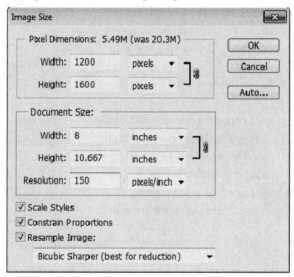

FIGURE 7-1.5 Image Size dialog – reducing file size

The final document might be a MS Word or Adobe InDesign file with 20-30 images like this in it. If all the files were 4-8MB each, it would quickly get slow and difficult to work with.

Selection Tools

The next step is to select the white walls so you can use other tools to adjust the color. Selecting portions of an image is an important and powerful feature in Photoshop. As you can see in the list of menus at the top of the screen, this feature has its own pull-down menu.

First you will use the *Magic Wand* tool to automatically select the three white sections above the door and window. This tool allows you to simply click within an area and the program will search out, in all directions, for the same color you clicked on. All pixels of the same color, which are connected, will be included in the selection. Keep in mind, a selection is defined by one or more closed boundaries.

The tricky thing about working with photographs like the one used in this example is the color on the same wall can vary due to lighting (both natural and artificial) and reflections. Therefore Photoshop provides a few options on the *Control Panel*, when the *Magic Wand* tool is active, to allow various amounts of color deviation. These setting may need to be changed from one area to another, even in the same image.

8. From the *Tools Panel*, click and hold down the mouse, on the **Quick Selection Tool** until the fly-out options appear (Figure 7-1.6).

9. From the fly-out menu, select **Magic Wand**.

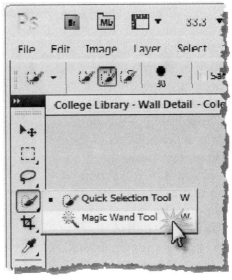

The tool is now active. Notice the options on the *Control Panel: Tolerance, Contiguous,* etc. You will not change any of these settings just yet.

10. Click in the upper left area, identified in Figure 7-1.7.

FIGURE 7-1.6 Selecting Magic Wand tool

Notice how the perimeter of the entire area has been selected. This is the fastest way to select an area with a consistent color.

Just so you know, the two vertical reveals are expansion joints which have been added to prevent cracking and buckling as materials expand and contract and/ or the building settles slightly.

FIGURE 7-1.7 Using the Magic Wand tool

By default you can only select one area at a time. Clicking the next area would automatically unselect the current area in favor of the new area. However, it is possible to add to the current selection by holding down the **Shift** key.

11. Hold down the **Shift** key and then click within the next area, just to the right of the first selection.

Notice, while holding down the **Shift** key a small plus symbol appears next to your cursor. This helps you know you are adding when you click. Conversely, if you hold down the **Alt** key, you will see a minus sign appear, indicating a click would remove an area from the selection.

With the next step you will see a problem arise and learn how to deal with it!

12. While holding down the **Shift** key, select the last area at the top of the image.

Right away you see a problem after the third selection (Figure 7-1.8). The coloring of the wood trim appears lighter in the photo just above the window (due to lighting and reflectivity of the finish). This caused the *Magic Wand* tool to select a portion of the trim as well. This is not what you want so you will have to reselect this area with a different **Tolerance** setting on the *Control Panel.*

FIGURE 7-1.8 Tolerance problem with selection

You could just press **Ctrl + Z** to undo the last command, but you will learn what to do when you want to get rid of a selection all together.

13. Pick **Select → Deselect** from the menu.

Nothing is selected now. Take a moment to notice the other options in the *Select* menu: *Inverse, Grow, Similar, Load, Save,* etc.

14. Use the ***Magic Wand*** tool to select the first two areas again (good practice).

Before clicking the third area again, you will adjust the tolerance downward to tell Photoshop not to allow as much deviation in the pixel color you click on.

15. Change the tolerance to **22** on the *Control Panel* (Figure 7-1.9).

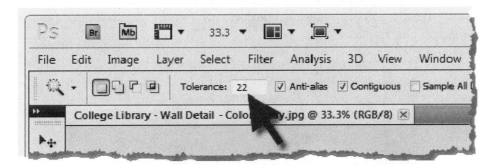

FIGURE 7-1.9 Change Magic Wand tolerance

16. Now click the third area while holding down the **Shift** key.

Next, you will select the two remaining areas between the door and window. The *Magic Wand* tool is a little tricky to use here due to the shadow lines created by the trim. This provides an opportunity to try another selection tool: the ***Polygonal Lasso Tool***. This tool allows you to pick a series of points, and the *Lasso Tool* adds a straight selection line between each pick until your last click – which needs to be back at the start point.

Note that the regular ***Lasso Tool*** is a freehand option which can be difficult to control, especially with a big fat mouse in your hand!

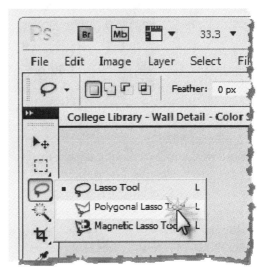

17. ***Zoom in*** on the portion of wall just above the sign – between the door and window.

18. Click and hold-down on the *Lasso Tool*, until the fly-out tool list appears.

19. Select the **Polygonal Lasso Tool** (Figure 7-1.10).

FIGURE 7-1.10 Polygonal Lasso Tool

Now you will click the four corners of the wall area.

20. Holding down **Shift**; click the four points as shown in Figure 7-1.11.

21. Holding down **Shift**; click the first point again to close off the selection area; the area will automatically complete itself when you click directly on the first pick point.

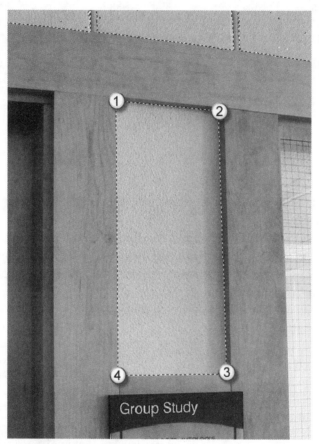

FIGURE **7-1.11** Using the Polygonal Lasso Tool

Now that you have spent all that time getting the selection just right, you won't want to go through that "pain" again, so you will save the selection. This will make it easy to restore whenever you want.

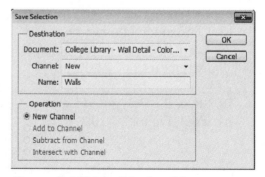

22. Pick **Select → Save Selection**.

23. Type **Walls** for the name and click **OK** (Figure 7-1.12).

FIGURE **7-1.12** Save Selection dialog

Now you will test the saved selection feature.

    24. Pick **Select → Deselect**.

    25. Click **Select → Load Selection**.

    26. Make sure "Walls" is selected for the *Channel* and click **OK**.

All five areas are now selected again. You are now ready to adjust the wall color.

Adjusting Colors

There are a number of ways to get different colors in an image using Photoshop. Some tools such as *Brush* and *Paint Bucket* will replace all the pixels in the selected area with a single color, totally removing all detail and shade variation. That would be undesirable. You will use another method to simply adjust the Hue and Saturation of the pixels in the selected area. Each pixel will get an equal amount of adjustment, thus keeping the overall variation intact.

    27. Select **Layer → New Adjustment Layer → Hue/Saturation…**

    28. If your selection area has been removed, load it again.

    29. Click the **Colorize** option (Figure 7-1.13).

FIGURE 7-1.13 Adjusting the wall color

You can now adjust the Hue and Saturation to achieve a wide variety of colors. Notice how the color variation and shadow lines are maintained.

30. Make the following changes to set the wall to a light yellow (Figure 7-1.14):

    a. Hue: **41**

    b. Saturation: **31**

FIGURE 7-1.14 Wall color adjusted

Now you will *Save*. When you do, you will notice Photoshop wants you to save the file as a PSD file format. This is a special Photoshop file format. Unlike JPG, TIF, PGN, etc., which can be viewed by most computers just using the operating system's built-in viewer, a PSD file requires Photoshop to view and edit the file. This format is now required because you are using *Layers* and Saved selections. The standard image formats have no way to save this information. They are mainly a collection of colored pixels.

31. Select **File → Save** (or **Ctrl + S**).

32. Save the file as **College Library - Wall Detail - Color Study.PSD**.

    a. After clicking *Save*, you may get a *Maximize Compatibility* option – unchecking this allows Photoshop to use all of its newest features and toolsets. However, older versions of Photoshop may not be able to open or edit the file.

Multiple Color Options

It is possible to use the *Layers* feature to set up multiple color options. This is much better than saving multiple copies of the file.

To do this you simply do the following:

33. In the *Layers* panel, click the **Eyeball** for the *Wall Color* layer (this is the adjustment layer).

This turns off the visibility of the adjustment *Layer*. Notice the original wall color is showing again. It has not been directly modified.

34. Repeat steps 27-30 to create another adjustment layer; be sure to:
    a. Provide a different name
    b. Select another color.

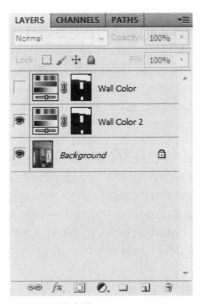

FIGURE 7-1.15
Multiple Adjustment Layers

Now you can toggle the *Layer* visibility on and off as desired to view the various options!

FIGURE 7-1.16 Another wall color option

Section 7-2
Working with Scanned Sketches

As the name implies, Photoshop is clearly designed to manipulate photographs. Of course, it can be used to view and manipulate a raster image. This would include scans, computer generated renderings, PDF files, and more. In this section you will take a look at how you can manipulate a scanned sketch.

This process of hand sketching and then using Photoshop to quickly add color and text is ideal. Once the hand sketch is done, Photoshop can be used to add the color. And, similar to the previous exercise, you can try various colors on your design. Another huge advantage is the ability to quickly correct mistakes and move on. If adding color by hand, with markers or watercolors for example, one slip of the hand could mean starting over.

Adjusting a Copy of the Original Scanned Image

The first thing you will do is open the scanned image and adjust its size and erase a few things, but only after making a copy so you leave the original intact! You should always do that so you can get back to the start again if needed – without having to rescan the image – if you even have the original!

1. Open the file **Community Center – Performance Hall.png** from the CD.

You will save the file in the Photoshop (PSD) format as you know you will be using Photoshop's features like *Layers*.

2. Select **File → Save As**.

3. Save the file on your computer's hard drive (or school server) as **Community Center – Performance Hall – Option A.psd**.

   a. Change the *Format* to **Photoshop** (Figure 7-2.1).

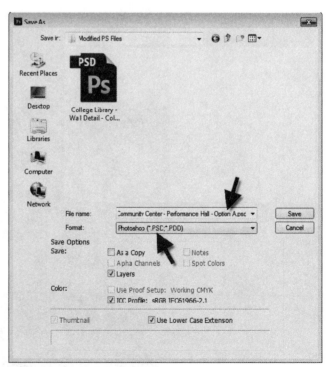

FIGURE 7-2.1 Saving your scanned file

Take a quick look at the image quality before you get started to make sure you have a decent quality image.

4. Select **Image → Image Size** from the menu.

As you can see, this image is about 8″ square which would fit on an 8½″ x 11″ sheet of paper. However, the resolution is a little low at only 96. We will assume, for this exercise, that you do not have access to the original anymore and need to use the features of Photoshop to help with this issue!

Before you make any changes, you will zoom in and visually investigate the quality of the lines in the scanned file (Figure 7-2.3).

5. **Cancel** the *Image Size* dialog without making any changes.

6. **Zoom in** to the top center peak of the image to see the current quality of the lines. *TIP: Use the magnifying icon from the* Tools Panel.

7. Now make the following changes in the *Image Size* dialog (Figure 7-2.2):

    a. *Width*: 6″
    b. *Resolution*: 300
    c. *Resample Image*: Bicubic Sharper
    d. *Click* **OK**.

8. Right-click and select **Fit on Screen** to zoom out; the *Zoom* tool must be selected.

9. Zoom in again, on the same area as step 6.

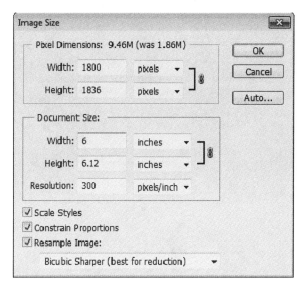

FIGURE 7-2.2 Changing image size

Notice how much smoother the line work is (Figure 7-2.4). This can save a lot of time if you scanned a bunch of images and don't have time to rescan them all. But it is best to scan them with a decent resolution to begin with.

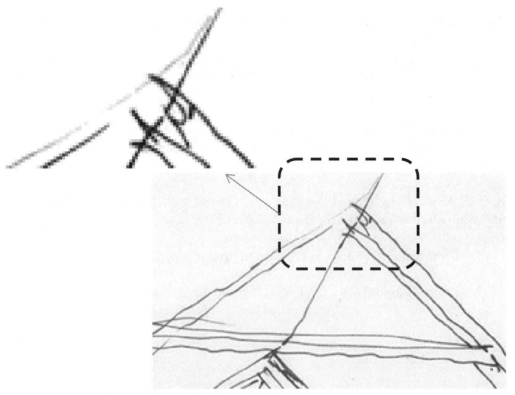

FIGURE 7-2.3 Scanned image original

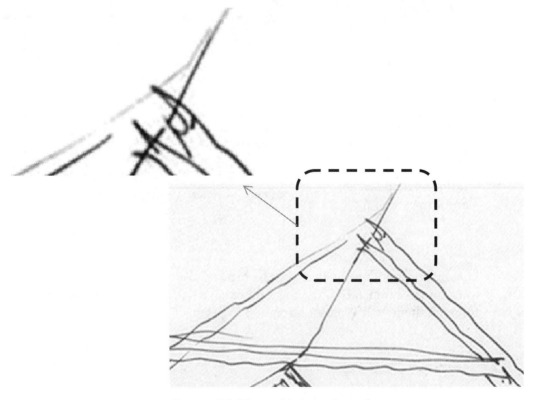

FIGURE 7-2.4 Scanned image enhanced

Removing the Background

An awsome feature of Photoshop is its ability to remove the background of your scanned image. The background is solid white, or whatever the color of your sketch paper. This, like the line work, was captured by the scanner.

The reason we want to get rid of the background is so we can add colors below the line work and not on top of it. The ability to add colors below the line work will also require the use of *Layers*, which are like transparencies. They are stacked one on top of another (the order can be adjusted). More on *Layers* in a moment.

To remove the background you will use yet another selection tool; ***Color Range***. This feature allows you to select all the pixels in the image which are the same color (or color range) as the one you click on initially. Once you have the entire background selected, you could change the color to a solid white, use *Hue/ Saturation* as before, or just hit the **Delete** key and remove all color. You will try the latter option, which essentially leaves the background transparent.

   10. Pick **Select → Color Range** from the menu.

A dialog appears which provides controls and a preview (Figure 7-2.5).

   11. Click in the background area of the image.

   a. You can click in the preview area or in the main image behind the dialog box.

   b. Be sure not to click on any of the lines. If you do, simply click again away from the lines.

The Fuzziness slider controls the range of colors selected. A low setting will restrict the variation in the color range – that is, only pixels which are nearly identical to the one you clicked on will be selected.

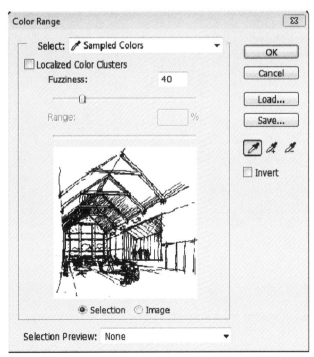

FIGURE 7-2.5 Color Range dialog

12. Click **OK** to select the entire background color.

13. Press **Delete** on the keyboard to erase all selected colors (or pixels).

14. Pick **Select → Deselect** from the menu.

15. **Save** your file.

Notice the background is now a checkered pattern (Figure 7-2.6). This indicates a transparent area; void of any color. This will allow you to create a *Layer* beneath this *Layer* and add color without overlapping the sketched line work.

FYI: See page 15-16 for more information on making the background transparent.

FIGURE 7-2.6 Transparent background

Cropping the Image

The following steps will show you how to crop an image. This is a quick way to remove a portion of the perimeter, which also makes the image smaller.

First, you will use the basic *Rectangular Marquee Tool* to select the area you wish to keep.

16. Pick the **Rectanglular Marquee Tool** (see image to the right).

17. Click two diagonal points to select the rectangular area shown in Figure 7-2.7.

18. Now select **Image → Crop**.

You have now cropped the image. If you go into the *Image Size* dialog you will see the size of the image is now smaller.

FIGURE 7-2.7 Rectangular selection – area to be cropped

Erasing Portions of the Image

Next, you will learn how to erase potions of the image. These steps will permanently erase pixels from the image – similar to the previous steps to remove the background.

19. **Zoom in** on the table pointed out in Figure 7-2-8.

20. Select the **Eraser** tool (see image to the right).

Notice on the *Control Panel* you have several options related to using the *Brush* tool. The thing you want to be most aware of is the brush options (Figure 7-2.9).

The *Eraser* brush options allow you to control the size of the *Eraser* "brush," that is, how much stuff gets removed with a single pass. You can also control if the edge is a hard erase, or a smooth gradiant erase.

When using the *Eraser* tool, you should start (i.e., press the mouse) and stop (i.e., let up off the mouse) often so if you mess up and erase too much in one area you can *step backward* (*Undo*) a smaller amount and not have to start the eraser process completely over.

FIGURE 7-2.8 Zoom in on table and erase it

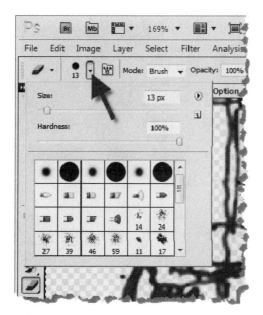

FIGURE 7-2.9 Eraser brush options

21. **Erase** the table so your image looks like Figure 7-2.10.

Zoom in and try to erase just the table, leaving the adjacent line work intact. If you accidentally erase too much, press **Ctrl + Alt + Z** to *step backwards* (or *Undo*).

You can use any of the selection tools you have previously learned to erase portions of your image.

Consider saving a copy of your image before erasing a large portion it just in case you need any of it back at some point.

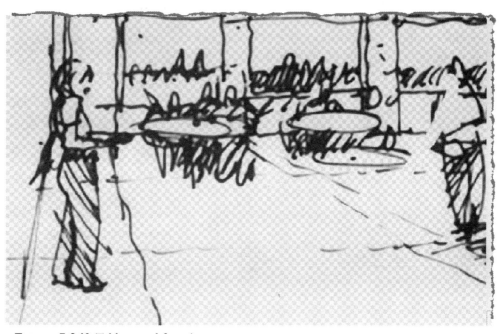

FIGURE 7-2.10 Table erased from image

Creating a Layer

Before adding color you will create a *Layer* on which to add the color. This will prevent the line work from getting overwritten. You will have to rearrange the order of the *Layer* stack so the color is under the sketch lines.

22. Click the **New Layer** icon in the *Layer* panel (Figure 7-2.11).

A new layer is created at the top of the "stack" as seen in Figure 7-2.12. You could rename the *Layer* to something like "colors" if you wanted to. To rename a *Layer*, you double-click on the name and type a new one.

23. Click and drag the *Layer* to the bottom of the "stack" as shown in Figure 7-2.13.

Layers have a lot more options than just controlling visibility and display order. If you select a *Layer* you can control the *Opacity* via the slider in the upper right corner of the *Layer* panel. This allows you to see through one *Layer* to another.

You can also double-click on the small preview icon to access a dialog with a ton of *Layer* related controls, as shown in the image below (Figure 7-2.14).

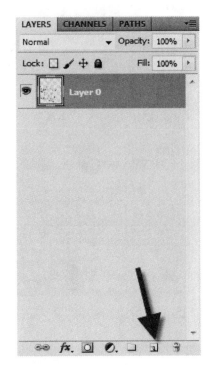

FIGURE 7-2.11 New layer

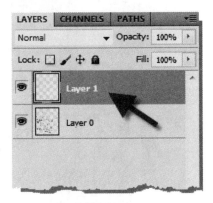

FIGURE 7-2.12 New layer

FIGURE 7-2.13 Moving layer

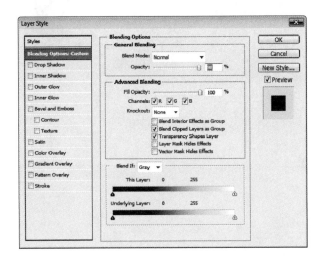

FIGURE 7-2.14 Layer Style dialog

Adding Color

You are finally ready to add color to your sketch!

The selected *Layer* is the *Layer* things are placed on when painting or adding text. You will make sure the new *Layer* is selected first.

24. Make sure **Layer 1** is selected in the *Layer* panel.

25. Zoom in on the roof truss in the back of the scene; this is the smallest one on the screen (due to the perspective).

26. Select the **Brush Tool** from the *Tools* panel (Figure 7-2.15).

Notice the various options on the *Control* panel (Figure 7-2.16). This is similar to the *Eraser* tool options, which is nice as the consistency helps with the learning curve.

The "brush preset picker" is opened in the image below. This allows you to pick a brush type and size quickly. You will do this next.

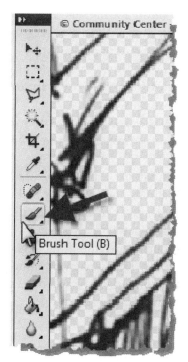

FIGURE 7-2.15 Brush tool

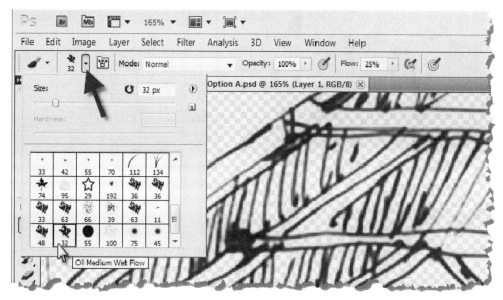

FIGURE 7-2.16 Brush options

27. Click the down-arrow to open the **brush preset picker** (Figure 7-2.16).

28. Select brush preset *Oil Medium Wet Flow -* **32** as shown in Figure 7-2.16.

This automatically sets the size of the brush to 32. This can be changed to a smaller (or larger) size via the slider at the top of the preset list.

The next thing you will want to do is select a color.

29. Click on the **Set foreground color** swatch on the *Tools* panel (Figure 7-2.17).

You are now in the *Color Picker* dialog (Figure 7-2.18). This allows you to quickly pick a color in a nuber of ways. Visually, you can click in the narrow vertical bar in the center to get within your main color range and then drag your cursor around in the large color window to fine tune the color. The preview swatches in the upper right show you a comparison between the previous color and the new one you are selecting.

FIGURE 7-2.17
Color selection

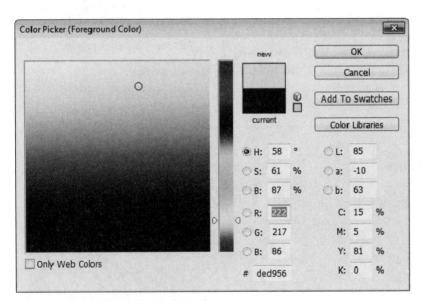

FIGURE 7-2.18 Color Picker dialog box

In addition to visually picking colors you can type in RGB/CYMK numbers, hue and saturation numbers, or click the **Color Library** button and pick from a vast library of industry standard colors – which can be calibrated to your monitor and printer.

It is also possible to get specific color inofrmation from paint manufacturers such as Sherwin-Williams. You can go to their website and get RGB values and type that into the *Color Picker.* Some companies also provide color palettes which can be used diredctly in Photoshop – an example of this is shown in the image below and at the following website:

http://www.sherwin-williams.com/pro/paint_colors/paint_color_samples /downloadable_palettes/index.jsp

FIGURE 7-2.19 Color information from paint manufacturer

In this exercise you will just visually select a light yellow color to represent a wood color for the exposed roof trusses at the ceiling.

30. Pick a **light yellow** color; your RGB numbers should be close to what is shown in Figure 7-2.18.

31. Click **OK** to close the *Color Picker*.

Now that you have selected your brush style and color you are ready to paint!

32. Color in the back truss by:

   a. Pressing down the mouse button and dragging within the lines of the truss.

   b. Take small strokes; that is, hold down the mouse button and drag for a short distance and then release the button, back up slightly and repeat.

   c. Keep your left hand (if right-handed) on the **Ctrl + Z** keys; this allows you to quickly press them to undo one stroke when you get outside of the lines.

Don't worry about getting outside the lines a little. This should not be worked on as if it were a work of art! You would never get anything done if approached from that perspective.

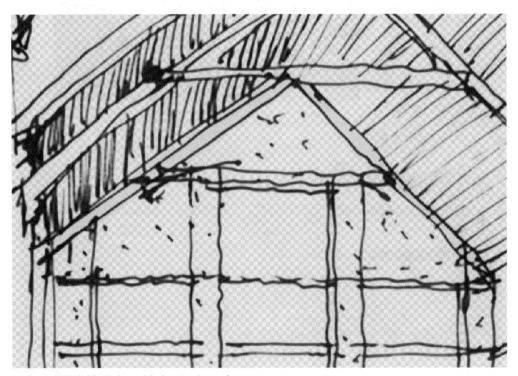

FIGURE 7-2.20 Color added to back roof truss

Using brushes and other draw and modify tools gets even easier when used with a pressure sensitive tablet or monitor. A monitor you can draw on is the best as your eye-hand coordination is one to one. However, they can be expensive.

When the *Brush* tool is active there is a toggle on the *Control Panel* that allows the pressure applied to a tablet/monitor to override the brush size settings. What that means is the harder you press, the fatter the line gets – just like with a real brush on paper! This feature is just being mentioned in passing and will not be covered here.

Now you will add color to the rest of the trusses.

33. Use the same brush settings to color the remaining trusses.

    a. You can change the size if needed for the larger (i.e., closer) trusses.

    b. Zoom in and out and Pan as needed.

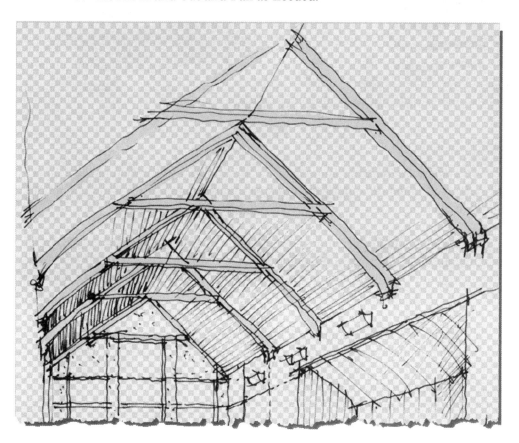

FIGURE 7-2.21 Color added to remaining trusses

Clicking the "Toggle the brush presets" icon on the *Control Panel* (while the *Brush tool* is active) gives you a nice visual on what the output for the brush presets are and an extensive set of controls to customize your brush (Figure 7-2.22).

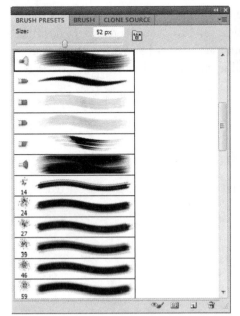
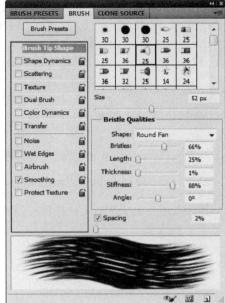

FIGURE 7-2.22 Brush panel options: presets and custom controls

Next you will create another *Layer* so you can add color to the ceiling. The *Layer* will be moved to the bottom of the stack so the color goes behind the line work and the truss color.

34. Create a new **Layer**, move it to the bottom of the list and rename it to "Ceiling" (double-click on the name and type) – Figure 7-2.23.

35. Adjust the color to a lighter yellow so it contrasts the truss color a little.

36. Select a different brush preset and adjust the size so it is larger (about 50).

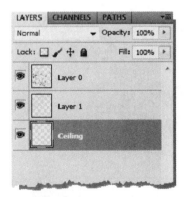

FIGURE 7-2.23 New layer

37. Make large sweeps from the back of the scene all the way to the front as shown with the arrow in Figure 7-2.24.

Because the color is lighter and the *Layer* is at the back, you do not have to worry about coloring over the trusses. Keep in mind you could create additional *Layers* to try other color options – toggling them on and off as needed.

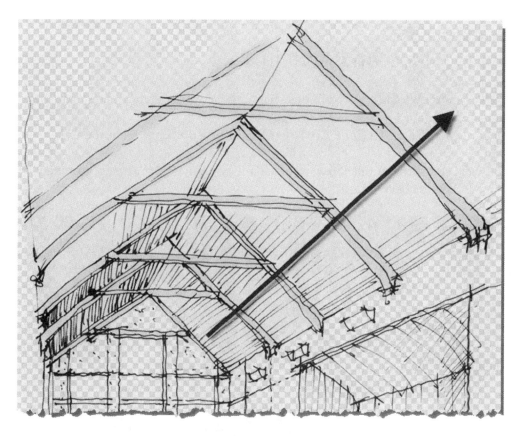

FIGURE 7-2.24 Adding color to the ceiling

You can continue this process to add color to the rest of the image. If you want to better contain color in a certain area, you can use one of the selection tools to define an area before using the *Brush* tool. Then, when you begin painting on the screen, the color will not extend out past the selection area. This can have an abrupt look if used with some of the more natural looking brushes. You can also flood the selected area with a solid color using the *Paint Bucket* tool.

While in the *Color Picker* you can move your cursor into the main canvas area and click to select a color from the image. This is helpful when you are trying to match a color from a photo or one you previously used. If you know you will be using a color in multiple locations, you may want to click the "Add to Swathes" button in the *Color Picker* dialog. This color will then be quickly selectable from the **Window → Swatches** panel.

38. Use these techniques to add color to the rest of the image.

39. **Save** when finished.

Section 7-3
Using Filters and Adding Text

The last exercise to be covered in this chapter is on using filters adding text.

1. Open the file **College Library – Reading Room.jpg** from the CD.

You will use a filter on this image to make it look a little more artistic, and then you will add text below the image.

FIGURE 7-3.1 Image to be used in this exercise

Photoshop has a number of filters which can be applied to an image (or selection) in order to achieve a special effect or style.

2. Select **Filter → Artistic → Colored Pencil** from the menu.

You are now in a preview mode where you can make adjustments which relate to the specific filter and the final results (Figure 7-3.2).

As you can see in the preview, the photograph now looks more like a sketch done with colored pencils. This is a nice way to present style concepts to a client without getting distracted by non-important details.

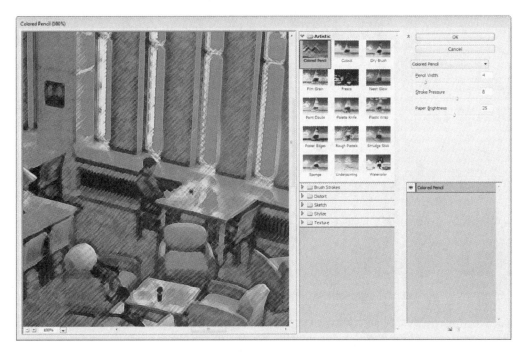

FIGURE 7-3.2 Applying a filter

3. Try selecting a few other filters in the preview mode to see what effect they have on the photo. Do not click **OK** just yet.

4. Select **Watercolor** and then **OK**.

The image has not been permanently modified to have a watercolor look. Be sure to save a copy of your original image before using a filter.

5. Select **File → Save As** to create a copy of the file.

6. Name the file **College Library – Reading Room – Presentation.PSD**

   a. Be sure to change the format to Photoshop (PSD).

Next you will add text. However, you would like some white space below the image to add the text – as a title. It is certainly possible to just add text over the photo anywhere you want, but you do not want to do that here.

To create white space below the image you will increase the overall canvas size.

7. Select **Image → Canvas size**.

8. Add two inches to the height and change the *Anchor* setting as shown in Figure 7-3.3.

9. Click **OK**.

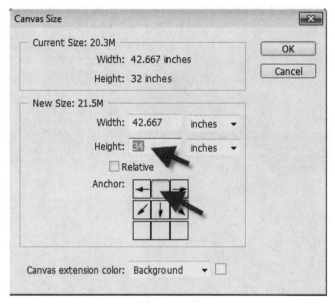

FIGURE 7-3.3 Adjusting the canvas size

Adjusting the *Anchor* position as you did will force the added canvas to the bottom of the image, rather than equally to all sides – which is the default (i.e., centered).

You now have two additional inches at the bottom of the image in which to add text (Figure 7-3.4).

FIGURE 7-3.4 Extra space added to bottom of image for text

Now you will add the text. When you select the *Text* tool, Photoshop will automatically add a new *Layer* on which to place the text. This is important as it lets you easily modify the text later if needed.

10. Select the **Text** tool from the *Tool* panel (Figure 7-3.5).

11. Click in the lower left corner of the image.

12. Type **TWO STORY READING ROOM.**

13. Click the **check mark** on the *Tools* panel.

Notice the other options on the *Tools* panel: font, text height, justification, color, etc. (Figure 7-3.6). Also, notice a *Layer* was automatically created.

FIGURE 7-3.5
Text tool

FIGURE 7-3.6 Text tool options on the control panel

FIGURE 7-3.7 Text added to image

To edit the text in the future, the *Layer* must be selected and the *Text* tool must be active. Then, you simply click on the text to modify it. If you don't click directly on the text, you may accidentally begin the process of adding another text object – simply cancel that and try again.

To move the text you need to make sure the *Layer* is selected and use the *Move* tool to drag the text around on the image.

14. **Save** your image.

Self-Exam:

The following questions can be used as a way to check your knowledge of this lesson. The answers can be found at the bottom of this page.

1. Photoshop offers several selection tools. (T/F)

2. Use *Image Size* to adjust the overall dimensions of an image. (T/F)

3. The *Magic Wand* tool finds a boundary based on a single pick point. (T/F)

4. What type of new layer was created to adjust the wall color? _____

5. Photoshop offers several ways with which to pick a color. (T/F)

Review Questions:

The following questions may be assigned by your instructor as a way to assess your knowledge of this section. Your instructor has the answers to the review questions.

1. Selections can be saved for future use in the image. (T/F)

2. It is possible to remove the background of a scanned hand sketch. (T/F)

3. Text is automatically placed on its own *Layer*. (T/F)

4. The *Eraser* tool does not permanently remove image data (i.e., pixels). (T/F)

5. When reducing the size of an image, you should set the resample option

   to: _____.

6. Selection amount in the *Magic Wand* tool is controlled by _____

7. Used to add space below an image: _____.

8. Feature used to apply an artistic style: _____.

9. The text height cannot be changed. (T/F)

10. You must have the *Layer* selected to modify things contained on it. (T/F)

Introduction to Hand Sketching

Every architectural drawing is drawn as if seen from a specific view; these views have specific names which you will learn in this chapter. Also, some architectural drawings are drawn "to scale", which means they are proportional to the real-world intended size of the building. And, just to make sure everyone is on the same page, we will cover some of the various graphics used in architectural floor plans which represent specific parts of a building — e.g., stairs, toilets, kitchen cabinets, etc.

This chapter will cover some fundamental information which is often relegated to classroom instruction. The authors felt it important to provide this information to ensure later discussions in this manuscript are clearly comprehended, especially for those using this book outside the classroom setting. If the reader is taking a class and the instructor also covers this material, that would be even better!

First, you will learn about the various views used to delineate an architectural design, starting with the 2D views and then the various 3D views. The use of line weights to make drawings "read" better is briefly introduced as well as the notion of "scaled" drawings which allows a sketch to be measured for reference or estimating purposes. Finally, the various graphic conventions used in architectural floor plans will be covered.

Architectural Drawing Views

Three dimensional objects are depicted on paper by 2D drawings of three or more sides of that object. These "three or more" 2D *Views* allow someone to interpret the 3D image in their mind. This section will review the various views used in architectural drawing and design.

The simple object below describes the standard views used to describe the 2D drawings that are created for a 3D object. Looking at the 2D drawings below and then at the 3D object above you should be able to visualize how each represents the object under consideration. Of course things can get more difficult with complex objects, especially when it comes to architectural objects (i.e., buildings).

The exercises at the end of this chapter are provided as a way to help you to think three-dimensionally. For some it just comes naturally, and for others it takes a little practice. One thing you will find interesting with the exercises that follow is that totally different looking objects can have identical 2D views.

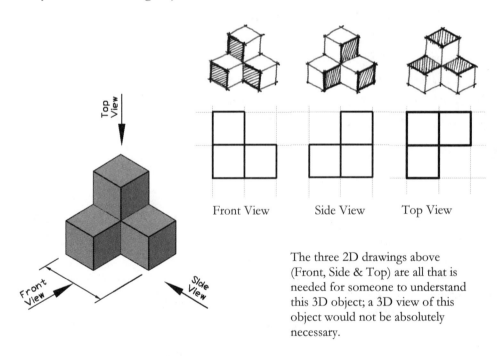

Front View   Side View   Top View

The three 2D drawings above (Front, Side & Top) are all that is needed for someone to understand this 3D object; a 3D view of this object would not be absolutely necessary.

Although you could imagine this object as an office building, the above example relates better to the world of *Mechanical Design and Drafting*. In the realm of *Architectural Drawing*, different terms are used to describe the views shown in the example above, and additional drawings, or *Views*, are often employed.

Exterior Elevations

The example below shows another simple object, but this time it clearly depicts an architectural example. In architecture, the vertical surfaces are illustrated in views referred to as elevations (exterior elevations to be specific); they are further defined by a direction modifier. For example, the exterior elevation which illustrates the walls facing south is referred to as the south elevation. Some "newbies" get a little confused because the view is actually looking north, but it looks at a wall(s) which is facing south!

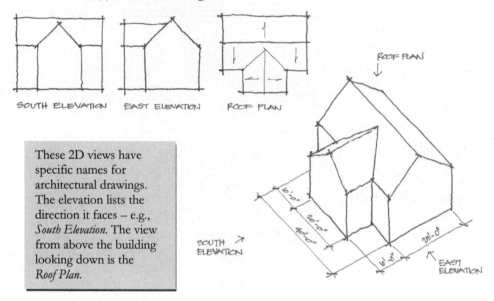

These 2D views have specific names for architectural drawings. The elevation lists the direction it faces – e.g., *South Elevation*. The view from above the building looking down is the *Roof Plan*.

The images below further demonstrate the concept of how an elevation is a projection of a three-dimensional building. The sketch artist will utilize various line weights, shades and shadows to suggest depth in an otherwise flat 2D drawing. (This is true for both hand sketching and technical drawings.)

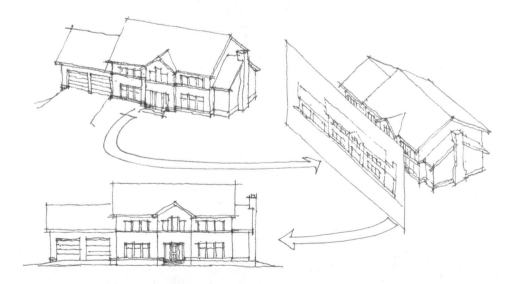

Floor Plans

In addition to the 2D views mentioned on the previous page which describe the outer-most faces of a building (i.e., Exterior Elevations), another set of 2D views reveal the elements within, called *Floor Plans* and *Sections*. Please read the information to the right in conjunction with the images shown below to learn more about these important views.

What is a Floor Plan – Image I
Imagine a plane which cuts through the building about 4 feet above the ground; this would be the cut plane

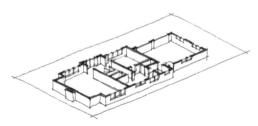

What is a Floor Plan – Image II
Imagine the portion of building above the "cut plane" being removed.

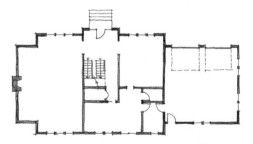

What is a Floor Plan – Image III
Result: Flattened 2D view from "cut plane" down.

2D Slices & Projections:

Architects use drawings to convey their ideas and design solutions to clients and contractors. This was true even when the Architect was the Master Builder and directly involved with the construction of a building. The drawings used today by contractors are legal, binding documents that the contractor must follow closely or risk legal or financial penalty. These drawings are primarily created using computers today, but for most of history, architectural drawings were created by hand drawing directly on paper.

The drawings created by an Architect or Engineer are typically 2D drawings, which makes sense as they are drawn on flat (i.e., 2D) pieces of paper. The 2D drawings, when considered as a whole, describe a building three-dimensionally. It takes instruction and practice to be able to create or even read these types of drawings, but the concept is quite simple. The 2D drawings are made up of what you might think of as slices or projections of the building in one of three axes: X, Y or Z.

One of the primary drawings used in architecture is the floor plan. As you can see in the illustration to the left, this drawing is a view from the top – totally flat – with the upper portion of the building cut-away (or ignored for clarity).

Floor Plans show the location of doors, windows, walls, stairs, cabinets, equipment, furniture and more!

Finally, imagine looking straight down on the cut-away building:
Another way to think about how a floor plan drawing relates to the actual building
is this: imagine taking a chainsaw and cutting horizontally, about four feet above
the floor, through the walls, all the way around your house (please don't actually
try this!). Then you remove the top portion with a crane. You then climb to the
top of the crane, which is positioned directly above the remaining bottom portion
of the house and you take a picture. That picture would look very similar to a 2D
floor plan of that house – only the picture would have some perspective distortion
where the floor plan would not.

Construction Documents:
The end result of a design project, in the drawing sense, is a set of formal drawings
(Construction Documents, or CD's) that become part of a binding legal document
a contractor will use to build your design. This formal drawing set is created on
the computer for speed and accuracy, but is entirely based on the earlier sketches
drawn by hand. The CD set may consist of 100's of sheets; the total number
depends on the complexity of the project and the level of detail required.

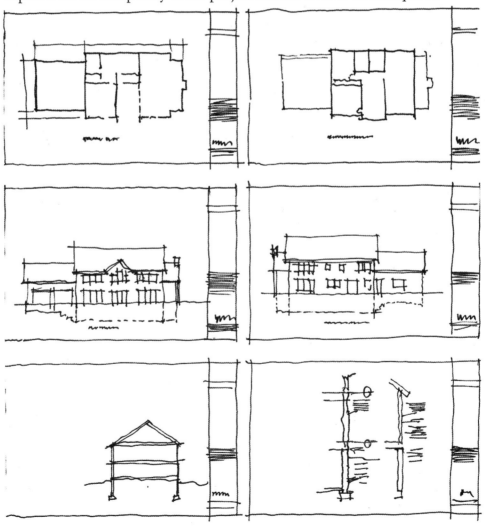

"True North" versus "Project North"

There are two more "big picture" aspects you should know about floor plans before moving on:

1. Drafted Floor Plans are always drawn to scale. This means that if you took the real version of the building and shrunk it, it would align with all the lines on the 2D floor plan drawing. The scale varies depending on the size of the building and the size of the paper; one example is ¼″ = 1′-0″ – this means that a line drawn ¼″ long on paper will equal 1′-0″ in the real world (a line 1″ long will represent 4′-0″ as there are four quarters in an inch).

   This is not as critical for hand sketches; however, an experienced designer can sketch [close to] proportionally accurate drawings. In other words, a 3′-0″ hallway is sketched about one-fourth the size of an adjacent 12′-0″ wide room. Proportionally accurate is more important than sketches being to scale.

2. With rare exception, modern drawings are oriented with project north upward on the paper; project north is not always the same as true north.

Project North Example:
The following real-world example illustrates the value of using the "project north" concept. In northern Minnesota, along the north shore of Lake Superior is a city which is generally stretched out parallel with the shoreline. As is turns out, all the streets run at an angle of almost 45 degrees off of "true north".

Rather than calling one end of the city the north-east end and the other the south-west end, a "project north" or plan north concept was embraced over time and one end is referred to as East and the other as West.

The "project north" concept, in this example, was implemented at a city wide level and has been subsequently used on all architectural projects.

Exception to the rule: the site plan is usually drawn with "true north" pointing straight up on the sheet, and the building rotated accordingly.

In conclusion to an overview of "project north" vs. "true north", the designer needs to be aware of N, E, S, W directions when looking at drawings and designing a building (especially, for example, if the roof is sloped and will be supporting solar panels so the maximum solar energy can be collected during the day). Plus, you will start seeing elevation drawings with directional labels in this book so this concept needs to be understood.

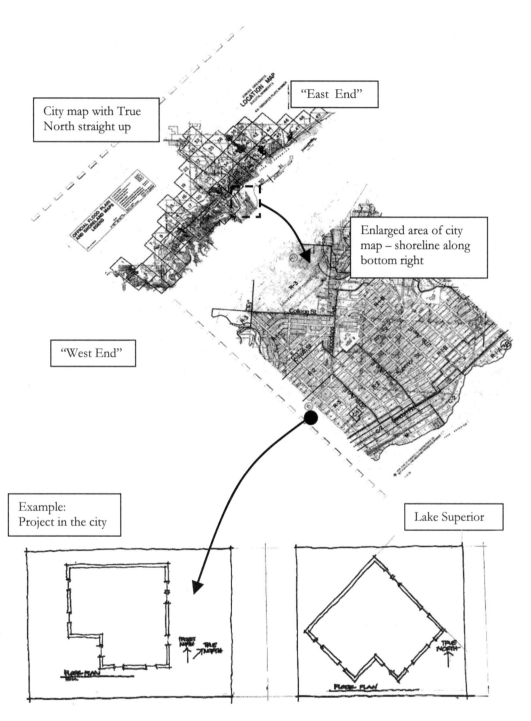

City map with True North straight up

"East End"

Enlarged area of city map – shoreline along bottom right

"West End"

Example: Project in the city

Lake Superior

Project North vs. True North:

The image shown above is a standard architectural drawing sheet with the plan rotated to align with the sheet. Project North is straight up on the sheet and True North is about 45 degrees off. The sheet to the right shows the plan positioned on the sheet with True North pointing straight up on the sheet which would make the project difficult to draw and hard to read angled dimensions and such.

Sections

Like a floor plan, Sections are a cut-away view. The section reveals vertical relationships within the building.

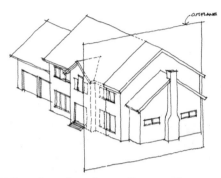

What is a Section – Image I
Imagine a plane which cuts through the building at a specific location.

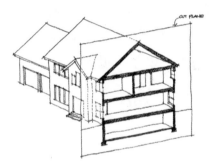

What is a Section – Image II
Imagine the portion of building in front of the "cut plane" being removed.

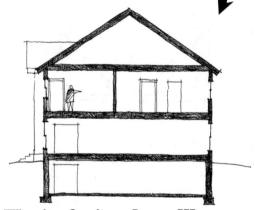

What is a Section – Image III
Result: Flattened 2D view from "cut plane" back.

Horizontal vs. Vertical Info:
Floor plans are the primary views used to convey relationships in the horizontal plane – for example, the distance between two walls, or the overall footprint of the building. It is not really possible to delineate relationships in the vertical plane – like the height from the floor to the bottom of a window (aka, the window sill).

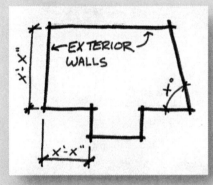

Elevations and Sections are the primary tools used to illustrate the various vertical relationships in a building – for example, the window sill, the distance between two floors or the roof's overhang.

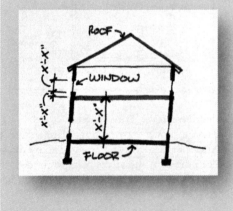

3D Views

Even though a good set of two-dimensional views can convey all required information to the contractor, both the client and contractor significantly benefit from one or more three-dimensional views

The image below is what you would refer to as a **Perspective View**. These types of views tend to be more life-like or photo-like than the isometric type 3D views covered below. Notice how the front of the building gets small as it moves back into the scene – even though the wall is the same height. Sketching this type of view will be a major focus of this book.

Example of a Perspective View

Another type of 3D view is an **Axonometric View** as shown in the example below. This type of drawing looks distorted as compared to the perspective view above; however, it can be drawn to scale (at least partially) so dimensions could quickly be derived from it. An axonometric drawing can be quickly drawn with a plastic 30/60 triangle (i.e., the sides of the triangle are 30 degrees, 60 degrees and 90 degrees) and a T-Square or parallel bar on a drawing board.

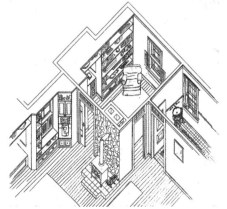

Axonometric example by **Anne Porter CID**

Line weights

You will not need to use this information just yet, but we will plant the "seed" now regarding the concept and application of line weights. Lines of varying thickness will help convey the depth of the image (which is important in both hand and computer drawings); here are a few concepts to keep in mind:

- The perimeter of major building masses should have a heavy line to make it punch out from the surrounding image.
- When buildings have multiple "major elements" the line weights should vary. For example, two building dormers in the same plane should be the same line weight, but the lines should get lighter as they step back (i.e., away from the viewer).
- The next heaviest lines should be between materials (e.g., lap siding to brick) and around elements like windows and doors. These lines will also get lighter as they step back into the image.
- The lightest lines will be the ones which represent the various building materials (e.g., shingles, siding, brick, etc.).

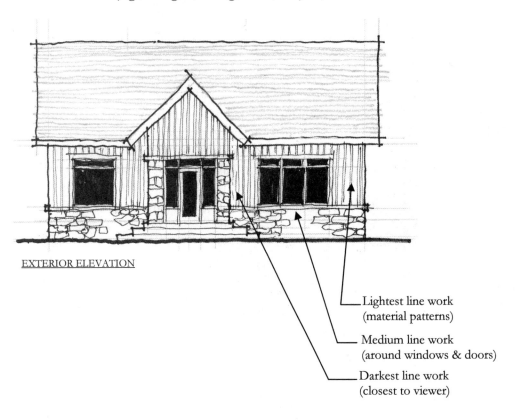

EXTERIOR ELEVATION

Lightest line work
(material patterns)

Medium line work
(around windows & doors)

Darkest line work
(closest to viewer)

Drawing Scale

Have you ever noticed the disclaimer on some cereal boxes which states that the picture has been enlarged to show texture of the product? They have intentionally made the product look larger than the actual size, or scale, of the product. Well, the opposite thing is done with architectural drawings. Architectural drawings are drawn at a fraction of the size of the real building, which makes sense as you would need a pretty big piece of paper to draw a building at actual scale. Rather than showing more detail (or texture), less is often shown for clarity. For example, the joints between the concrete blocks are not shown nor are the individual studs; instead just a representative space is shown with a hatch pattern to graphically represent each material type (concrete, studs, concrete block, etc.).

Not all hand drawings are drawn to scale. The early sketches are quick and loose and do not lend themselves to the time consuming task of laying down an architectural scale (not a ruler) and marking a specific length.

There are two main issues related to scaled drawings.
- **First** you need to assure your building will be buildable and meet the various building codes. If you did not draw to scale you could not be certain, for example, that all the furniture would fit in a particular room or that a sink/stove/dishwasher would fit into a length of countertop along a certain wall.
- **Second** you are constrained by the size of paper you intend to use. It is ideal to make the drawing as large as possible on the page, which allows for more detailed line work and notes and dimensions. However, only certain scales are typically used for certain types of drawings – like for plans, for example.

Here are the most used scales:

Architectural	Engineering
1/16″ = 1′-0″	1″ = 10′-0″
3/32″ = 1′-0″	1″ = 20′-0″
1/8″ = 1′-0″	1″ = 30′-0″
3/16″ = 1′-0″	1″ = 40′-0″
1/4″ = 1′-0″	1″ = 50′-0″
3/8″ = 1′-0″	1″ = 60′-0″
1/2″ = 1′-0″	1″ = 80′-0″
3/4″ = 1′-0″	1″ = 100′-0″
1″ = 1′-0″	1″ = 150′-0″
1 1/2″ = 1′-0″	1″ = 500′-0″
3″ = 1′-0″	1″ = 1000′-0″

Note: ′ means FEET and ″ means INCHES

The image below will be used to cover how a scale is used and one method of determining what scale a drawing is (assuming you did not draw it).

Floor plans are typically drawn at ⅛″ = 1'-0″ or ¼″ = 1'-0″. So, assuming you did not draw this closet, you will try to determine what scale the drawing is. Is this closet drawn at ¼″ = 1'-0″ or is it drawn at ⅛″ = 1'-0″? Below the closet are two architectural scales (top two) and a ruler (the bottom one).

Question: how wide is the closet door if drawn at...

⅛″ = 1'-0″ _____   ¼″ = 1'-0″ _____

You will notice that each half tick on the ¼″ scale equals six inches; you can see that the closet door is two ticks or 1'-0″ wide (6″ x 2 ticks). Now looking at the ⅛″ scale we see that each tick is 1'-0″; thus, the closet door would be 2'-0″ wide if drawn at ⅛″ = 1'-0″.

Although possible, it is not likely that the closet door is only 1'-0″ wide. Even a 2'-0″ wide door is on the narrow side. So, we can conclude that the scale of this drawing is ⅛″ = 1'-0″. Knowing this you can see that the overall size of the space is 4'-0″. **FYI:** *It is helpful to know that most doors on commercial projects are 3'-0″ wide, meeting the requirements for accessibility.*

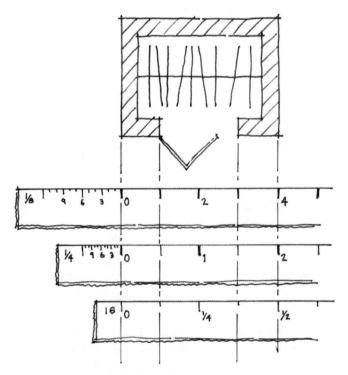

This image is enlarged for clarity and therefore is 'Not to Scale' in this book.

To make sure you get what is going on here, take a look at the image below. This is a sketch of a ¼″ scale (you do not always have to write or say the *equals a foot* part) and a ruler. This makes it clear what is meant by a ¼″ = 1'-0″; every quarter of an inch on the paper relates to 1'-0″ in the real world. Notice how 1'-0″ on the ¼″ scale aligns with ¼″ on the ruler above it? The 2'-0″ mark on the ¼″ scale aligns with the ½″ mark on the ruler – because (2) quarter inches equal 2'-0″ (or ½″ on the ruler). On a ¼″ scale drawing everything is scaled down to 1/48th of its actual size.

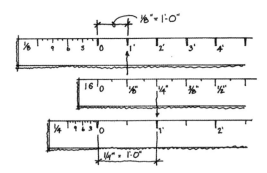

A contractor uses this information (i.e., drawing scale) to determine the quantities and cost of a building. So you can imagine how important it is to label drawings with the correct scale!

<u>Which Scale to Use</u>?
The next logical question is how is the correct scale selected? The list below indicates the most common scales used for each type of drawing. Ideally the largest scale possible would be used – the limitation being the size of the paper.

Common drawing scales used:

Floor Plan:	⅛″, ¼″
Enlarged Floor Plan:	¼″, ½″
Exterior Elevations:	⅛″, ¼″
Interior Elevations:	⅛″, ¼″, ½″
Building Sections:	⅛″, ¼″
Wall Sections:	½″, ¾″
Details:	½″, ¾″, 1″, 1½″, 3″

The details are the largest scale drawings because they represent a smaller part of the building (e.g., a roof edge vs. an entire floor plan) and show lots of details (e.g., flashing, rebar, fasteners, rubber roofing).

Although drawing to scale has a more limited role in hand sketching, it is still mandatory that the architectural designer understand this concept.

There are several types of scales (i.e., a tool for measuring distance) which can be purchased, so you need to understand the options before getting one.

Format/Units
First of all, there are architectural, engineering and metric scales. The engineering scales are used mainly by *Civil Engineers* and *Landscape Architects*. However, it is handy for the architectural designer to have one when drawing site plans. The metric scales are largely used by designers outside the United States, but are used on certain projects (e.g., US federal and military projects require them).

Shape/Size
Drawing scales come in all shapes and sizes. You can buy short ones (6" to 12" long) that are easy to carry around in a shirt pocket, briefcase or purse. In addition to being portable, the smaller scales are handy for measuring details and parts of larger drawings – for example, the clearances around a door in a floor plan.

These scales also come in sizes up to 36" long (and longer) for drawing and measuring larger drawings. A scale this size can be used to measure the full length of a building plotted out on a sheet of paper (e.g., 24"x36").

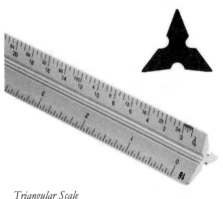

Triangular Scale

In addition to length, you should also consider the shape of the scale. Scales generally come in two shapes; triangular and flat. Each shape has its advantages and both are handy to have around.

The triangular shaped scale, shown to the left, is easy to pick up, lays flat on the drawing and has the most scales on it due to the numbers of sides (6 total) given the shape.

Flat Scale

The flat scale, shown to the left, has the advantage of being portable as mentioned above. This scale can be a little more difficult to pick up off the drawing surface compared to the triangle which always has an edge pointing up with continuous grooves on each side making it easy to grasp. This scale only has four edges compared to the six on the triangle. It really comes down to preference more than anything, but many designers have and use both regularly.

Most architectural scales have two scales superimposed over each other – for example, ¼" and ⅛" share a common side of a triangular scale. Working from left to right is the ⅛" scale and from right to left is the ¼" scale. This means you have to pay attention to which numbers you are reading as one set is for the ⅛" scale and the other set is for the ¼" scale. The two sets of numbers are offset from each other to help keep things straight. The two scales on a face are always compatible in that one is twice the scale of the other; e.g., ½" and 1", ⅜" and ¾", 1½" and 3".

Looking at the image below, the arrows point at the numbers that relate to the 1" = 1'-0" scale. Notice how the other numbers are offset and are getting larger from the other direction (these would be for the ½" scale). The finer ticks to the right of 0 are the inches.

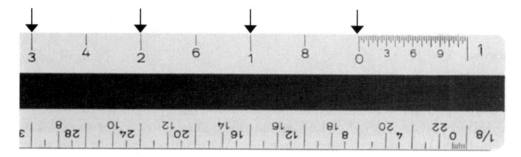

When you are measuring something, you align the closet whole foot number on one end and then see where the other end falls on the "inches" scale. In the example below the table is 2'-3" in length for a 1" = 1'-0" scale.

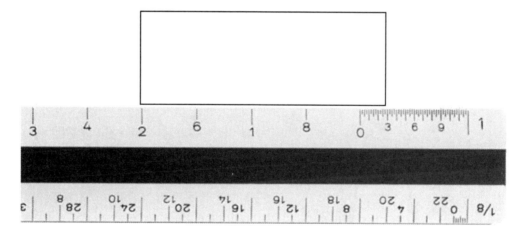

All architects and designers need to have a few drawing scales. Even the architectural technician who often mainly draws using the computer needs to be able to quickly measure the length of various lines on the printed page. At the very least, the scale is used to verify the plotter/CAD program printed the drawing the correct size.

Drawing Symbols/Graphics

When sketching Architectural drawings you need to be aware of a few basic graphic conventions for the major building elements like doors, windows, stairs, cabinets, and such. The drawings presented here can vary a bit from one designer/firm to another as far as line weight and embellishments, but for the most part everyone does it pretty much as shown here. Of course, we are talking about hand sketching here; when things get further along and are drawn in CAD/BIM, the symbols are more standardized and consistent.

When sketching preliminary floor plans, the walls, doors and windows are usually the only things drawn until you find a layout that looks like it will work. Then that option is refined with additional architectural elements like cabinets, plumbing fixtures (toilets, sinks, etc.), appliances and then even furniture.

Doors

Doors are an important part of any building design; their locations determine circulation, privacy, code compliance and more. In a floor plan, doors are usually shown open 90 degrees and an arc is added to indicate the swing. The swing arc is the path the door travels across the floor. Imagine attaching a piece of chalk to the outer edge of the door so it touched the ground and then you open the door; the line left on the ground by the chalk is the swing arc. The door is shown in the open position to indicate which direction it opens, which is important for circulation and code compliance, and to ensure the door does not conflict with other things such as cabinets, toilets, etc.

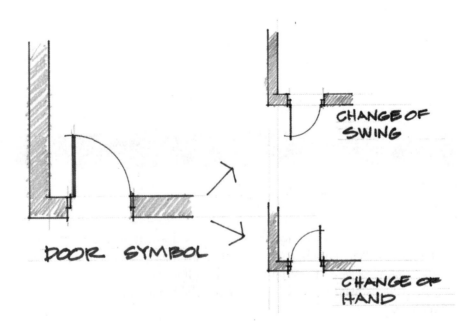

Here are a few additional door graphics you might see or use in any given floor plan. Notice most show the door in an open position and have a swing arc line. Those that do not have a swing do not swing open. On commercial projects, as opposed to residential, the door frame is always shown.

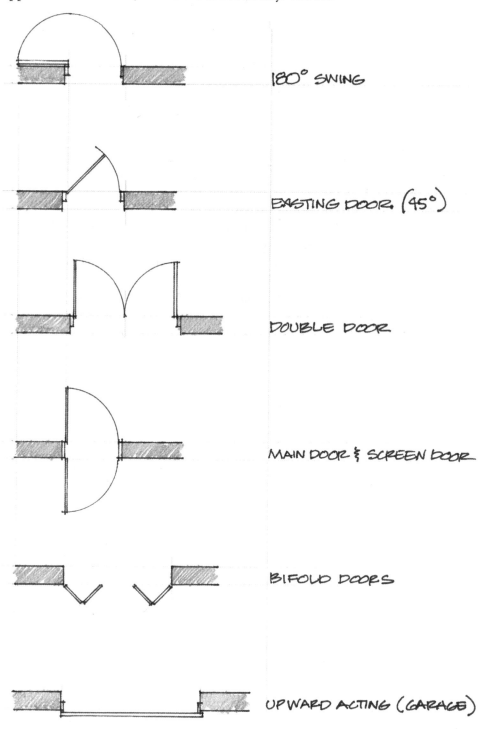

180° SWING

EXISTING DOOR (45°)

DOUBLE DOOR

MAIN DOOR & SCREEN DOOR

BIFOLD DOORS

UPWARD ACTING (GARAGE)

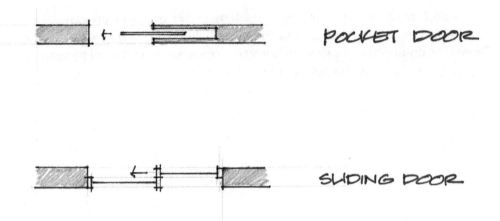

Windows

Another type of opening is the window. Early in the design process a very generic window is sketched – one line for each side of the window and a line parallel with the wall to represent the glass. As things become more developed, you can start adding mullions and frame depth and "location-in-wall" information.

> *FYI: All sysmbols drawn in this section have been hand drawn with a straight edge to make them crisp and less ambiguous. However, you will likely want to just sketch them by hand without the aid of a straight edge as that will slow you down. You can leave the straight lines for CAD/BIM.*

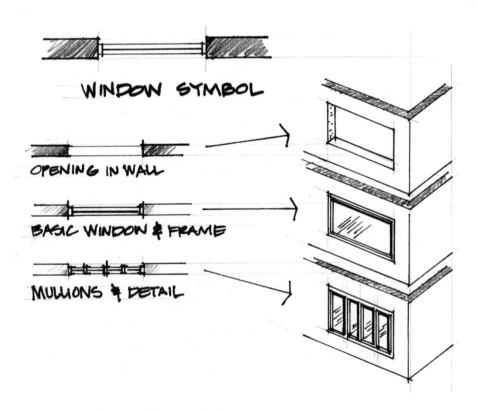

Plumbing Fixtures

As mentioned previously, plumbing fixtures are added once the plan becomes more finalized. It does not make sense to take the time to sketch in every little detail early on when you are still trying several different ideas. However, it is a good idea to show the plumbing fixtures (even in the sketching phase) so you don't forget how much room you need for the various toilets, sinks and such. Experience really helps here as the number of fixtures is based on various code requirements, and due to accessibility rules you may need twice the space you originally imagined. Figuring this out after the plan was thought to be "set in stone" and the structural, mechanical and electrical designers have begun their drawings is BAD! However, things are always changing right up until the last nail is hammered into the finished building, so it would not be totally unexpected.

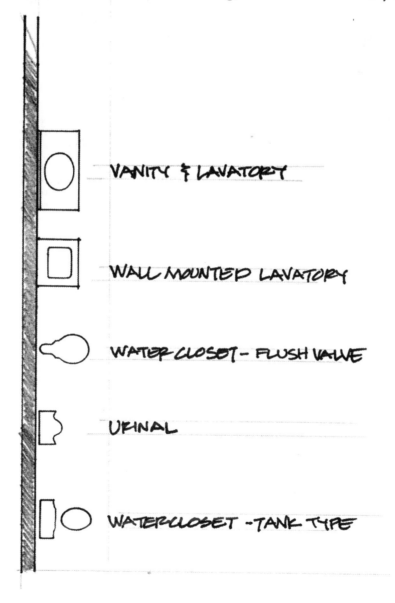

Vertical Circulation: Stairs

Any building, residential or commercial, which has more than one floor or level has a stair with rare exception. Stairs take up a decent amount of floor space so you need to show them from the beginning of the design process and they need to be shown correctly. "Shown correctly" means the correct number of steps are shown (which meet building code) to get you from one floor to another – given the specific floor-to-floor height. You may not always know the exact distance between floors so you have to make an educated guess until you have more information.

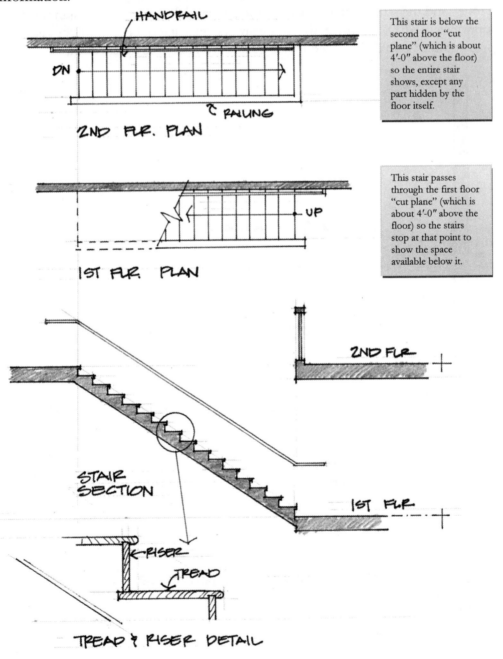

This stair is below the second floor "cut plane" (which is about 4'-0" above the floor) so the entire stair shows, except any part hidden by the floor itself.

This stair passes through the first floor "cut plane" (which is about 4'-0" above the floor) so the stairs stop at that point to show the space available below it.

Below are a few additional stair layouts. Many more scenarios could be shown but these cover the basics. Additional vertical circulation would include elevators, and space for their required machine room, and escalators.

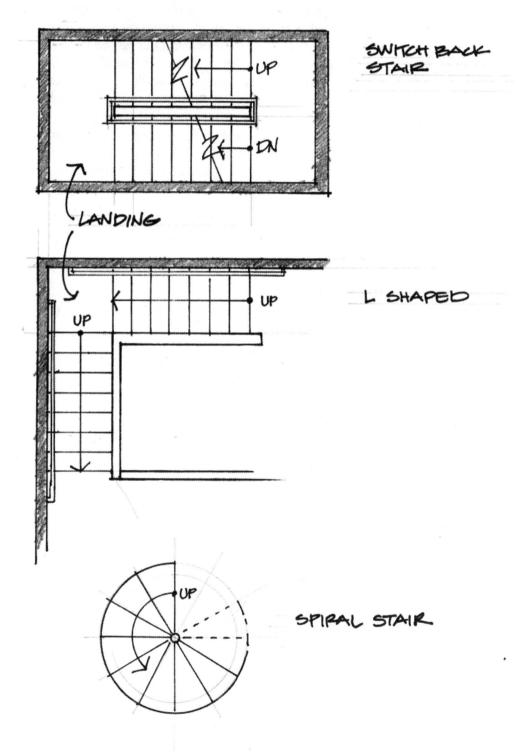

SWITCH BACK STAIR

LANDING

L SHAPED

SPIRAL STAIR

Casework: Cabinets

The goal in most architectural floors plans is to show anything that is fixed, built-in or otherwise not moveable; cabinets are one such thing. A few standard graphic conventions have been developed to show the various layered components of cabinets in a floor plan. Referring to the sketch below, and the one on the next page, you see the cabinets sitting on the floor, called **Base Cabinets**. They are drawn with solid or continuous lines. Base cabinets are typically 24″ deep. Next you have the cabinets above the base cabinets and attached to the wall, called **Wall Cabinets** (or Upper Cabinets). Wall cabinets are usually 12″-14″ deep and are drawn with a dashed line to indicate they are above. **Appliances** (i.e., refrigerator, range, dishwasher, etc.) are also shown and sometimes their doors are shown "dashed-in" while in the open position to make sure it does not conflict with something else.

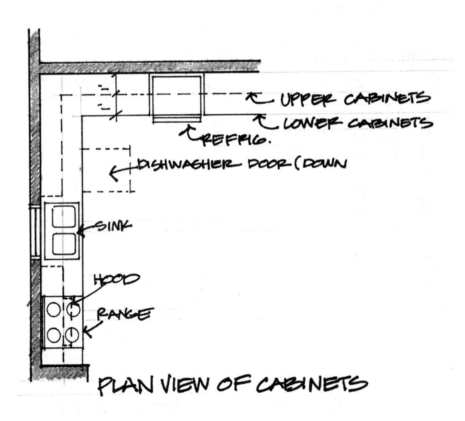

The information provided in this section just skims the surface on this topic. For an extensive study, you are encouraged to take a look at the **Architectural Graphic Standards** (Wiley, ISBN: 978-0-471-70091-3). Most every architect and architectural designer has this reference book which covers a large array of information, e.g., waterproofing, building details, masonry construction, gutter sizing, sports fields and much more!

This is not something that is usually hand drawn these days, but it is shown here to help you understand what exactly is being shown and discussed in the floor plan sketch on the previous page.

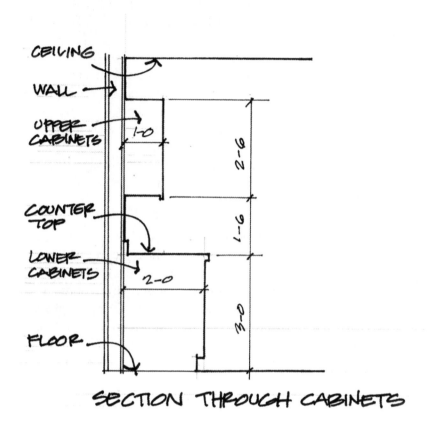

SECTION THROUGH CABINETS

Summary

This first section presented several fundamental concepts you need to know to get started in the world of creating architectural hand drawings. It is highly recommended that you complete the exercises that follow this chapter to make sure you "get it". If you have problems with the exercises, you should flip back through this section to see if you missed something. Also, the information here is meant to give you the knowledge and confidence to tackle the remaining chapters in this book. *NOTE: It is recommended that you complete the chapters in order as they generally build upon each other. Finally, be sure you make time for reading and working on the exercises if you want to be really good at architectural drawing!*

The Line

The line is the beginning of all architectural drawing. It must define the edge of a wall, the corner or it is a part of a number of lines that defines a *hatch* or a *tone*. In short, it is the most basic "definer" that we use and hence the QUALITIES of this line can be very important.

The line must be done with an economy of time and effort. The sketch artist cannot waste too much time overanalyzing the technical aspects of each line one is drawing. Architectural projects often have tight budgets and short schedules – clients do not typically have bottomless pockets and would like to start utilizing their new facility as quickly as possible. Spending excess time sketching can eat into the design professional's profits and delay the project. So, the longer it takes to get your ideas on paper, the greater chance you have of that idea slipping away or you have less time to think about additional ideas.

Oh, and in the "real world" you are on the clock! Your boss is not going to pay you to just sketch all day and not get anything else done! The typical design professional still has to make time in the day to create the meeting minutes for the meeting with the client yesterday, meet with a product representative about a new roofing system they are promoting, and the list goes on and on. Thus, the problem is not so much wasting time sketching as it is not having enough time, so one is forced to use their time wisely.

What better way to analyze the fundamentals of the architectural lines than to use an architectural sketch of a six year old?

The sketch to the right clearly presents itself as a sketch of a building; it has walls, roof elements and a door. A hatch has even been added to better define the walls and perhaps a specific material.

A few key goals of this section are to plant the seed about ways to draw horizontal and vertical lines that are indeed horizontal and vertical, as well as equally spaced, when needed. Also, the line thicknesses change for various parts of the sketch.

Of course these are not things a six year old need concern himself with, but those reading this book most certainly should!

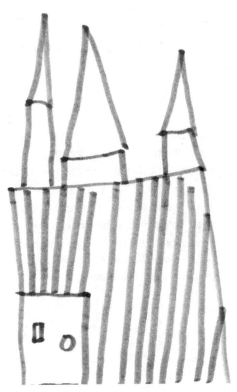

Six year old's sketch; Image by Carter Stine

The Horizontal Line

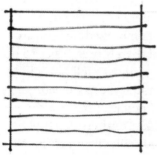

A handful of comments can be made about the horizontal line in the context of hand sketching – particularly freehand sketching. You are encouraged to read through this material and not just jump ahead to the exercises, especially if your instructor assigns the questions at the end of the chapter!

The most challenging thing about drawing a horizontal line is drawing a horizontal line; the line does not have to be perfectly straight but rather close to horizontal overall. Many are challenged with the eye-hand coordination required to keep a line horizontal on the paper when they are first learning to sketch. The main reason has to do with how your body is designed and the result is that you have to adjust your wrist and/or elbow as you move your pencil across the paper (this is not really a problem for vertical lines – discussed a little later).

Therefore, the natural "arc" of the hand can limit stroke lengths. At a certain point you find the need to make an adjustment in your hand position to keep your horizontal line on track. This results in a "kink" in your line. Rather than a "kink" that tends to look like a mistake you can overemphasize the transition by lifting the pen/pencil and leaving a small gap – even adding a little extra pressure at the beginning and end of each stroke…

Another method that can be employed when developing horizontal lines is an intentional (even exaggerated) squiggle in the line. This can effectively hide the "adjustments" that are needed to keep the line on track (i.e., horizontal).

A squiggly line intentionally added at the roof edge.

The Vertical Line

Unlike the horizontal line, the vertical line is not so much limited by the "arc" of the hand and therefore is easier to do. You still need to practice a little eye-hand coordination to keep the line vertical. These lines are often drawn downward, unlike "drafted" vertical lines which are usually drawn from the bottom up.

Drafted means a drawing was created with tools such as straightedges, triangles, and parallel bar in order to create accurate, crisp lines. In contrast, a **Sketched** drawing does not employ much more than the pen as illustrated in the image below.

Even though vertical lines are easier to draw than horizontal lines, you may still want to add gaps between smaller strokes, which will add a little "snap".

Your vertical lines can be straight or have some intentional squiggle which allows for more fluid movement.

Lines to Avoid

In order to get a better feeling for the qualities of a "good" line we will point out some less desirable lines and techniques. No one is suggesting that there is a "right way" and a "wrong way" to create architectural drawings – but, honestly, there are "good" drawings and "not so good" looking drawings; some that are generally clear and easy to understand and some that are ambiguous and amateurish. So the goal here is to point you down the path that most seasoned architectural designers travel and find success.

One line to avoid is the "scrubbing" line. This would be great as the outline of a lion, but architecturally you would rarely use a line like the one below. This resultant "scrub" type line is often the natural inclination if one has to assemble a series of line stokes.

Another line to avoid is one that starts out weak, then heavy and then weak again. A line should usually be constant in thickness and can even have its start and end points emphasized so it appears very intentional.

When lines come together to form the corner of a wall in a floor plan or the peak of a roof in elevation, architects and designers usually extend the lines so they cross – which develops an unmistakable corner. Most sketches are not meant to be works of art, rather they are a tool in which to communicate a design solution to other people (usually the client or the public), so drawing "outside the lines" is actually encouraged! If you take a look at the image below, you will find this line lacks consistency and crossing corners (a good example will be shown next). Finally, notice how the shape below is simply four individual lines – looked at individually you can see the "weak" line just mentioned above.

Good Lines

To balance things out we will now take a look at a few positive attributes you should be shooting for when sketching a line. Keep in mind we are talking about freehand sketching at the moment, not lines generated with the aid of a straight edge (i.e., drafted). You are shooting for "good" lines, not "perfect" lines...

You are encouraged to have a sketch book open and lying beside you as you read so you can try a few techniques. This will give you a little practice before you get to the <u>exercises</u> which need to be turned in (if using this book in a classroom setting). In your sketch book, try these concepts with both a pencil and a pen; many designers typically use a pen for most exploratory sketches as the lines are always crisp and you don't have to stop and sharpen the pencil.

Directly below is a sketched rectangle which has clearly defined corners and nice consistent lines. Notice that the lines usually start and end with a little heavier dot that is created by applying extra pressure. This line was created with a pencil; using ink is even easier to emphasize the ends.

As previously discussed in the section on horizontal lines, the wrist has a natural tendency to pivot. Therefore, this natural pivoting of your hand tends to want to arch, thus the ease with which the arc can be drawn (but not without some concern for accuracy if you need it).

Angled Lines and Hatching

The next logical topic for discussion is straight lines which are neither horizontal nor vertical: that is, angled lines. These lines are often used for contrast in a sketch – to shade one side of an object so the various faces stand out from each other – or to represent shadows. Taking this concept a bit further, we find this technique being used in more technical drawings to represent various materials – we refer to this as hatching.

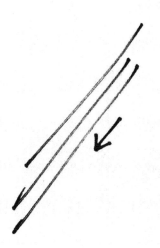

The **Diagonal Line** is typically drawn in a downward stroke.

The diagonal line is a basic building block of shading and hatching patterns. You can create many different looks by varying the spacing or angle and pencil or pen weights.

One way to very quickly control a series of diagonal lines and turn into a hatch is to place a triangle, straight edge or similar clear ruler and draw a series of closely spaced diagonal lines against it... creating an open, yet crisp edge.

Connecting strokes on a diagonal line is fairly difficult and not that pleasing visually. It is often easier to use very short strokes and slightly change directions as shown here. As you look at the older illustrations using pens, you will often see this sort of technique and will come to appreciate the tonal qualities it can impart.

The **Cross Hatch** is quite simply the overlay of two diagonal directions. Often the second (or cross) hatch can be only partial or over a certain area, giving depth and variety to the effect.

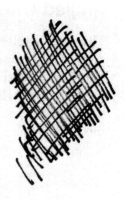

Below are a few other variations on hatching. The upper left box shows more of a "technical" hatch in that it is used on details and working drawings (often referred to as Blue Prints – even though they are not blue anymore). The lower left and middle right are the result of rubbing the lead over the paper while it has a heavily textured material beneath it; this results in a consistent and interesting pattern.

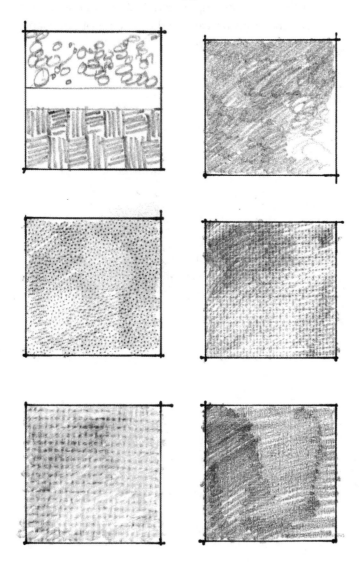

Gesture Drawing

One of the biggest hurdles many have to becoming decent delineators is moving the instrument (pencil, pen, etc.) quickly and loosely on the paper. Too often the would-be designer is sketching slowly and overanalyzing even the earliest strokes. Therefore the next discussion, and subsequent exercises at the end of the chapter, are designed to address this challenge.

Gesture drawing is the process of sketching quick, playful lines on paper while leaving the pen in contact with the paper most of the time. The goal is to create a close approximation of an object (real or imagined) with an economy of time.

With practice your gesture drawings will start to have the proper proportions and poses that will enhance the "scene" of your perspective drawings later on in this book. Again, right now this is just a pragmatic exploration in putting pen to paper!

Architecture is really about the interplay of people and buildings; drawing a building with no people is like drawing a car with no tires. Quickly sketched human forms give your drawings scale and life.

The exact way in which a *gestured person* is drawn is really up to the individual, but a few tips will be provided here to help get you started. With a little practice and effort you can develop your own style, which can be one of the "trademarks" of your drawings.

Sketching a basic figure, perhaps like the one shown below, can start with a head oval (which is often aligned with the horizon line), then the quick body trunk which morphs into the legs with no feet. Next you add arms that omit the hands. The position of the arms and legs often imply a certain activity (walking, sitting, pointing) or situation (assembly, excitement, peace). Finally one might choose to add hatch or tone with diagonal lines (just covered) or swirly lines which give the figure dimension; and maybe some are hatched and others left as outlines which creates contrast and can imply racial diversity amongst the buildings occupants.

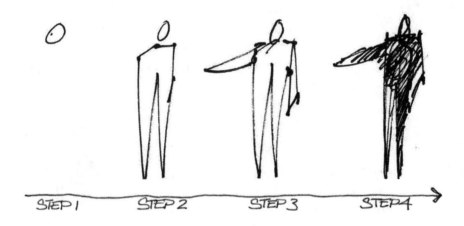

Similar steps can be used to create a gesture drawing of a seated person. Focus should be placed on the larger body elements such as the torso, thighs, calves, etc. Next you can add "props" like a chair or a briefcase (see example on previous page) to give the figure additional dimension or meaning.

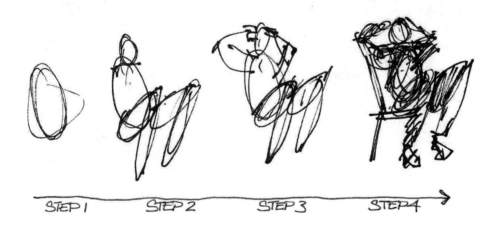

Remember to stay fluid and work very quickly. In fact this exercise should focus on speed to capture the essential "massing" of the human form. If you are working through this book in a classroom setting, you may be asked by the instructor to do some in-class exercises where everyone has, let's say, one minute to sketch a person being displayed on the overhead projector. Several images can be displayed and each drawn within the time constraint. Of course you can do this on your own using a magazine and your sketch book. Either way this would be great practice before trying the gesture exercises at the end of this chapter.

Just as people can be quickly "gestured" in a drawing, so too can building masses, forms and ideas be rapidly done. Below is an example of a small building; note the multiple quick lines and no scrubbing. Practicing in a sketchbook on small, simple buildings, in conjunction with great speed will help develop an ease with the medium (i.e., paper) and tools (e.g., pen or pencil).

Quick simple bold lines portray the building, the tree and the land form.

Gesture sketching just for fun…

Image directly above by Architect Alan Anderson

The images on this page provide examples from two architects' sketch books.

The image above, by co-author McNeill, is a loose lunch-time sketch of a visiting ship in the Duluth harbor.

The image to the left is a page with multiple studies nestled together on one page; these quick sketches are meant for practice and therefore do not need to be neatly arranged on separate pieces of paper.

Even architects with years of experience find time to practice…

Using the gesture technique in sketching up a floor plan is an all important tool to place an idea on paper. Note the door drawn over the wall lines. This is not a problem (and no need to erase anything); just darken the walls to the side of it to emphasize the opening. This, again, is a very quick exercise intended for study and analysis – not a drawing you would likely show a client (unless you where meeting with the client and sketching in front of the client).

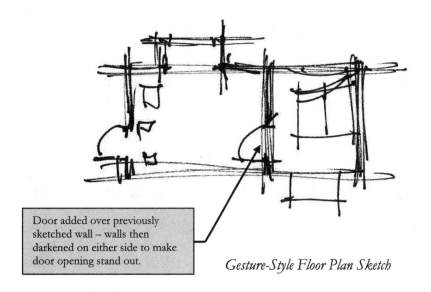

Door added over previously sketched wall – walls then darkened on either side to make door opening stand out.

Gesture-Style Floor Plan Sketch

In addition to getting ideas onto paper there are a few additional reasons for employing this "gesture" type sketching method for buildings and floor plans. One is when walking through a building for the first time (maybe you will be designing an addition or remodeling); by sketching the location of walls and doors you are enhancing your memory of each space by putting pencil to paper. Taking digital pictures certainly helps, but architects, designers and technicians usually have the ability to think three-dimensionally, so sketching reinforces one's grasp of a space. Once back at the office, the sketches can be reviewed for the purposes of writing a memo about the meeting or to develop an estimate for your services.

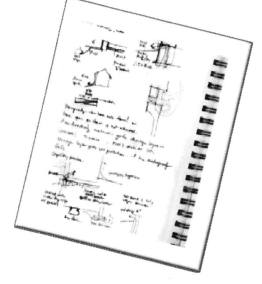

Also, quick sketching is helpful when attending seminars. This sketch book page (to the right) is from a Radon Gas presentation. The sketches may never be directly looked at again, but simply having sketched it helps one engrave that concept or image in their mind for future retrieval.

Hand Lettering

The art of hand lettering is not as admired as it once was. Most of what you read these days is presented in typed format, generated using a computer and printer. There is certainly nothing wrong with computer generated lettering, and some of us really benefit from the spell-check functionality! However, the would-be architectural designer would do well to practice hand lettering and develop a lettering style. The designer will often find one's self sketching in front of the client or contractor and should be able to create clean legible text that looks professional.

Most designers are rather particular about their lettering style; this also applies to their signature. It is interesting that many designers have two lettering styles – one for presentation drawings and the other for personal and inter-office notes. The latter is barely legible, even by the author! The "sloppier" lettering style has to do with the fact that the brain works faster than the hand and pen – so designers, much like doctors, tend to have lots of horizontal lines that appear to jump up and down and roughly form words (this is a bit of an exaggeration, but you get the point)!

A presentation-type lettering style is usually preceded by two light horizontal lines which are used as guidelines; the typical text height is 3/16″ for notes (when generated by a computer, like a CAD system, the text height is often 3/32″; due to the consistency and accuracy of the computer and printers it is still easy to read and takes up less room. This may seem elementary, but it helps to create nice, crisp, horizontal lines of text where the tops and bottoms are well proportioned and aligned.

The instrument used to generate the letters is just as important as the style. As you can see below, the top example in which a **pen** was used produced a bolder and crisper look as compared to the second example created with **pencil**. The third example used a heavy **felt tip pen**. So you may have created a sketch in pencil but maybe the text should be in pen to make to "punch out" more; or if you sketched in pen, maybe the text is done with a heavy felt-tipped pen.

ABCDEFGHIJKLMN
OPQRSTUVWXYZ ABCD
EFGHIJKLMNOPQRST

ABCDEFGHIJKLMNO
PQRSTUVWXYZ ABCDE
FGHIJKLMNOPQRSTU

ABCDEFGHIJK
LMNOPQRSTUV
WXYZ 123456789

Most architectural hand lettering is uppercase. Beginning on the next page you will see the lettering style of a few different architects. Notice the various little embellishments that make each unique. In the exercises at the end of this chapter you will have the opportunity to practice hand lettering. Throughout this section on hand sketching, you should try to place an emphasis on hand lettering, labeling drawings and even just adding your name and the date to any pages to be turned in.

In the past, primarily before computers were common place, all text was hand written. Text, such as titles, firm names and such, was often generated with a pen or pencil and an aid, such as a stencil or transfer sheet. With modern technology most all of the formal title can be generated by the computer, which makes for a clean, crisp and professional presentation. Hand lettering for formal presentations should be limited to notes and minor labels. Much like the way this textbook was prepared, one can scan hand sketches and place them in a document with computer graphics and text.

Hand sketched image with computer generated text; also take note of the "gesture" people.

Image Used by Permission

Below (and on the next page) are several examples of hand lettering styles:

ABCDEFGHIJKLMNOPQRSTU
VWXYZ ABCDEFGHIJKLMN
OPQRSTUVWXYZ ABCDEFG

Example #1: *Dan Stine (as a student in1992)*

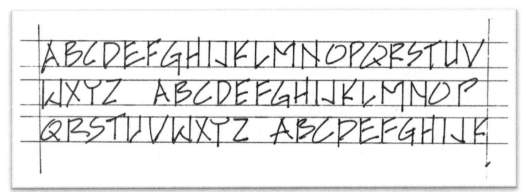

Example #2: *Larry Turbes*

Example #3: *Alan Anderson*

Example #4: *Craig Schneuer*

Example #5: *Mark G. Poirier*

Another example, in the sketch below, is hand lettering used to note materials and list lengths. Notice that zero inches are always listed and everything is capitalized.

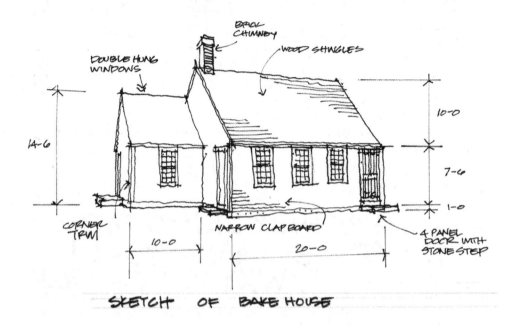

Lines and Hatching applied

Below are two birch bark study sketches which use several of the techniques discussed in this book, including lines and hatching.

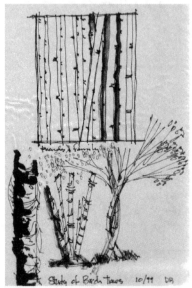

Birch Study Sketches by **Darryl Booker***,*
Associate Professor, North Dakota State University

Self-Exam:

The following questions can be used as a way to check your knowledge of this lesson. The answers can be found at the bottom of this page.

1. Every project has a True North. (T/F)

2. All sketches are drawn to scale. (T/F)

3. Less detail is typically shown for clarity. (T/F)

4. The natural "arc" of the hand aids in drawing horizontal lines. (T/F)

5. Line work closest to the viewer is heavier/thicker. (T/F)

Review Questions:

The following questions may be assigned by your instructor as a way to assess your knowledge of this section. Your instructor has the answers to the review questions.

1. 3D objects are depicted by three or more 2D views. (T/F)

2. Window sills are often dimensioned in floor plan views. (T/F)

3. The Architectural equivalent to Top View: _____ _____.

4. The type of drawing that looks most life-like: _____.

5. One of the primary views used in architecture: _____ _____.

6. Hand lettering is mostly uppercase in architectural drawings. (T/F)

7. Name of drawing type that looks down on walls and floors:

   _____

8. Construction Drawings are used by the contractor to build from. (T/F)

9. A 3D view drawn to scale: _____.

10. Did you remember to write your name at the top of the page? (Y/N)

Notes:

Instructions: Chapter 8 Exercises

These exercises are meant to help you look at a drawing on a piece of paper, which of course is a 2D drawing, and visualize its 3D shape. Sometimes you cannot fully comprehend a 2D drawing's complete 3D shape unless you have more than one view in which to reference. All views provided should have adequate information for you to complete the exercise.

The instructions provided below are for the exercises on the following pages – specifically, the Chapter 8 Exercises.

Match the small top, front and side views with the proper isometric view (i.e., the two large views). Write the *view type* (top, front or side) and the *isometric name* that view corresponds to (one example shown on the first exercise). Place a star on duplicate views for both isometric views; meaning the top view, for example, looks identical even though the 3D shape is clearly not identical.

The graphics below are repeated from the chapter as a reference.

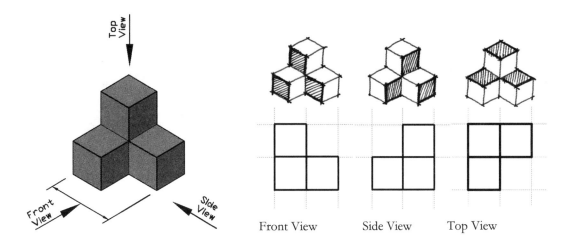

Front View   Side View   Top View

~blank page~

NAME_____DATE_____

Exercise 8-1

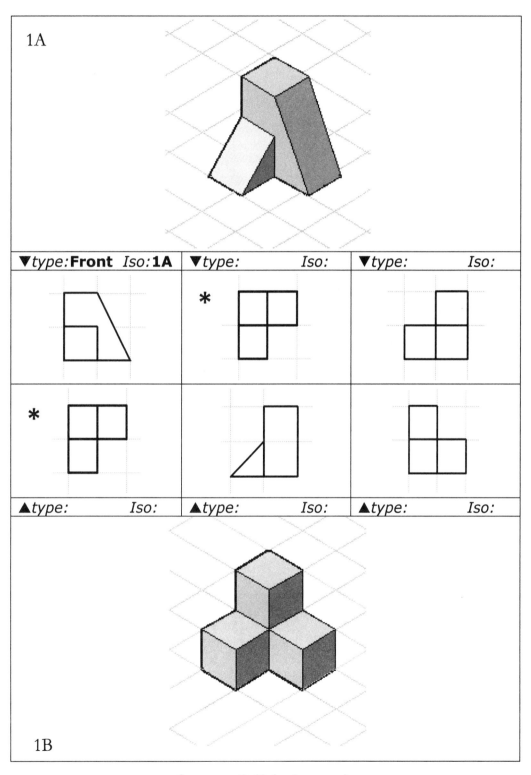

1A

▼type:**Front** Iso:**1A**	▼type: Iso:	▼type: Iso:
	*	
*		
▲type: Iso:	▲type: Iso:	▲type: Iso:

1B

See page 8-43 for instructions.

~blank page~

NAME_____DATE_____

Exercise 8-2

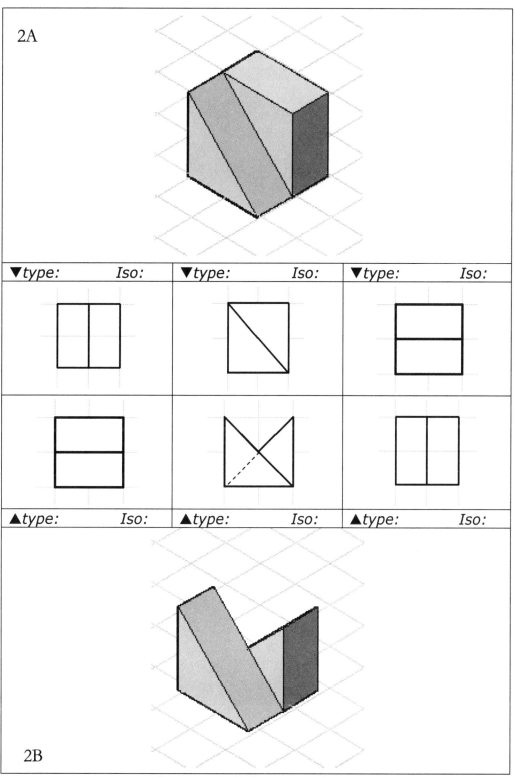

~blank page~

NAME_____DATE_____

Exercise 8-3

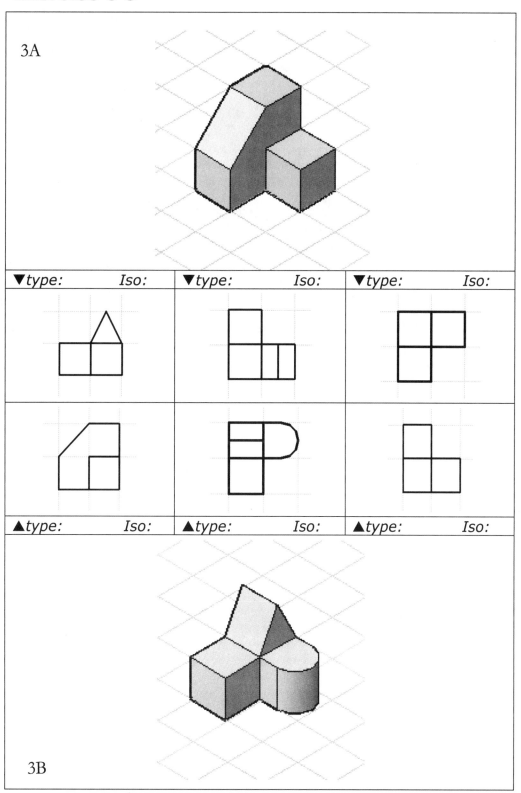

3A

▼type: Iso: ▼type: Iso: ▼type: Iso:

▲type: Iso: ▲type: Iso: ▲type: Iso:

3B

See page 8-43 for instructions.

~blank page~

NAME_____DATE_____

Exercise 8-4

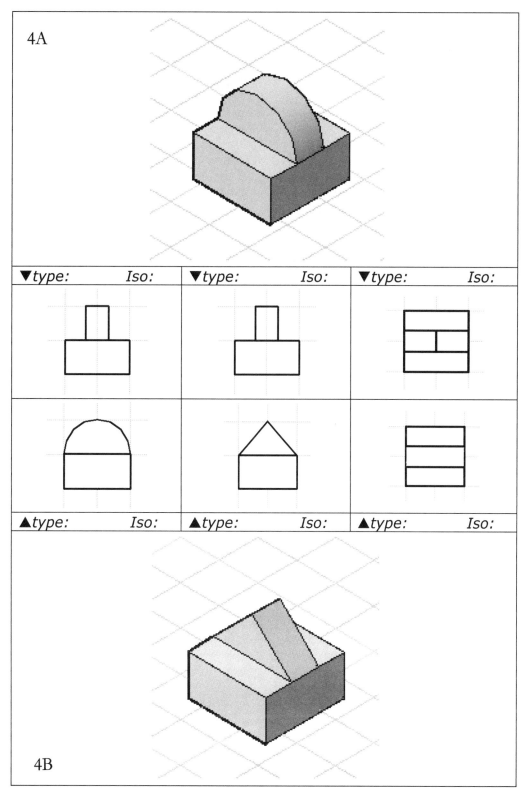

See page 8-43 for instructions.

~blank page~

NAME_____DATE_____

Exercise 8-5

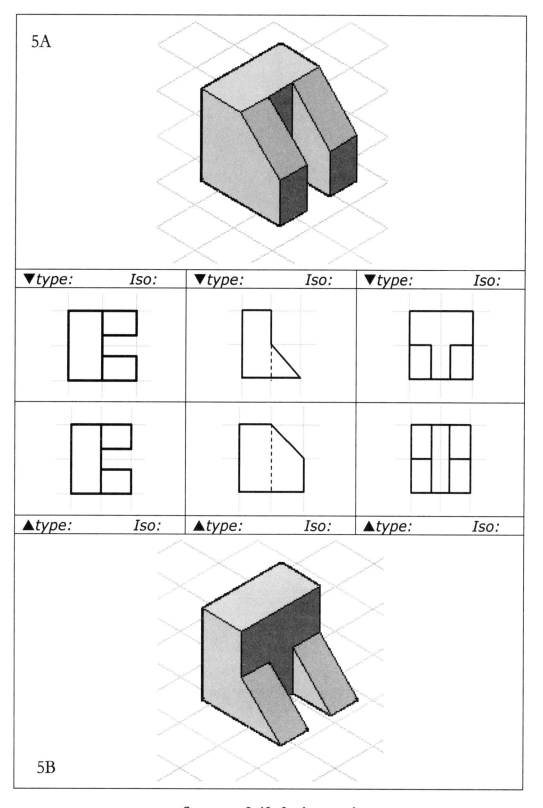

5A

▼type: Iso: ▼type: Iso: ▼type: Iso:

▲type: Iso: ▲type: Iso: ▲type: Iso:

5B

See page 8-43 for instructions.

~blank page~

NAME_____DATE_____

Exercise 8-6

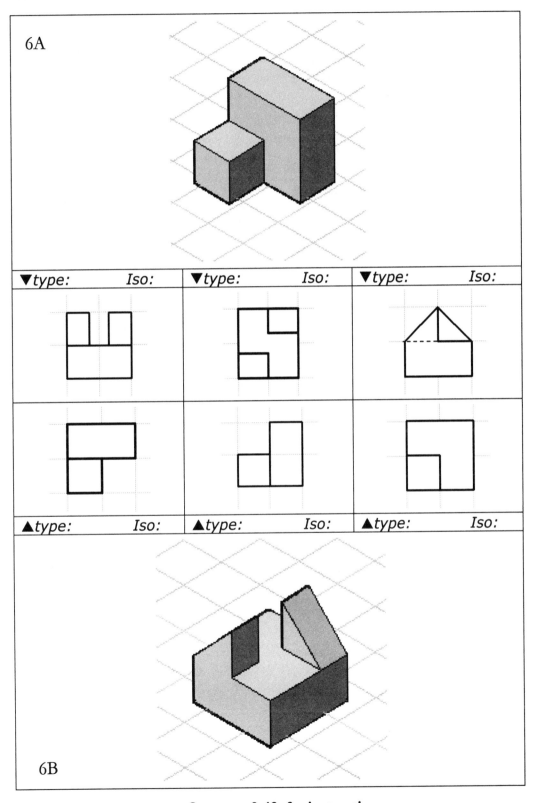

6A

▼type: Iso: | ▼type: Iso: | ▼type: Iso:

▲type: Iso: | ▲type: Iso: | ▲type: Iso:

6B

See page 8-43 for instructions.

~blank page~

NAME_____DATE_____

Exercise 8-7

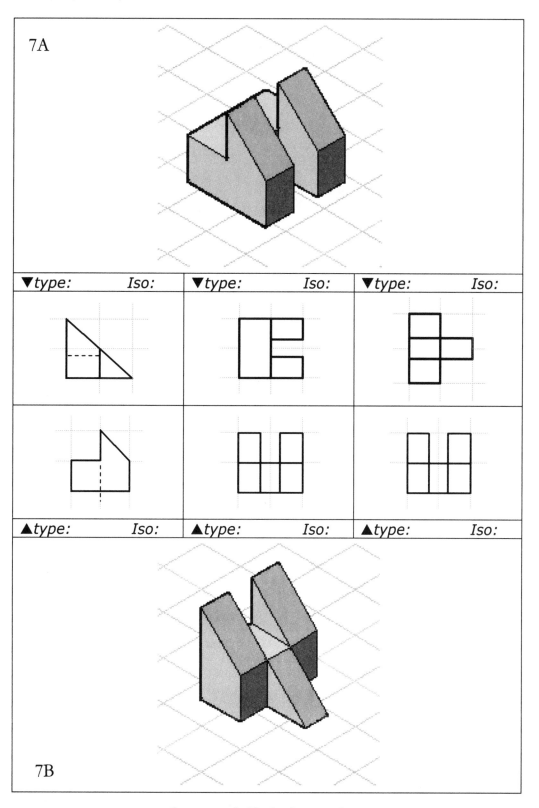

7A

▼type: Iso:	▼type: Iso:	▼type: Iso:
▲type: Iso:	▲type: Iso:	▲type: Iso:

7B

See page 8-43 for instructions.

~blank page~

NAME_____DATE_____

Exercise 8-8

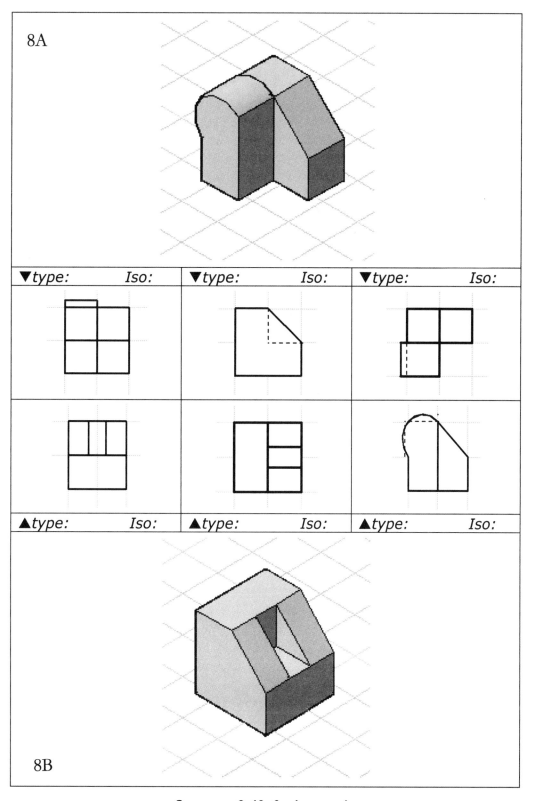

8A

▼type: Iso: ▼type: Iso: ▼type: Iso:

▲type: Iso: ▲type: Iso: ▲type: Iso:

8B

See page 8-43 for instructions.

~blank page~

NAME_____DATE_____

Exercise 8-9

This is a lightly drawn floor plan of a cabin or small home. Take a felt tipped pen, and using the conventions for windows, doors, cabinets & bathroom fixtures, sketch them in – using a straightedge or freehand – your choice. Be creative in your placement! Darken over the lightly drawn walls and infill or "poche" the walls with red or black pencil. Add hand written text to label the rooms.

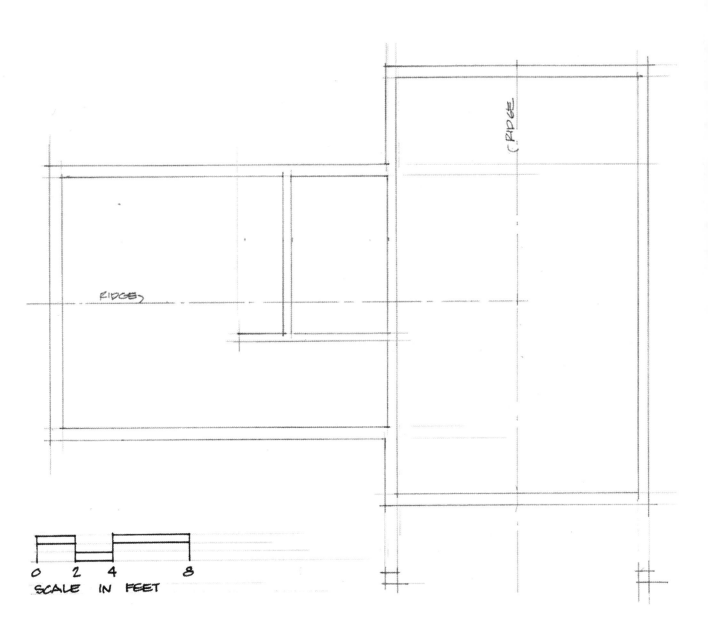

RIDGE

RIDGE

0 2 4   8
SCALE IN FEET

~blank page~

NAME_____DATE_____

Exercise 8-10

It is recommended that you tear these pages out at the perforated edge, one at a time, before you use them so you can lay them firmly on a smooth surface as you work. You can then add your name and date above and turn in to your instructor.

It is important to learn to handle your pencil and/or pen properly to create the desired line or shape. The following tasks will walk you through several fundamental steps in sketching. <u>Only use a pencil (or pen) for these "Chapter 8" exercises (no straight edges)</u>.

Equally Spaced Horizontal Lines using a pen

In this first task you will draw equally spaced horizontal lines. One goal is to learn how to move your hand as you draw so the line stays horizontal; the other is to visualize where to place your pencil on the paper so the next line will be equal distance as compared to the previous lines. *The lines do not have to be perfect, so do this quickly!*

Next draw equally spaced horizontal lines, making them twice as close (in spacing) as the previous example. *Do this quickly!*

~blank page~

NAME_____DATE_____

Exercise 8-11

Equally Spaced Vertical Lines using a pen
Follow the space steps in the previous exercise, but sketch vertical lines. Do not simply turn the page 90 degrees and sketch horizontal lines; this is often not possible as the paper is too large or it is taped to the drawing board. Do this three times in the boxes provided. You may want to try it a few times in a sketch book or on the back of some old printer paper first.

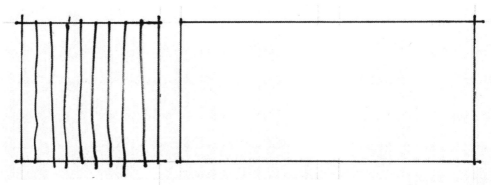

This is the example   Draw equally spaced vertical lines
using a consistent line weight.

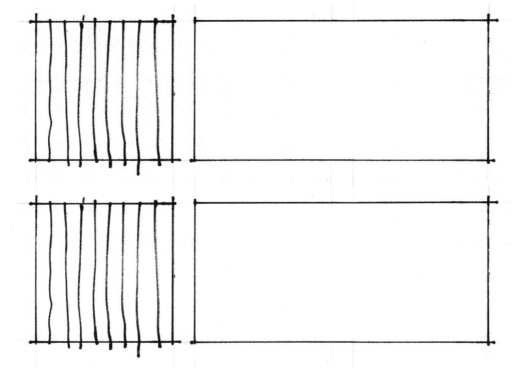

~blank page~

NAME_____DATE_____

Exercise 8-12

Equally Spaced Vertical Lines using a pencil

Here you will sketch additional vertical lines - the only difference is that you will use a pencil rather than a pen. Take the time to note the difference in line quality and tone.

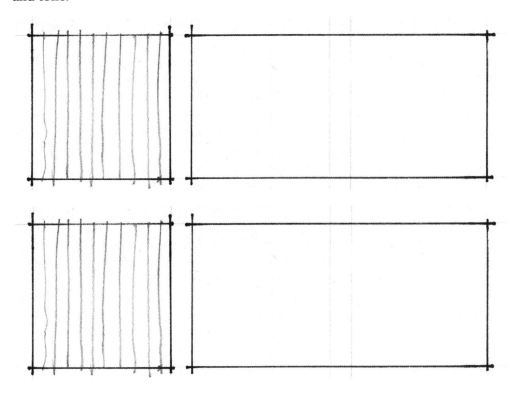

In this last box, apply varying degrees of pressure to vary line weights.

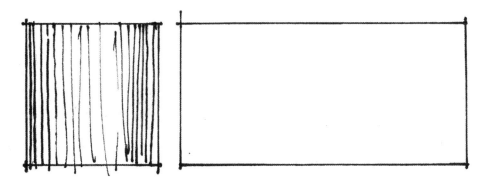

~blank page~

NAME_____ DATE_____

Exercise 8-13

Tightly Spaced Vertical Lines using a pen

Here you will sketch additional vertical lines – the objective is to use the finest tipped pen you have and sketch closely spaced lines. This should still be done quickly while moving lightly! A series of lines like this can be used to represent the texture of a buildings material (e.g., brick, lap siding, corrugated roofing) or shades and shadows in a more abstract way.

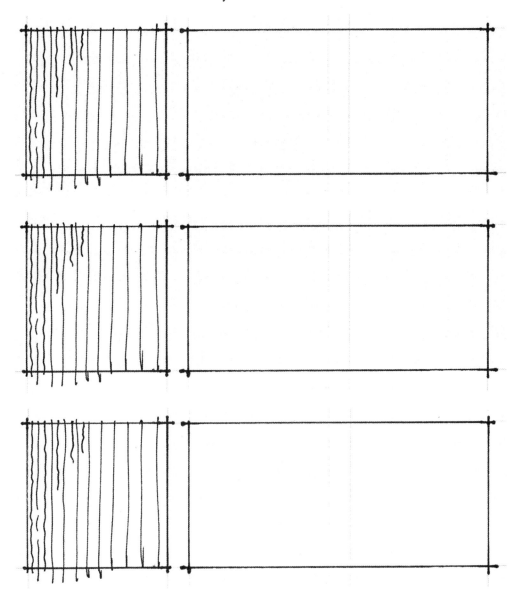

~blank page~

NAME_____DATE_____

Exercise 8-14

Long Vertical Lines using a pen
Continue to practice sketching vertical lines that are evenly spaced – pick your spacing. Don't be afraid to add a little squiggle to your lines as discussed previously in this chapter. Remember: move quickly and only free-hand.

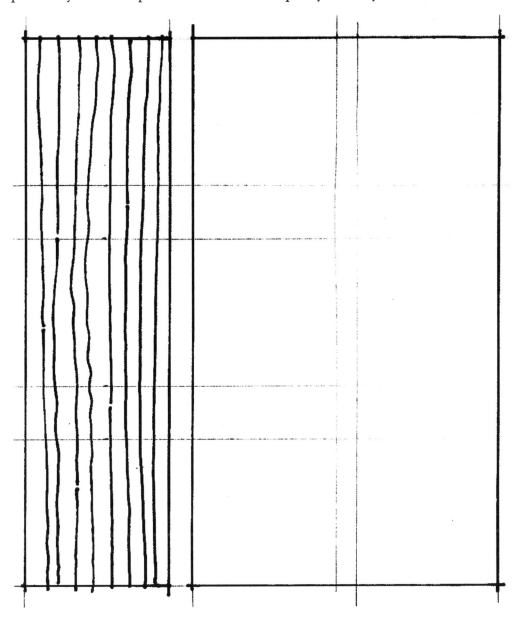

~blank page~

NAME_____DATE_____

Exercise 8-15

Equally Spaced Diagonal Hatch

In this task you will draw equally spaced diagonal lines. Follow this pattern to complete the other two tasks below (on this page).

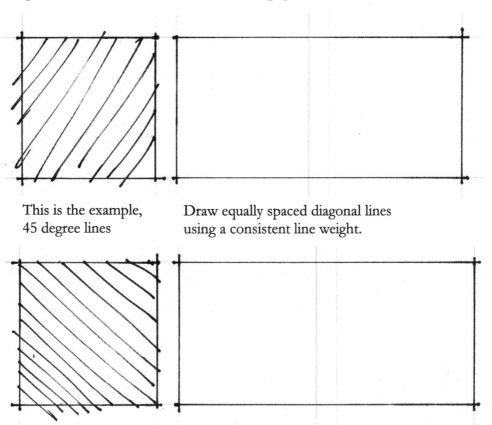

This is the example, 45 degree lines

Draw equally spaced diagonal lines using a consistent line weight.

Irregular Diagonal Hatch

Using quick hand movements, sketch an irregular hatch pattern as shown below in the example square (on the left).

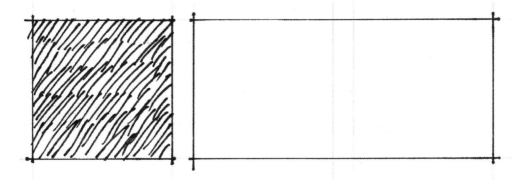

~blank page~

NAME_____ DATE_____

Exercise 8-16

Additional Hatch Patterns

Draw the hatching as shown in the space provided.

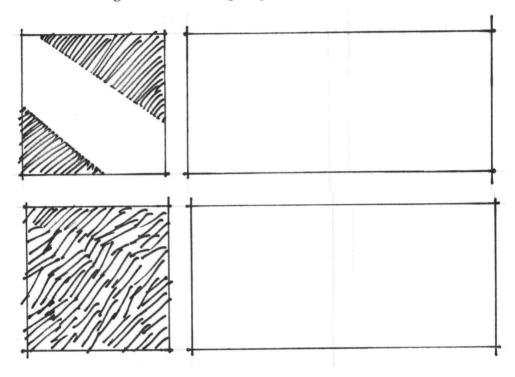

Cross Hatch

Add a set of diagonal lines (45 degrees) in each direction. This pattern is used in sketches to represent shadows and glass; in details it is rigid insulation.

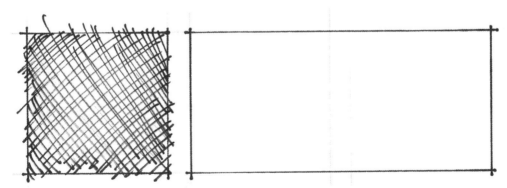

~blank page~

NAME_____DATE_____

Exercise 8-17

Additional Hatch Patterns

Sketch the hatch patterns shown in the space provided to the right. The top example, as you will recall from this chapter, shows gravel over an earth hatch pattern. The bottom example is the result of "rubbing" the pencil over the paper with a heavily textured material below the paper – which means you should first remove the paper from the book and place over a heavily textured material to complete this exercise!

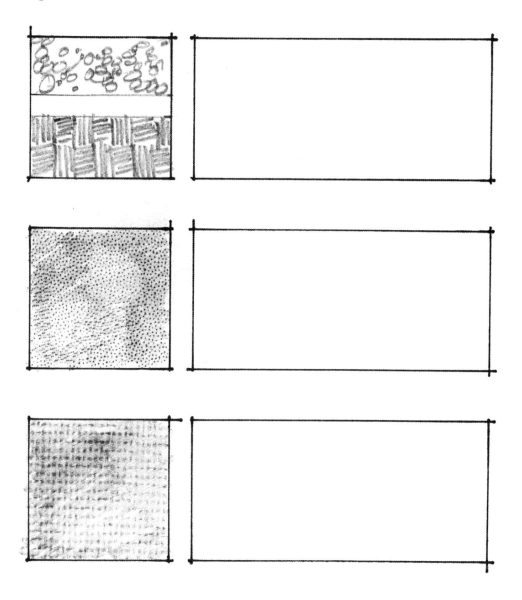

~blank page~

NAME_____DATE_____

Exercise 8-18

Additional Hatch Patterns

Sketch the hatch pattern shown in the space provided to the right. Use the techniques covered in this chapter.

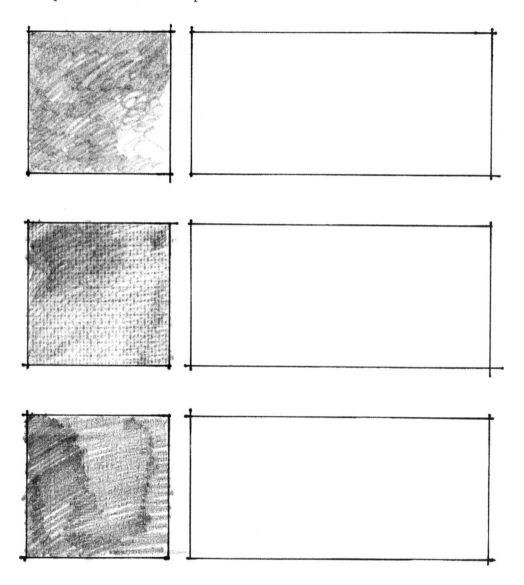

~blank page~

NAME_____DATE_____

Exercise 8-19

Equally Spaced Long Horizontal Lines

In this task you will draw longer horizontal lines – the goal is to pay attention to not resting your palm on the paper; rather keep it moving with the pencil and anticipate any adjustments needed to keep the line horizontal. Try to keep things fast and loose – do not erase anything.

More Horizontal Lines

Continue drawing long horizontal lines in the boxes below. Try this technique for creating equally spaced lines: sketch the first line in the middle and then draw the next line centered between that line and the edge. Continue this process in each direction until you cannot add any more lines.

Aligned Horizontal Lines

Follow the steps in the previous box, but make the lines line up between boxes. Try drawing one continuous line, lifting your pencil to skip to the next box.

~blank page~

NAME_____ **DATE**_____

Exercise 8-20

Equally Spaced Long Vertical Lines
Same as the previous tasks, just vertical lines. Line work like this is often used to represent materials on the surface of your building, for example: brick, siding, roofing, etc.

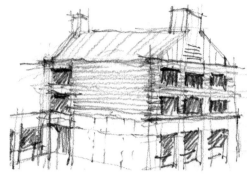

~blank page~

NAME_____DATE_____

Exercise 8-21

Quickly Sketch Circles

Use the square to aid in drawing an accurate circle – focus on a quarter of the circle at a time. Each quadrant of the circle fits the midpoints of the edges of the squares.

FYI: You will apply this technique again later in the book, but onto a surface in perspective.

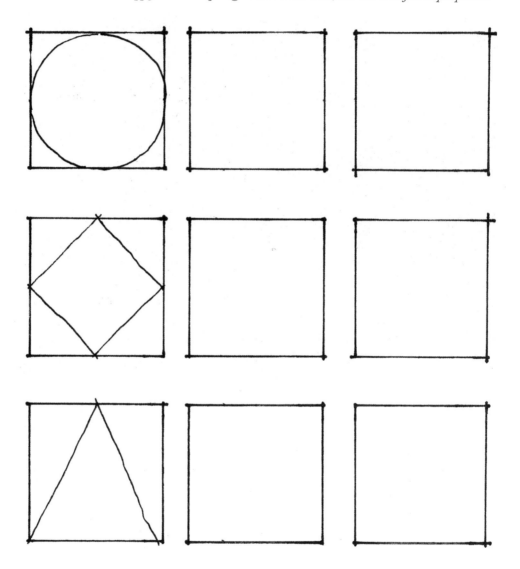

~blank page~

NAME_____ DATE_____

Exercise 8-22

Practice Gesture Drawing: People
As discussed in this chapter, you need to practice quick and loose sketching of people and small simple buildings. These gesture drawings should each be done in less than two minutes.

Quickly sketch the figures above in the boxes below.

~blank page~

NAME_____DATE_____

Exercise 8-23

Practice Gesture Drawing: People
As discussed in this chapter, you need to practice quick and loose sketching of people and small simple buildings. These gesture drawings should each be done in less than two minutes.

Quickly sketch the figures above in the boxes below.

~blank page~

NAME_____DATE_____

Exercise 8-24

Practice Gesture Drawing: People

As mentioned in the previous exercise, these gesture drawings should each be done in under two minutes.

~blank page~

NAME_____DATE_____

Exercise 8-25

Practice Gesture Drawing: Buildings

Try sketching this small building in a gesture type format; try using a felt tip pen and give yourself about 8-10 minutes tops. Don't worry about the little details.

~blank page~

NAME_____DATE_____

Exercise 8-26

Practice Gesture Drawing: Buildings

Try sketching this small building in a gesture type format; try using a felt tip pen and give yourself about 8-10 minutes tops. Don't worry about the little details.

~blank page~

NAME_____DATE_____

Exercise 8-27

Practice Gesture Drawing: Floor Plans

Quickly sketch a "gesture" floor plan of the space you are in. Note doors and windows but move quickly – get it down! Again, this is an exercise in time efficiency. Give yourself 8-10 minutes of time to complete the drawing.

~blank page~

NAME_____DATE_____

Exercise 8-28

Practice Architectural Lettering

Use the space provided below to practice hand lettering. For this exercise you will just write the alphabet as many times as will fit in the space provided. Looking back at the samples shown in this chapter, try to imitate 2 or 3 of them, put a star (★) by the style you like best.

~blank page~

NAME_____DATE_____

Exercise 8-29

Practice Architectural Lettering

Transcribe the paragraph below while applying some of the concepts discussed previously in this chapter; your lettering should all be uppercase.

A *green roof* is one which has vegetation growing on it. The value in this type of design is multi-fold. First, the roof reduces the load on the storm water system as the rain water is mostly retained on the roof to "feed" the vegetation. Second, the structure does not absorb as much solar radiation, thus requiring less energy to cool the building. Next, the green roof provides for insect and bird life which would otherwise be displaced by a new structure. It should be pointed out that a green roof weighs more than a traditional roof and thus requires a stronger building structure and during drought-like weather the vegetation needs to be irrigated – both of these things cost more but are often outweighed by the savings derived from the benefits previously mentioned.

~blank page~

Formulating Design Solutions

In this chapter we will talk about the design process used to formulate design solutions. Before the first line is drawn, the designer needs to collect sufficient data in order to make meaningful decisions. The focus of this book is drawing so we will not get too deep into the technical stuff.

The start of many *commissions* (i.e., a design job where you get paid) begin with a person's desire to start or grow a business, or a family wishing to remodel, expand or build a new home. At some point, using one of a variety of methods, they hire a designer to help them realize their vision. Once a contract is signed, the designer (or design team) can begin meeting with the Client to collect data about the project.

Another important preliminary step is to analyze the property on which the building will be built; the designer can determine the maximum buildable area based on local zoning ordinances and building codes.

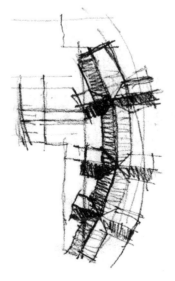

Once a sufficient amount of data is collected and the site has been considered, the designer can begin to develop design solutions using the type of quick sketch studies covered in the previous chapter. Sometimes the designer will go through hundreds of design iterations in an attempt to fit the pieces of the puzzle together just right. A good designer will develop a solution that complies with government regulations, the client's requirements, is aesthetically pleasing and is technically sound (i.e., it keeps the rain, wind and snow out!).

To recap, the list below highlights many of the things a designer must factor into their design in order to reach an adequate solution:

1. Client Requirements
    a. Budget
    b. Program (more on this later)
    c. Timeline
    d. Sustainability
    e. Aesthetics
2. Government Regulations
    a. Zoning ordinances
    b. Local Building Codes
    c. State Building Codes
    d. National Building Codes
3. Climatic Conditions
    a. Hot/Freezing
    b. Rural/Urban
    c. Valley/Mountains
4. Site Conditions
    a. Wetlands
    b. Rivers/Lakes
    c. Ledge Rock
    d. Soil (clay, sandy, etc.)
5. Political/Cultural

A section of code books in an architectural office

The Program Statement

One of the first things a designer, or design team, does is to meet with the client and develop a *Program Statement*. A program statement is such an important step in the design process, it is almost hard to put into words. This document reveals the pieces to the puzzle needed by the designer before they can begin sketching the first lines. This document is derived by one or more meetings between the designer and the client, where many questions are asked about the spaces needed, what will be happening in these spaces and when. The client typically has a pretty good idea about what spaces are needed – for example, one might say "I need three offices, one for each of my sales people". Additionally, the designer's experience and knowledge of the various building codes will reveal other rooms required like recycling rooms, toilet rooms, mechanical and electrical rooms.

In addition to the function and number of rooms, the ideal square footage for each room is specified. These numbers might come from the client, whose intimate knowledge of the business helps select the size, or from the designer, who may have designed previous buildings of the type under consideration.

In the end, a document is created (see the example on the next page) that lists each room and its ideal size. This document can then be used to put together preliminary construction costs and design fees. If the client's budget is sufficient, then the project can move forward, and the designer has a firm understanding of the client's needs.

Sometimes the *Program Statement* includes an **Adjacency Matrix**. This matrix is used to dictate when one room needs to be close to another room. For example, in a hospital project, the Emergency Room needs to be close, if not connected, to the X-ray department so patients are not traveling great distances. Conversely, some rooms may need to be separated by a great distance; for example, a music recording studio wants to be remote from the mechanical room or any other noise producing spaces.

On the next page you will find an example of a project program that acts as a preliminary design tool – which forms the puzzle pieces – when laying out a floor plan.

The next section in this chapter begins a dialogue on sketching charts and diagrams. The conclusion of this discussion talks about Bubble and Block Diagrams – the information from this program is used to create the "bubbles" and "blocks" used in those diagrams.

Sketch by **Alan Anderson**; Duluth, MN

STEEL CITY COMMUNITY CENTER
Architectural Program

Common Spaces	Total SF
Welcome Area (Waiting/Reception)	400
Multi-Purpose Room	900
Public Restrooms (Adult/Child)	300
Staff Lounge	100
* Kitchen	200
Maintenance - Storage	100
Sub-Total	2,000

Shared ECFE and Pre-School Spaces	Total SF
Shared Meeting Room	400
Resource Area/Book and Toy Library	300
* Classroom Equipment Storage	300
Staff Office Space	500
Interview/Conference Rooms (2 @ 100 SF each)	200
Staff Resource - Work Room	150
Sub-Total	1,850

Steel City School District	Total SF
Preschool Classrooms (2 @ 800 SF each)	1,600
Preschool Classroom	1,000
Parent Room	500
Sub-Total	3,100

Pre-School	Total SF
Preschool Classrooms (2 @ 900 SF each)	1,800
Sub-Total	1,800

Oakey County - Adult/Family Services	Total SF
Waiting	150
Reception/Office (2 workstations)	150
Counselor Offices (3 @ 100 SF each)	300
* Basic Education Classroom	800
Fuel Assistance/Foodshelf Office (2 workstations)	150
Foodshelf	400
Loading Dock	150
Weatherization Office	100
Weatherization Work Room	150
Sub-Total	2,350

Total Assignable Area (80%)	**11,100**
Total Non-Assignable (20%)	**2,775**
Total Gross Area (100%)	**13,875**

* Negotiable areas (i.e., first to be cut in size or out of Program).

Site Development	*Total SF*
Parking (60 cars plus school bus drop-off)	12,000
Playground	1,000
Service/Delivery @ Loading Dock	1,000
Total	14,000

A few comments will be made about the program statement before moving on. The types and number of rooms are clearly identified and the desired size is also listed. All of the desired spaces are referred to as "assignable area" in contrast to "non-assignable area" which accounts for required spaces such as mechanical rooms, electrical and data rooms.

In addition to specific building elements, the site development has its major features mentioned so they can be considered in early design concepts. For example, maybe the multi-purpose room should be near the playground.

As the project proceeds, the design team will revisit the program statement and add a column showing the actual square footage. It is not practical to expect the design would ever achieve 100% square footage compliance with the program, but each room should be within an agreed upon percentage (e.g., 9-10%).

The sketch below does not relate to the discussion at hand, but is provided in an attempt to fill whitespace in the book with "inspirational" drawings. Enjoy!

Sketch by Steve **McNeill**

Diagrams

We are all familiar with typical diagrams of everyday life, such as the *Pie Diagram*, the *Graph* and the *Bar Chart* as shown below. You see these diagrams in newspapers, magazines, science books and computer programs like *Microsoft Excel* and *Quicken* (by Intuit). These basic diagrams aid in dissecting and disseminating information. Architectural designers also use these types of diagrams in their practice. Here you will take a look at how this fundamental concept can be used within the context of sketching to break down large chunks of information to aid in the decision/design process.

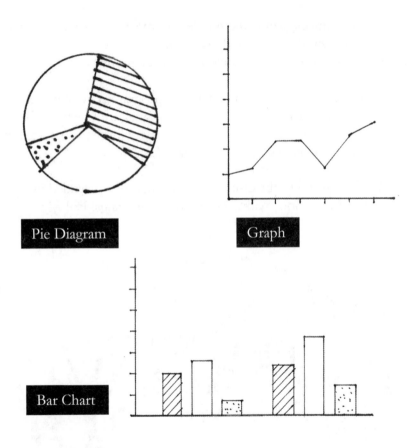

Pie Diagram

Graph

Bar Chart

Your skills with these diagrams, or proto drawings as we refer to them, can enable you to express ideas pictorially, define decisions and even organize large complex tasks such as reports, term papers and drawing presentations.

Project Storyboard

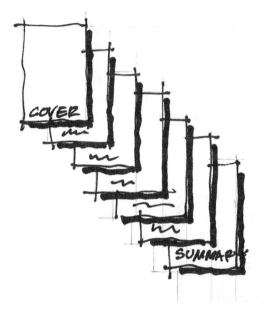

We often find that *Reports*, *Proposals* and *Text* documents can be organized as shown in the image to the left.

Note each element or area has a title which describes, and represents, a portion of work that must be done to complete a project.

When shared with staff, this Project Storyboard helps people to focus on the elements rather than feel overwhelmed by the project as a whole.

Each element above may in fact be complex in and of itself, and thus may need to be broken down further. For example, each section above could represent the work required by the various disciplines on a specific project: Architectural, Structural, Mechanical, Electrical, Civil, Food Service Consultant, Fire Protection, etc. Thus, each section is analyzed and diagramed to indicate the various tasks required by each discipline in order to complete the project.

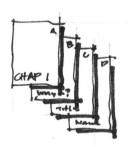
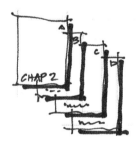
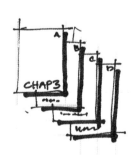

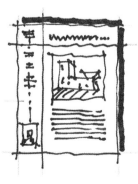

When considering the pages in a book (such as this one) or in a school report, you may use storyboarding to visualize the information you think will fit on each page. This will help you determine how many pages are needed overall and how best to divide up the work when working in a group. These images may be as small as the one shown to the left or may be a full-size page.

Storyboards are very useful in the planning of *Plan Sets* or *Drawing Presentations*. The sheets required can be piled up or tiled (see both examples below).

The first example below graphically lists each sheet and a label is added. This would be a breakdown for boards needed for a presentation or a very early preliminary "stab" at the number of drawings needed for a set of Construction Drawings (the set of drawings the contractor bids and builds from). The designer could sketch this in a sketch book or on 8½″ x 11″ bond paper (copy machine paper).

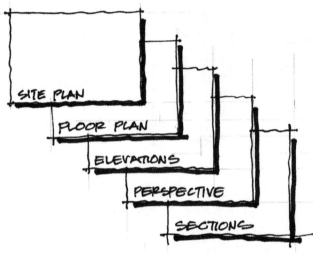

Not only is a sheet study useful for dividing up the work for your staff, but it is also used to determine the amount of time required to complete the project. Many designers use past projects to determine the average amount of time needed to complete one sheet. Therefore, when calculating the time needed to do a new project, a storyboard can be used – taking the number of sheets multiplied by the hours needed per sheet (so: 6 sheets x 40 hours = 240 hours).

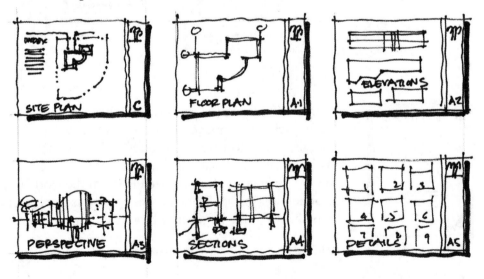

The *Sheet Storyboard* (which some like to refer to as the *Cartoon Set*) requires a certain amount of experience to know which drawings and details would be needed on any given project type. Additionally, the approximate amount of space required by each drawing can be hard to know for sure, so more or fewer sheets may be required and should be taken into consideration (especially when using this method to calculate fees and budgets).

So you might be thinking to yourself, why not just list the project components in a check list? Well, for some reason the visual process seems very effective for teams as well as the individual in adding clarity to the task at hand; designer-types often think better visually whereas engineers like to use lists more. These little pictures, storyboards, or vignettes are very powerful! Not to mention, if a potential employer sees a few examples of this in your portfolio (*i.e., examples of your work*) they will think it's cool and hire you (well, maybe – but it sure can't hurt).

Decision Tree

Architectural practice involves, more than anything, getting decisions on where, what, how and how much to build. A very useful "thinking diagram" that clarifies visually much talk and discussion is the *Decision Tree*. There are many types of decision trees, but the basics are covered here.

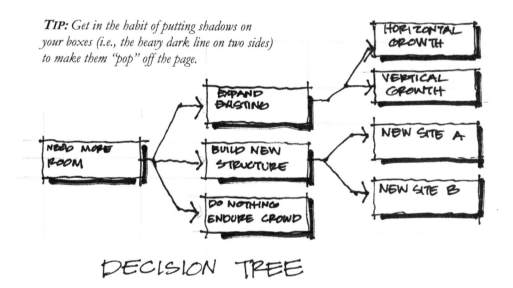

TIP: Get in the habit of putting shadows on your boxes (i.e., the heavy dark line on two sides) to make them "pop" off the page.

DECISION TREE

The example on the previous page shows the analysis of a problem – a business or home owner "needing more room". Given that problem, they have at least three options: *1)* Expand their existing facilities; *2)* Build a New Building; *3)* Do nothing and live with the inconvenience and lost revenue. From those three options, each then has its own set of options – for example: within the context of expanding, one could expand vertically (add additional floor) or horizontally (if the site was large enough). As you can imagine, this could go on and on until the utmost detail was revealed about each possible option, including timelines, costs, risks and rewards. The final result is the ability to make an informed decision.

The *Decision Tree* can be combined with small diagrams and sketches to almost instantly portray options. This type of sketching can often be done right in front of the client, utilizing the knowledge of both the designer (knowing codes and construction issues) and the client (knowing budgets and timelines), with an economy of time!

The drawing below shows the same Decision Tree as the one on the previous page, but with sketches rather than words. Assuming enough preliminary information exists to create the sketches shown below, then you can see how much more revealing this Decision Tree would be compared to the one on the previous page.

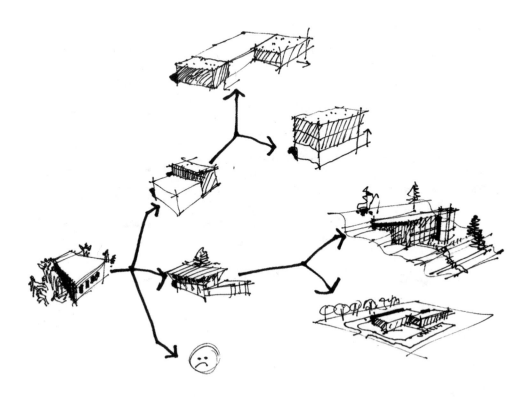

Circulation Diagrams

Buildings are largely composed of two basic functions: 1) *Activity Areas* such as living rooms, offices, cafeterias, etc., and 2) *Circulation Areas* such as hallways, corridors, lobbies and exit passages. It is often necessary to analyze the "paths" people follow to get from one space to another in an effort to determine if the path is efficient (e.g., distance) and unobstructed (e.g., not crossing other paths) – this can be done with a *Circulation Diagram.*

A building's circulation areas can be simple or complex. In either case it is possible to study the flow as "piping", "networks" or "vessels" similar to our veins and arteries. These circulation areas are often diagramed using width to indicate volume, as shown in the diagram below. As people exit the corridor (for example, they enter a room) the "load" on the corridor is reduced and as people enter the same corridor (for example, a hallway connects to it) the "load" increases. So, at some point the corridor may need to be very wide at the heaviest load, but as the load dwindles (usually at the extremities) there may be an opportunity to make the corridor narrower, allowing more space for the adjacent rooms or even reducing the size of the building.

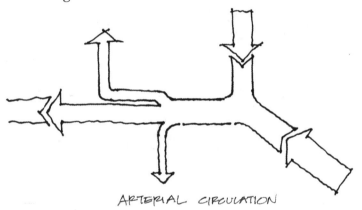

ARTERIAL CIRCULATION

The above example is a sketch of a linear circulation diagram and a closed loop diagram is shown below.

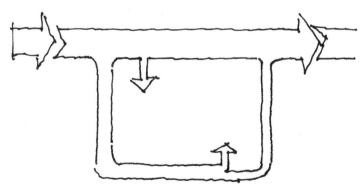

LOOP OR NETWORK CIRCULATION

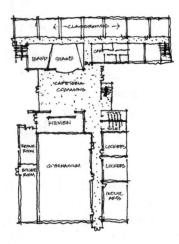

Now you will take a more realistic example of a Circulation Diagram, using the school building floor plan shown to the left. A quick look at the plans reveals the following components: the north (i.e., top) block contains the classrooms and offices, the center area houses the cafeteria/auditorium with an adjacent kitchen, while the south portion contains the gymnasium and locker rooms.

In both images on this page, the circulation areas are *Hatched* with a *Stipple* pattern (which is a series of random dots made with the tip of a pen or pencil).

In the floor plan below the circulation diagram reveals the path students would travel from the classrooms to the cafeteria and then to the playground and finally back to the classrooms. Notice how the diagram lines start out narrow and then get thicker as the students converge near the center. The overall circulation is fairly smooth but it is revealed that the toilet rooms are in a rather inconvenient location which may discourage students from washing their hands before eating!

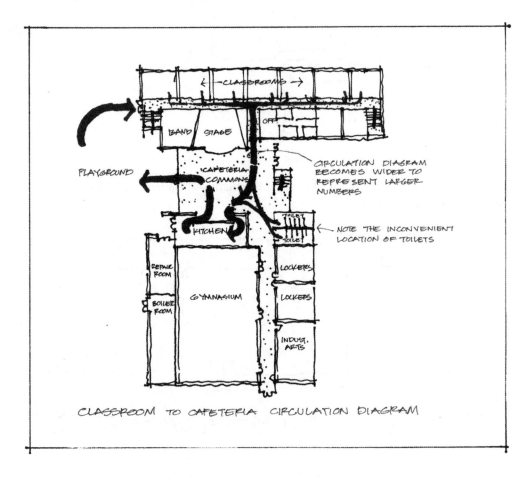

CLASSROOM TO CAFETERIA CIRCULATION DIAGRAM

It may have surprised you that the designer is concerned about whether a student washes his hands or not, but this is a good example of the subtle effects the built environment can have on its occupants; not only circulation, but equipment noise, natural daylight, air quality and finishes.

Now let's consider the same school building and diagram the circulation for a situation where large numbers of students are released to lunch from both the classrooms and the gymnasium area at the same time. As you can see, things get pretty messy as paths cross and the students coming from the classrooms are even less likely to wash their hands now that another obstacle has been put in their way, that is, a large and hungry group of students!

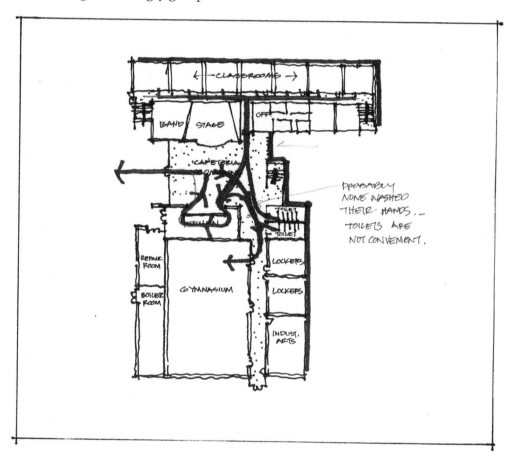

Circulation diagrams are also used to verify building codes are complied with – which require a certain number of exits and widths based on several factors. The authors often work in one State which required a plan diagram to be submitted.

In conclusion, the Circulation Diagram might reveal the need to develop another design solution. Maybe another bank of toilets can be added near the classroom, or it might be that the entire floor plan needs to be revisited. Another outcome might relate to the building's operations, where the client makes the decision to offset the time when the students are released from the classrooms and the gym.

Concept Diagrams

With most of the puzzle pieces in hand (program, site, etc.), the designer can generate a *Concept Diagram* which is meant to convey the project's "big idea". Below is an example of a concept drawing for a new office complex at a manufacturing facility. The elements are simple shapes that do not have to relate to the actual shape of the building. (In fact, that is not usually even known at this stage of the design.) Again, you may think of these as the major pieces to the puzzle, with this sketch being used as a visual thinking exercise. This kind of drawing may be created in front of the design team and/or the client.

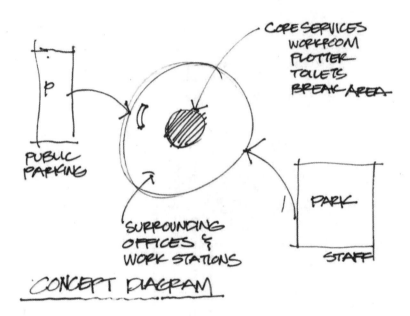

Form Diagrams

The *Form Diagram* is an example of small thumbnail sketches meant to study the basic shapes and proportions the building could take. Looking at the image on the next page, we have taken the *Concept Diagram* (from above) and further developed it into this new drawing (the Form Diagram) – which looks at the impact of the various design goals such as elongation in the East-West direction; lots of exterior skin for windows, but a simple rectangular composition which allows daylight to reach deep into the building. Also, the intent to try and locate much of the "core" components near the center of the building is shown. The "core" components might be spaces such as toilet rooms, mechanical rooms, and other rooms that do not required natural light; thereby placing more of the occupied spaces directly on an exterior wall and in line with natural lighting – which reduces lighting loads/costs and makes the space more enjoyable for its occupants.

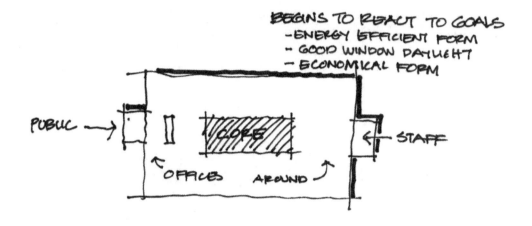

FORM DIAGRAM 1

The next iteration of the Form Diagram takes the ideas developed above and slightly modifies them as shown in the image below. Not every sketch needs to be a completely "ingenious" new idea – a few may be, but not all will be. The best design solution is often found by trying many options and refining them as problems arise or new information comes to light. Notes are added to help recall how this diagram was achieved, which is really helpful when you are going back through 20-30 options and wonder how you got to that point originally. The notes added should be simple statements identifying what is different about that sketch from the previous one. Finally, notice how heavy black lines on two common sides suggest a shadow and give the sketch a sense of three dimensions.

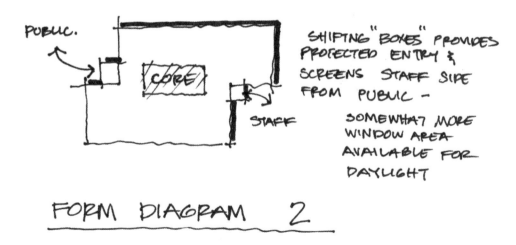

FORM DIAGRAM 2

Further "branching" of ideas often leads to a consideration of the growth options for a given design. Is there an option that allows for growth for the given design that also fits on the site? After studying a few options, is one found that looks less like an addition with minimal impact to adjacent areas when considering circulation and day lighting? This future growth study may reveal that the site is inadequate for a client's long term growth and another location should be found on which to build, or maybe the building's structure needs to be designed to support additional floors.

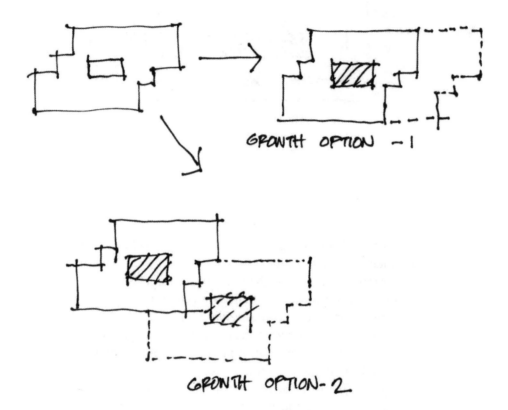

GROWTH OPTION – 1

GROWTH OPTION- 2

At this point, none of these sketches need to be to scale (meaning you should not expect to place a ruler or scale on the drawing to see how big the building is). You will have to validate these very preliminary options later in conjunction with the *Program*. Here you are just playing around with ideas in your sketchbook based on early information collected.

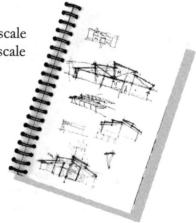

Thumbnail Diagram

The *Thumbnail Diagram* can be set down onto the paper. The example below is similar to a *Decision Tree* diagram discussed earlier, but here you are starting from a "decided" point on that decision tree. Notice the upper-left potion of the image below represents the outline of the second Form Diagram on the previous page. With a specific form in mind, you can extend construction "rays" up from the corners and depict the basic.

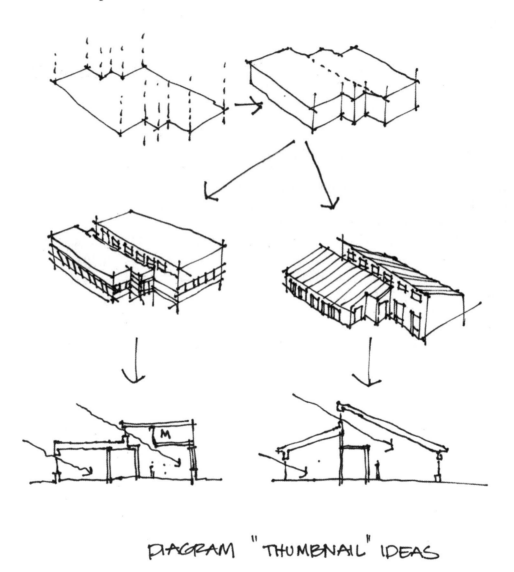

DIAGRAM "THUMBNAIL" IDEAS

The basic "massing" form can be used as an "underlay" and then branched out into two very different building forms for consideration. Each form has a unique cross-section which is sketched below each option to start to think about the structure and to illustrate how the sun's rays penetrate into the building through window openings.

Note that these are quick *Sketch Book* ideas, but if you were to enlarge them on a photocopier and post them on a wall, they could act as your "thinking storyboard" of how this design came to be. Some firms have what are called *Design Critiques* which allow the larger design team, or colleagues, to hear about your design and to challenge certain decisions or draw out certain issues not previously considered. These *Thumbnail Diagrams* are perfect for the early design critique process.

Building Section Thumbnail Diagram

In addition to the building section concept just introduced on the previous page (which looked generically at volumes and not so much at constructability), thumbnail sketches often study what is happening with the structure in a building section. The sketches below are abstract diagrams, in that they are only showing the structural components of the building (i.e., the roof beams, columns and footings), which omit the architectural elements such as the walls and roof. A sketch like this opens up discussions of economy and flexibility. Little stick figures are added to suggest the scale of the structure. This type of analysis would likely be done in conjunction with a Structural Engineer, who is ultimately responsible for the structural design.

3 BAY STRUCTURE
MORE COLUMNS / LESS FLEXIBLE

2 BAY STRUCTURE
– MORE FLEXIBLE / MORE COST

BUILDING SECTION STUDY

Light/Sun Ray Diagram

Architecture for many of us is, at its simplest, a manipulation of light and space. A cross section study that analyzes the sun's path is frequently done to study how well lit, or not, the space may be.

This sketch applies the rule-of-thumb which says good daylight of space can occur up to 2½ times the height of the window opening. The diagonal line shown is what we will refer to as the *Sun Ray Line.*

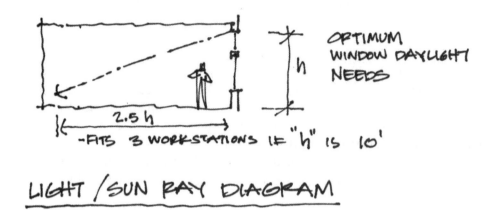

Below is a section generated as part of a real design process. This early sketch begins to reveal the thickness of building elements like walls, floors and the roof. The structure is loosely implied and minimal information is added (for internal use only, e.g., the roof slope and light ray data).

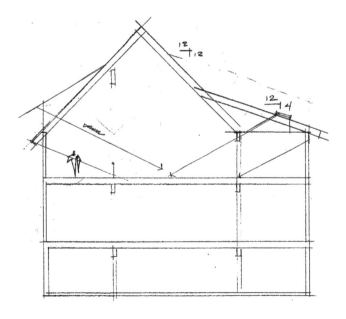

Bubble Diagram

The *Bubble Diagram* is probably one of the most used diagrams in the Architectural Profession when it comes to design layout of a building. It is a quick way to start thinking about where various rooms should go in a building. As you can imagine, a circle is quicker to draw than a square or rectangular shape – no corners!

The circles are not so much to scale as they are proportionally correct relative to each other. So if a Living room needed to be 800sf and a Dining room 400sf, your circle for the living room would be twice the size of the dining room. All the circles should be labeled so you can refer back to them later and make sense of them.

Arrows can also be added, as shown in the sketch below, to indicate relationships of circulation. So an arrow connecting two spaces (i.e., circles) may indicate the two spaces need to be near each other (like the mudroom and the garage), or it may indicate a desire to walk from one room directly into another (by a door or opening in the wall between the two rooms). This is helpful when you are trying several options; you may be tempted to move a room that should be near another room that you were not planning to move, which would create a problem.

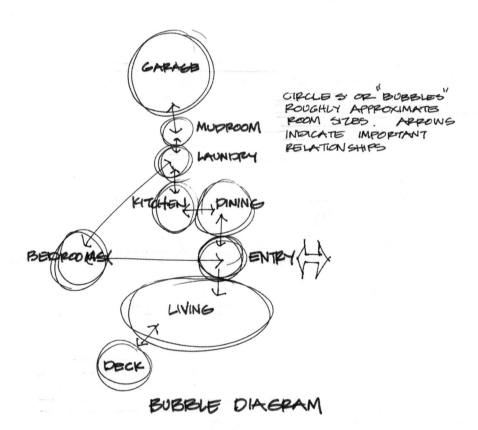

Block Diagram

The *Block Diagram* is different from the previously covered *Form Diagram* in that the Block Diagram deals with individual spaces and the Form Diagram entire buildings. This type of diagram is the next step from the *Bubble Diagram*.

This is a great diagrammatic drawing to show the client and get their initial impression, because 1) it does not take too much time so if big changes are needed it will not be a problem, and 2) the client will not think the drawing is done and won't be afraid to request changes. A computer drawn plan loaded with dimensions would give the impression that the drawings are set in stone and cannot be changed, causing the client to possibly compromise on a change that otherwise might not have been a problem.

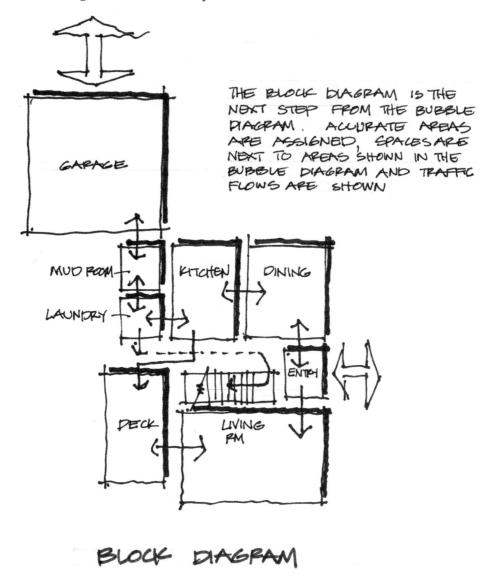

BLOCK DIAGRAM

The drawing below is the result of an overlay sketch based on the *Block Diagram* shown on the previous page. Some would prefer to show a drawing like this to a client rather than the more abstract sketch shown on the previous page – it really comes down to preference. On larger projects where there are more client meetings, you may show both: the Block Diagram at an earlier meeting and then this loosely sketched floor plan at a follow up meeting.

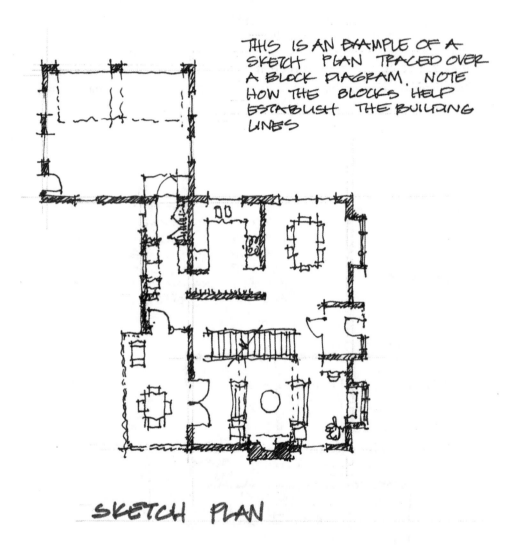

THIS IS AN EXAMPLE OF A
SKETCH PLAN TRACED OVER
A BLOCK DIAGRAM. NOTE
HOW THE BLOCKS HELP
ESTABLISH THE BUILDING
LINES

SKETCH PLAN

Tracing Paper

A favorite "tool" in the architectural designer's toolbox is *Tracing Paper*, which is also referred to as Bum-Wad. Tracing paper is a quick and easy way to clean up a drawing or start another design option based on a previous option; this would be a design iteration. Tracing paper is very lightweight and easy to see through, which makes tracing the page below it easy. If you did not have tracing paper, you would need to use a light table, which many designers have, but is usually inconveniently away from their desk as it is shared by the office.)

Tracing paper is available in two forms: by the sheet or on a roll. Most designers use tracing paper from a roll, often having a handful of roll widths on hand. The nice thing about a roll is that you are able to tear off a piece of paper of any length that you need. This is especially useful when working on two-point perspectives and your vanishing points are widely spaced. The final sketch-over can then be done on a smaller piece of sketching paper (or higher quality paper) where the actually vanishing points do not need to appear.

The image below shows the tracing paper concept using the sketches from the two previous pages. It is handy to use drafting tape to hold the various overlays into place to keep them from moving around.

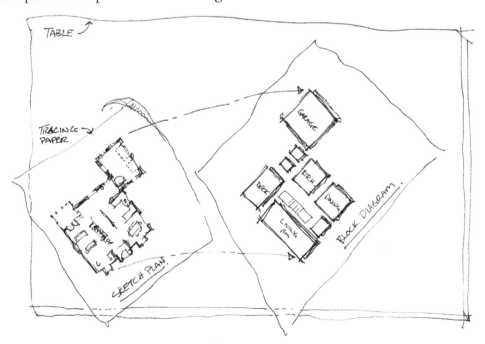

Site Planning

Preliminary site planning is typically done via hand sketching in order to look at several options quickly. Often these early sketches will be based on a survey drawing prepared in a CAD program; this will show the property lines, streets, existing buildings, utility locations (power, water, sewage, phone, cable, gas, etc.), and contours (which show the slope of the land).

A **Site Analysis Diagram** is an important step in understanding the land in which a building is be built. The building design should not even be started before this drawing has been done as it will determine where certain rooms should go and the location of windows. This diagram is also indispensible when considering "green" design options such as daylighting and passive solar design.

Looking at the sketch below, you can see several elements overlaid on the *Site Analysis Diagram*. A few of the items often found here are (in no particular order):

- Street Access
- Sun pattern
- Winter Wind direction
- Property lines

- Setbacks (code buildable area)
- Existing Trees
- True North
- Direction ground slopes

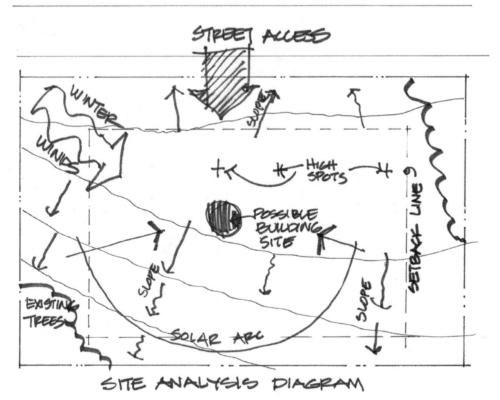

SITE ANALYSIS DIAGRAM

Actually determining sun angles and wind direction is beyond this book's scope.

Once the *Site Analysis Diagram* has been completed and the preliminary drawings for the building done, a **Basic Site Plan** can be drawn to show the client how the building will work on the site.

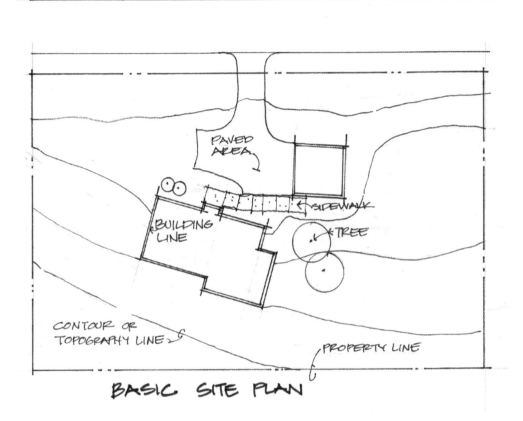

BASIC SITE PLAN

A few points about the graphics of the sketch above include:
- The buildings are just shown as outlines, no need to show interior walls. For larger, more complicated, buildings it is helpful to indicate where the exterior doors (both people doors and garage doors) are so the sidewalks and driveways can be properly located.
- Things are clearly labeled; property lines, paved areas, trees. Existing items, such as trees, roads, buildings, etc., should be labeled as such.
- New contours are shown (compare to sketch on previous page) to indicate how the rainwater will be dealt with as well as a rough idea about how much earthwork will be needed (i.e., cut and fill). This text is not meant to be a study in site design, but we will quickly mention that a good site design sheds rainwater away from any buildings (all sides) and tries to equalize the amount of cut and fill to minimize earthwork costs.

While the *Site Analysis Diagram* and the *Basic Site Plan* are shown to the client at meetings to determine if their needs are being met, a ***Rendered Site Plan*** is sometimes generated as a formal presentation to the owner/client, users and/or the public. The exact techniques on how a site plan is rendered can vary quite a bit. This type of sketch may be produced by the architect, a landscape architect, or a civil engineer depending on how the design team is structured.

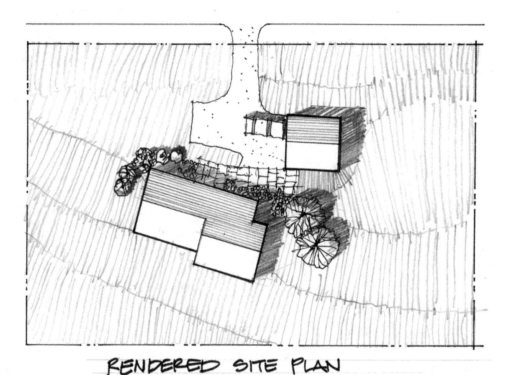

RENDERED SITE PLAN

Above is an example of a typical Rendered Site Plan. Its main features are:
- Lineweights to distinguish between materials and convey depth.
- Shadows to indicate solar impact at a specific time of year.
- Some surfaces/materials are hatched or highlighted; for example:
  - The roofing has parallel lines which usually indicate shingle roofing; and to distinguish between adjacent sloped surfaces one slope is often hatched differently (or not at all in this case) to make things more clear.
  - The paved driveway has a stipple hatch pattern, which is nothing more than several randomly placed dots.
  - The ground and its slope are highlighted by the light hatch pattern that runs continuous and perpendicular to the contours (water always flows perpendicular to the contours).

Self-Exam:

The following questions can be used as a way to check your knowledge of this lesson. The answers can be found at the bottom of this page.

1. *Cartoon Sets* can be used to determine how much time will be needed to design a building. (T/F)

2. An *Adjacency Matrix* lists nearby buildings. (T/F)

3. *Diagrams* can be used to break down large chunks of data. (T/F)

4. A _____ diagram shows how people move around in a building.

5. Which diagram conveys the project's "big idea"? _____.

Review Questions:

The following questions may be assigned by your instructor as a way to assess your knowledge of this section. Your instructor has the answers to the review questions.

1. A *Program Statement* is an important part of the design process. (T/F)

2. The *Decision Tree* is mainly used by architects to determine which type of pencil to draw with. (T/F)

3. A *Commission* is a job for which you are paid. (T/F)

4. What is collected from a client at the beginning of a project: _____.

5. A _____ _____ lists the rooms needed.

6. *Project Storyboards* are useful in the planning of plan sets. (T/F)

7. Complex problems are made more manageable via *Diagrams*. (T/F)

8. An experienced designer can approximate how many sheets will be needed in a drawing set by creating a *Cartoon Set*. (T/F)

9. A *Rendered Site Plan* is often the first type of site plan drawn. (T/F)

10. Early design idea sketches and diagrams should always be to scale. (T/F)

Self-Exam Answers:
1 – T, 2 – F, 3 – T, 4 – Circulation, 5 – Concept

Notes:

NAME_____ DATE_____

Exercise 9-1

Storyboard Exercise – Data

Take a report or similar document and diagram it into sub-components; break the information into bite sized chunks. If you are at a loss, diagram your daily class schedule or this textbook. Do your work in the empty square below.

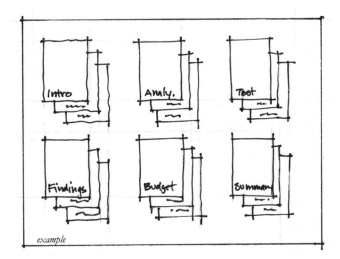

~blank page~

NAME_____ DATE_____

Exercise 9-2

Storyboard Exercise – Drawing Set

Using the information you learned in this chapter, create a Storyboard (or Cartoon Set) to show approximately how many sheets would be needed to document the existing conditions of the building pictured below (i.e., a Record Set). Assume the building is symmetrical, the floor plan will fit on one sheet and two of the four elevations will fit on a sheet. Try to represent the building shapes.

~blank page~

NAME_____DATE_____

Exercise 9-3

Decision Tree

Create a decision tree for an event, perhaps an important event such as a wedding or a trip. Pick something with lots of options. Use the back side of this page if you need more space. Make a small "+" or "-" below each option to indicate a good option versus a bad option. Place a star by each decision you actually made (or would make if you where to do this thing). The stars will identify a "path" taken or to be taken.

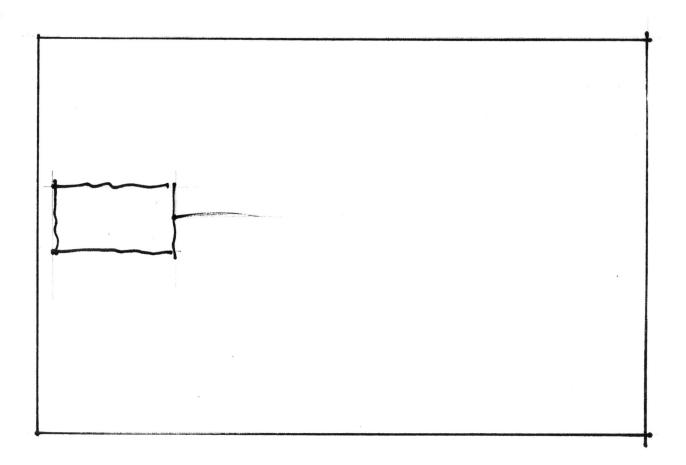

~blank page~

NAME_____DATE_____

Exercise 9-4

Pictorial Decision Tree

In this exercise you will create a decision tree using graphics to represent a decision (e.g., sketch an air plane to represent flying to a location). Use the decision from the previous exercise for this exercise. Make sure you get all the decisions along the prefered (or starred) path. Add as many of the other decisions as possible after that.

~blank page~

NAME_____ DATE_____

Exercise 9-5

Circulation Diagram

Create a circulation diagram showing student "flow" from the gymnasium to the Locker rooms (for both male and female students) and then back to the classrooms (classrooms are located on both the first and second floors). Try using a colored pen or felt tipped pen if you have one.

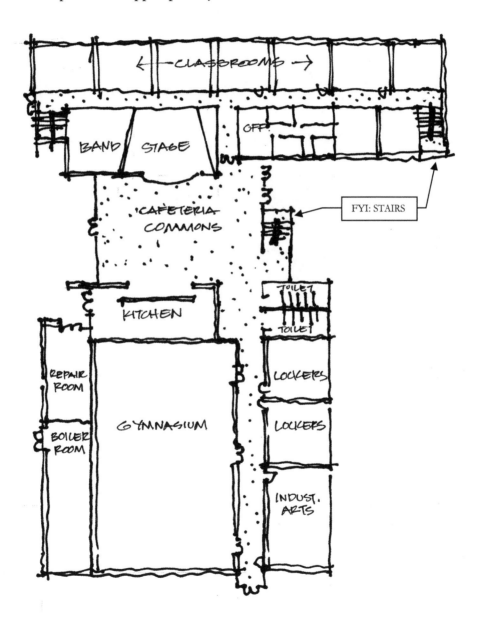

~blank page~

NAME_____ DATE_____

Exercise 9-1

Bubble Diagram
Quickly layout the floor plan using the various rooms provided below. Make sure each bubble is proportionately the correct size (relative to each other). Each space should be labeled. Note: the "bubbles" should all touch each other, as if their edges were common walls.

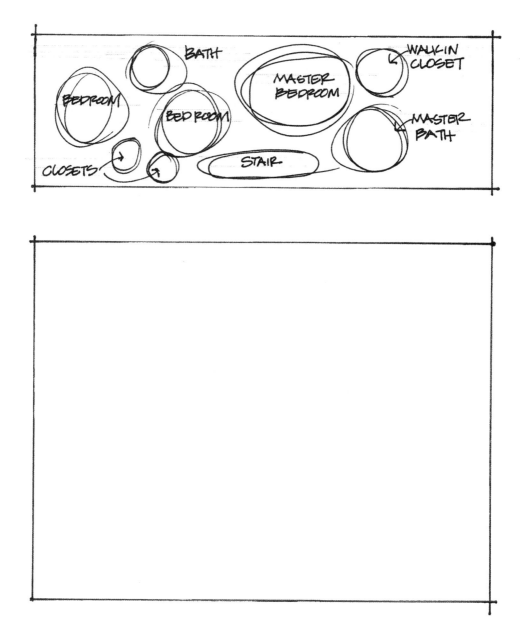

~blank page~

NAME_____ DATE_____

Exercise 9-2

Block Diagram

Use the "puzzle pieces" shown below to layout a second story floor plan of a single family home. Follow this mini-**program**: north is up, each bedroom must have windows, the south side has a lake view, provide minimal hallway space, and the master bedroom must have a view of the lake. Space between spaces implies circulation, i.e., hallways.

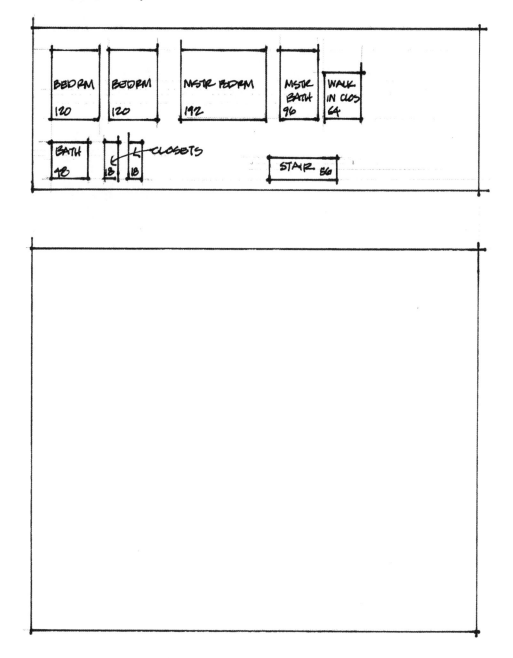

~blank page~

NAME_____ DATE_____

Exercise 9-3

Building Section Study

Analyze the photo below and develop a simple building section based on what you think is going on inside. Your section should cut through the middle (in the shorter direction) and through the tallest part. Show windows and doors in section if you are cutting though them. Do not worry about scale but try to be as proportionally correct as possible. Also, add the Sun Ray line.

~blank page~

NAME_____ DATE_____

Exercise 9-4

Building Section Study

This is a sketch of a New England village tavern, done with a felt tip pen and then a sepia Prismacolor® pencil over textured board. Draw a diagrammatic section through the "salt box" shaped tavern. Note that the tavern is built into a hill. Show the walkout level on the one side and the front porch (and street) on the other.

~blank page~

NAME_____ DATE_____

Exercise 9-5

Site Diagram

Take this house and garage and place them on the site plan shown below. Indicate the driveway from the road to the garage and also show sidewalks as needed. Use the graphic scale and notice the north direction. Add neat hand-written notes to label the house, garage, driveway and sidewalk.

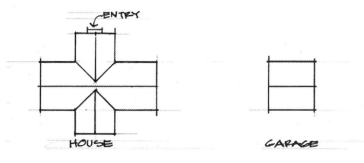

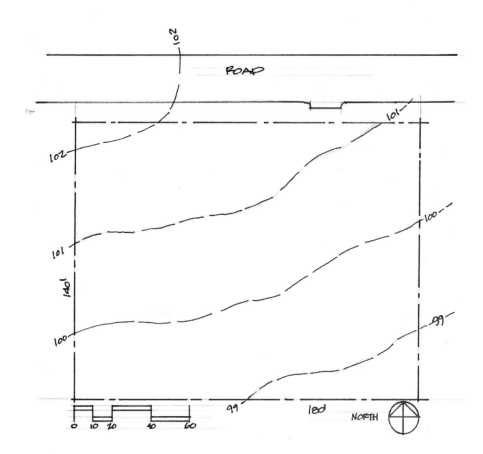

~blank page~

Chapter 10

One – Point Perspective
and Digital Tools

*The dramatic one-point perspective is introduced in this chapter. The person viewing
a one-point perspective often has a sense of being immersed in the image. As with
the two-point perspective drawing type, the one-point represents a real-life
representation from a specific vantage point – stay tuned and learn all about it!*

The sketch below shows a simple example of a one-point perspective. The partial
floor plan sketch beside the perspective is the basis of the sketch. Using this
technique, you can quickly create a sketch that helps you to visualize the space
three-dimensionally. From here you might adjust the floor plans or add color and
present it to your client for their approval.

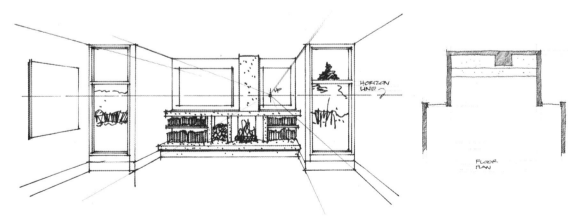

The next two paragraphs introduce two techniques covered in this chapter.

The basic components of a one-point perspective

The process of creating a one-point perspective will be described first in this chapter. The mechanics are very simple and do not take much time to master. Like anything, it just takes practice.

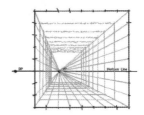

Establishing depth in your perspective

Another topic to be presented is developing a three-dimensional grid which can be used to more accurately sketch items in perspective (in terms of depth from the viewer). This is a very rigid process and often only used for more formal presentation drawings. Note that the location of the Diagonal Point (DP) will establish the depth of the view; when positioned correctly, the view will have the proper feelings of scale and proportion.

Understanding One-Point Perspectives

The photo to the left shows a hallway which should help you see how a one-point perspective relates to the real world.

Below is the same image with the *Vanishing Point* discovered; which was done by projecting the perspective lines until they converge with a straight edge.

Vanishing Point lines derived from a photo...

Notice the one-point perspective has three types of lines (with few exceptions):
1. Perspective lines
2. Vertical lines
3. Horizontal lines

The sketch below is formatted in a similar fashion to one previously presented in two-point perspective. As you can see, however, the circle does not really define a point of distortion for one-point drawings. Again, items completely above the *Horizon Line* are as seen from a "worm's eye" perspective and below the *Horizon Line* as seen from a "bird's eye" view.

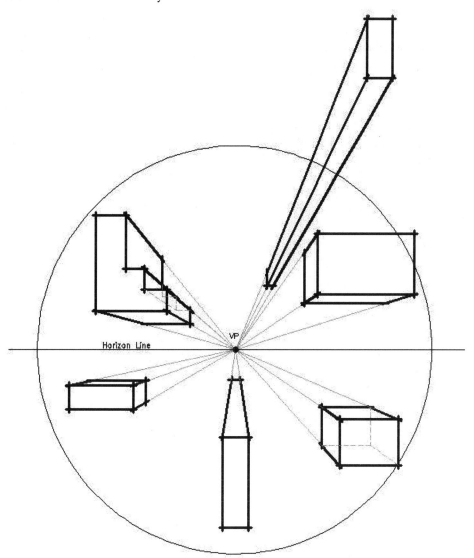

The next two pages provide step-by-step instructions on setting up a one-point perspective and establishing a grid which allows proper proportions and scale to be achieved.

Step A:
Start with a proportionally accurate outline of the space – walls, floor and ceiling.

Step B:
Locate the *Vanishing Point* (VP) in a location that will best depict your design. Next, add the four vanishing lines as shown.

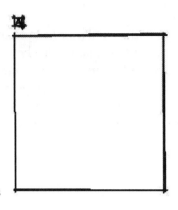
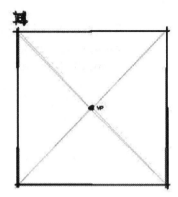

Step C:
Sketch the bottom horizontal line; this line will determine the depth of the space. Now you can project the vertical lines up and then add the top horizontal line.

Step D:
Darken the lines which define the space. People are often added to instill a sense of scale; notice how the heads align at the horizon.

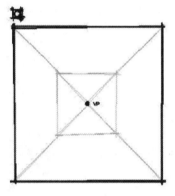
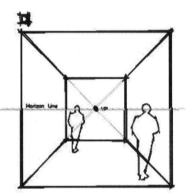

Step A:
Same as step 'A' above.

Step B:
Locating the VP to the right can help to direct focus to the left– maybe you have some built-in cabinets on that wall!

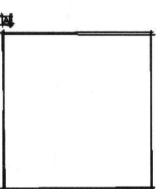

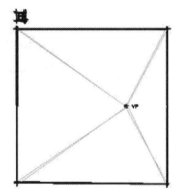

Step C:
Same as step 'C' above.

Step D:
Same as step 'D' above.

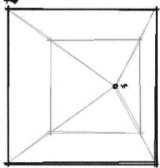
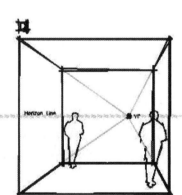

This page shows you how to more accurately establish depth in your sketch. Note the *Diagonal Point's* (DP) placement has an impact on the look and feel of the drawing. You may have to experiment to achieve desired results.

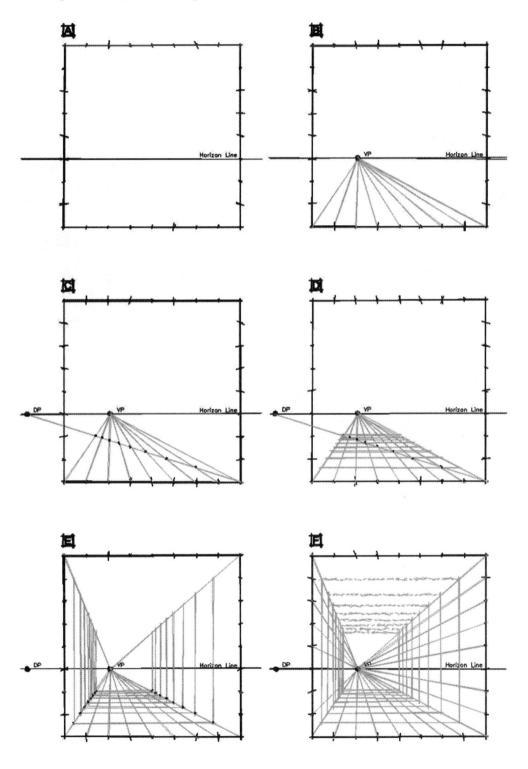

Here are two photographs that demonstrate real one-point perspectives. Keep in mind that perspective drawings are meant to simulate reality.

Now that you have the basics down regarding one-point perspectives, you can apply those techniques to create a one-point section/interior elevation based on the floor plan below.

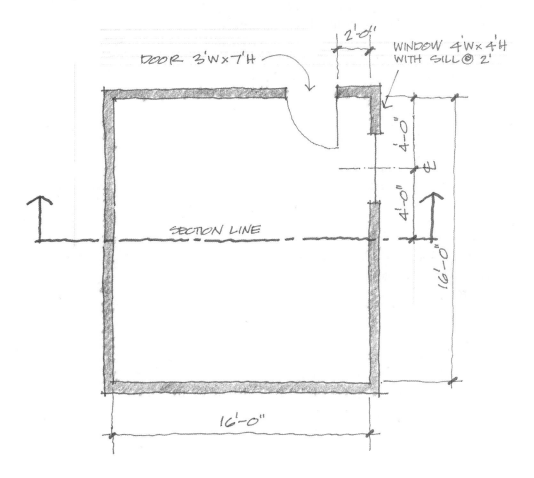

First you start with a section which has been drawn to scale…

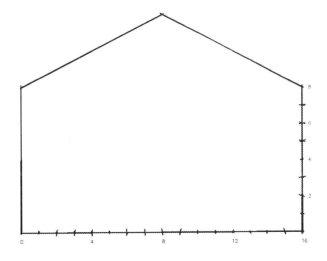

Developing a one-point perspective

Read though the following steps and
then try them with the "starter" image
in the exercise section following this
chapter.

1. Sketch the five perspective lines –
    from VP to corners.
2. Add the horizontal line – its
    location will define the depth of
    the space.
3. Sketch two vertical lines.
4. Locate the center of the back wall
    with a perspective line, and then
    add a vertical line up to the ridge
    line.
5. Connect-the-dots: add the last two
    sloped lines at the back edge of
    the roof.

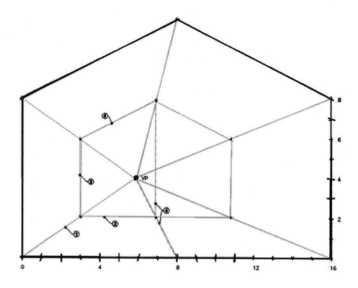

In this exercise, everything drawn
at the Cut Plane is to scale, both
vertically and horizontally.

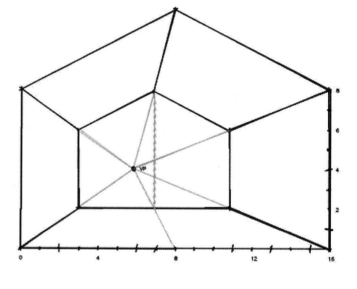

1. [See floor plan on previous page.]
    Sketch perspective lines to define
    door width and location.
2. Locate height on adjacent wall.
3. Then project over onto back wall.
4. Add vertical lines as shown.

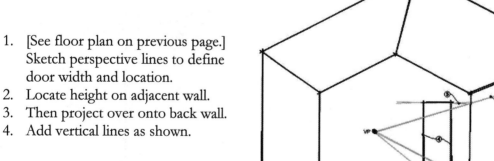

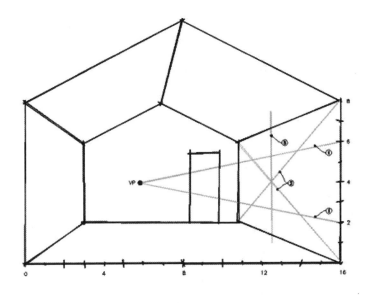

Now you will add a pair of windows to the east wall:

1. Add the two perspective lines to determine the window head and sill locations.
2. Sketch an 'X' to find the center of the wall.
3. Add a vertical line at center of wall.

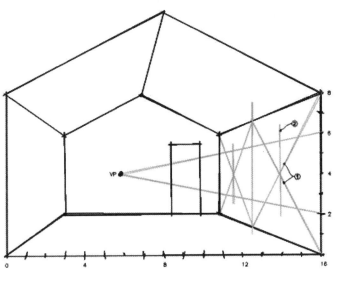

You know the window is 4' wide and the wall in this view is 8' wide (see plan view on previous page), thus you can divide the spaces as previously covered:

1. Sketch 'X's in the two spaces.
2. Add a vertical line at the intersection of each 'X'.
3. You now have the extents of the window defined and can be darkened for clarity.

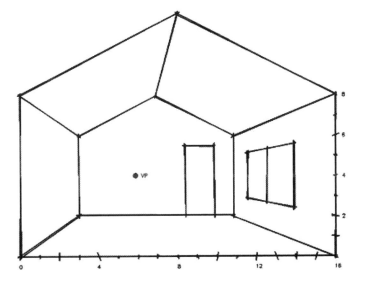

The final step is to darken the major lines and add embellishments, like window and door trim, wall's base, etc.

You will get a chance to practice this in the end of chapter exercises.

Once you have learned to create one-point interior elevations, you can easily apply that technique to creating one-point floor plans. This type of perspective drawing allows you to quickly think about the design of an entire room, rather than just one corner (i.e., two walls).

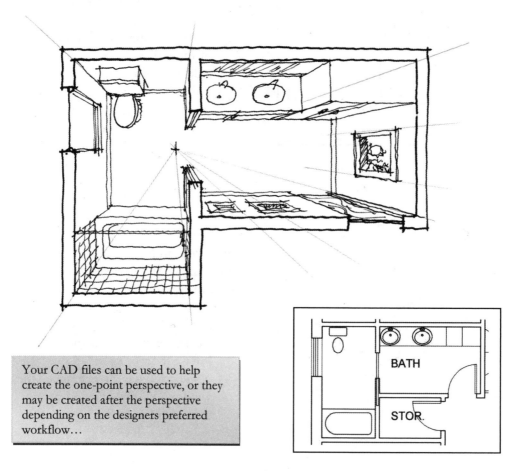

Your CAD files can be used to help create the one-point perspective, or they may be created after the perspective depending on the designers preferred workflow…

Simply sketch the footprint of the room, pick a *Vanishing Point* (VP) and then project the walls up and add features. See the next page for examples on various VP locations and how they affect the resultant perspective.

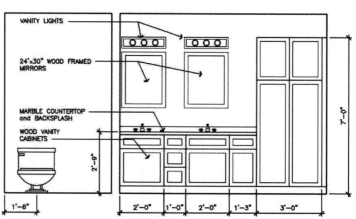

Plan or Elevation and VP location...

You need to think about the information you want to convey in your one-point perspective before you start drawing. Without thinking through to your desired result, you could find you have wasted a lot of time if you get started too quickly. If you want to highlight a lot of detail on the wall then you should do a perspective from an elevation vantage point. If you want to show overall relationships and circulation you could create a plan-type perspective.

In the example below you see a rough sketch of a kitchen floor plan (on the left) and (3) plan-type and (3) elevation-type one-point perspectives. Notice the various *Vanishing Point* (VP) locations and what they show and don't show.

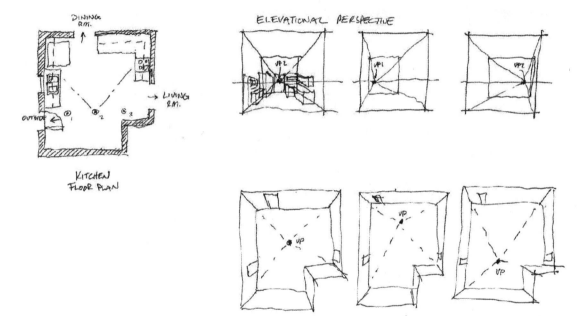

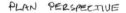

The 1-point sketch to the left is a field sketch of a restaurant in Europe. Notice this one-point perspective captures the essence of the space with minimal detail: the forms in the ceilings, the shape of the chair backs, the layout of the tables, the quantity and location of light fixtures.

Below is an example of the melding of a digital CAD drawing and a hand sketch. Simply print out a floor plan or building section, lay a piece of tracing paper over and begin producing a one-point perspective. Picking the *Vanishing Point* is very important – you want to make sure no major features are hidden. Once the *Vanishing Point* has been established, you can then project lines from the VP through the various corners within the floor plan. The first line you draw to represent the top-of-wall will dictate all others via the "connect-the-dots" process.

This concept even works for 3D programs such as Revit Architecture. You can print out an exterior perspective of the building and then hand sketch various siding and window options quickly without having to meticulously lay out each in an exacting computer program.

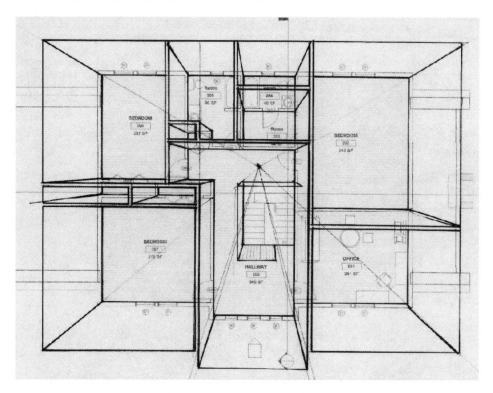

The image below is an example of a student's work using one-point perspective drawings to convey design intent. These sketches have been assembled onto a foam-core board to facilitate a presentation, in which case the board is placed on an easel. Most of the time, these days, a digital projector and Microsoft PowerPoint would be used to streamline the process and allow for much larger images to be displayed for the client.

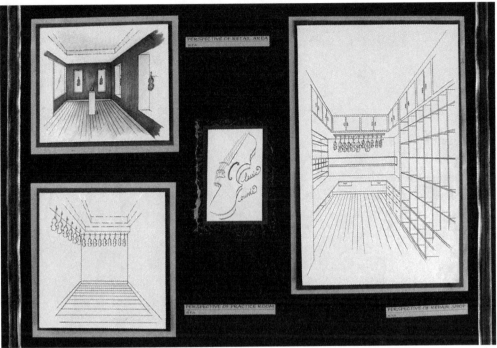

One-point perspective examples by **Anne Porter** CID

Three-Point Perspective

Just as the two-point perspective is generally more realistic than the one-point perspective, there is a third *Vanishing Point* that occurs in most settings. The third *Vanishing Point* can be above or below the object being viewed. As you will see on the next page, the 3rd VP is below the object when the object is being viewed from above – and vice-versa when viewed from a worm's eye view.

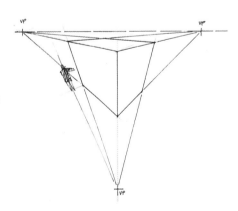

Many architectural perspective drawings omit the third *Vanishing Point* to simplify the process and to remove the slight distortion that would otherwise distract from the main intent of the piece; which is to convey design intent. Rather than a third

Vanishing Point, all lines which would normally be defined by the 3rd VP are drawn vertical. This is done with a parallel bar (or T-Square) and a 90 degree triangle.

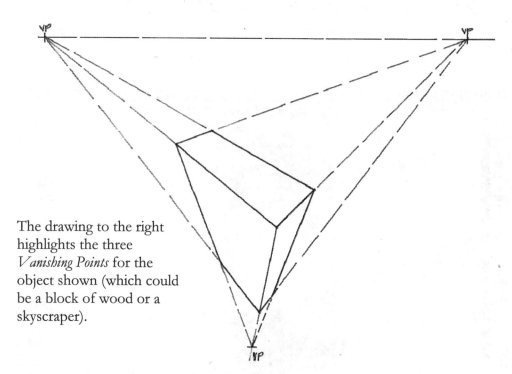

The drawing to the right highlights the three *Vanishing Points* for the object shown (which could be a block of wood or a skyscraper).

Below is a photo demonstrating a 3-point perspective. The smaller image to the right reveals the third *Vanishing Point*. When the object is viewed from below, the 3rd VP is above. Note: this photo is slightly distorted due to the camera lens.

Digital Sketching Techniques

Even though hand sketching is a great tool in and of itself, most designers often find ways to speed the process along. Remember, they still have meeting minutes to deal with! This section will reveal a few such digital hybrid sketching tricks which may make your task a bit easier.

Every modern design utilizes a computer in one way or another. The trick is determining when to sketch something by hand and when to use the computer. The two extremes are: you spend too much time sketching and have to recreate a significant amount of graphical information in your Computer Aided Design program (CAD; AutoCAD or Revit Architecture, for example) with little time to spare; or you jump right into the CAD program and try to do all your designing there, rather than employing the fluid sketching process which allows for several design iterations, and ultimately gives you the most options and the best design solution. The best scenario is to find the proper balance between the two, CAD and sketching, and in fact they overlap quite a bit.

The subsequent pages will introduce you to a few digital sketching techniques utilized by co-author McNeill regularly on real-world projects. Just to make it clear, you will not be required to use a computer or any software in this chapter. The exercises will try to explain the process at a high level, rather than step-by-step, so you understand what can be done. Additionally, the exercises will have the "digital" base-work done and then you do the sketching part.

Machu Picchu by
Duane Thorbeck FAIA

Photographic Fako-Blendo

As previously mentioned, and perhaps you already knew, a perspective drawing mimics what is seen by the human eye. Photographs also capture the perspective qualities we see, so with a digital camera you can snap several pictures of an existing building or interior space as the basis for a perspective sketch. This works great for additions and remodelings, as well as being the springboard for ideas on a totally new project. An example of each will be presented for your enjoyment!

Interior One-Point Perspective

In this example you may have an existing space, a computer lab shown, which you want to remodel. Or, maybe you are developing drawings for a new building but have a collection of photographs and one or two have the look and feel you are generally going after in your design. In either case, you can use the following process to quickly develop a great looking sketch with a minimum of time and effort:

Step-by-step process:

1. Take a picture with a digital camera.
2. Print the photograph as large as possible on 11"x17" paper.
3. Tape the photo to your drawing board.
4. Tape a fresh piece of tracing paper on top of the photo.
5. Discover the *Vanishing Point* by projecting lines from the picture back.
6. Hand trace the major elements you wish to retain in the photo.
7. Embellish the sketch with new ideas; this example shows the ceiling raised, indirect lighting and exterior windows added.

Exterior Two-Point Perspective

Another way in which to apply the *Photographic Fako-Blendo* technique *(**FYI:** Fako-Blendo is a made-up word, in case you were wondering)* is on an exterior perspective. Just like the previous interior example, this could be utilized on both new and remodel building projects. The example below (and continued on the next two pages) shows how you can use this method to delineate the design of a new building based on an existing, similarly proportioned building.

Below you see the photo of the building used as the underlay, and below it you see the end result. The next two pages show the intermediate step to this process.

This intermediate step, which has been expanded across two pages to show more detail, reveals some of the preliminary work required to modify the building pictured. First, the two *Vanishing Points* were discovered by projecting lines back until they all intersect at two points. Next you "connect the dots" between the two *Vanishing Points* to document the *Horizon Line*.

Once you have the *Vanishing Points* located, you can use them to add new elements to the sketch such as the cross-gable shown roughed in here. Note that the *Vanishing Points* do not need to be in the picture (as you can see in the refined sketch on the previous page), but they do need to fit on your desk (or your neighbor's desk); so make sure you plan accordingly!

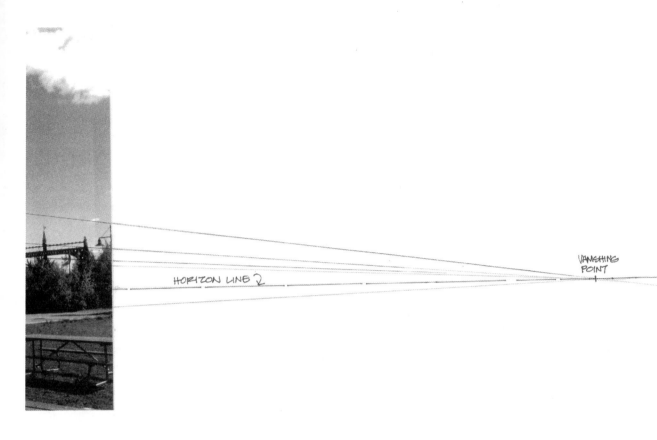

Don't just copy it...

One point we would like to make clear is that we are not, in any way, suggesting you directly copy or plagiarize anyone's work. Rather, the main idea is that you see a space or building, and you can visualize your design generally fitting that mold. From there you rework the "clay" until you are happy with the outcome, which usually does not look too much like the original (of course classrooms only vary so much, but our example is still quite different).

This workflow is not too far removed from common practice in which an architect looks through several magazines and marks pages that catch the eye. Then the pages may be attached to a board and referenced from time-to-time during the design for inspiration.

Digital Camera Photograph Perspective

The images below represent a visual introduction to the *Digital Camera Photograph Perspective* process which will be explained in more detail starting on the next page.

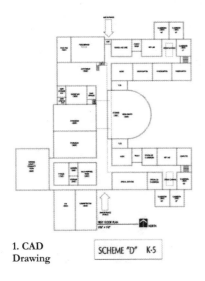

1. CAD Drawing

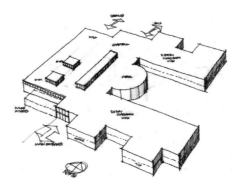

4. Sketch Overlay: Option "A"

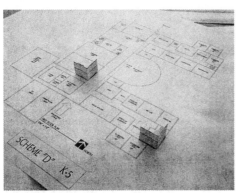

2. Photo of CAD Drawing

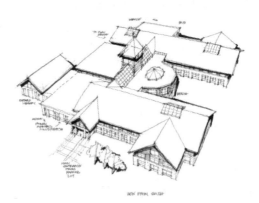

5. Sketch Overlay: Option "B"

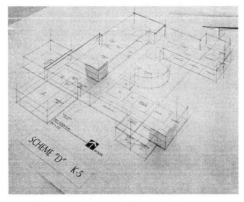

3. Sketching on Printout of Photo

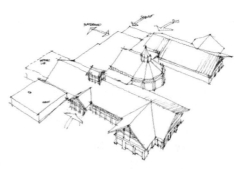

6. Sketch Overlay: Option "C"

Digital Camera Photograph Perspective

This is one of co-author McNeill's favorite perspective methods simply because it is fast, accurate in perspective and allows for the building and site to be depicted together. The process starts with a building floor plan (the ground level) or site plan (see sketch below). This plan is taped onto a table; vertical elements such as wood blocks, cardboard, etc., are positioned to act as "story poles" by which one can judge heights. Next, pictures are taken using a digital camera (see example on the next page). You can select many different vantage points and angles to best portray the project.

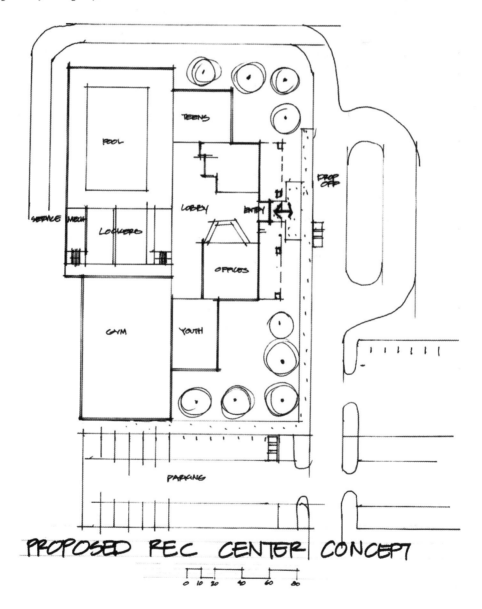

PROPOSED REC CENTER CONCEPT

Once you have selected an image, it can be sent to a printer or plotter and enlarged to create a drawing background; 11″x17″ paper is a common/convenient size.

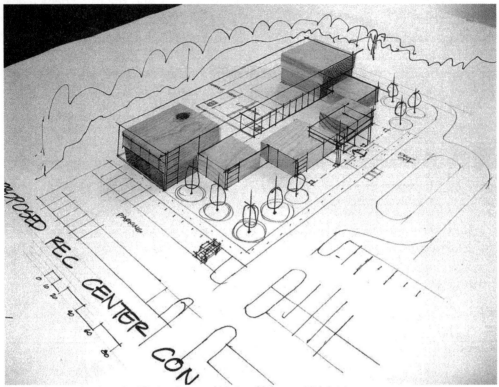

Digital photograph taken of a 2D site plan; wood blocks added to establish height.

The image is drawn upon to establish the major building forms, typically in block fashion. You will note that there is no *Vanishing Point* or *Horizon Line* to guide your perspective lines. Rather you will find lines in perspective that are from other site or building elements that guide your perspective lines to an accurate angle. The vertical wall elements will portray the third *Vanishing Point* direction into the ground. You may wish to follow this angling or simply draft the walls as if all are vertical and parallel to each other for simplicity (this is the most common option used).

Any number of sketch and drawing types can then be produced over this base with tracing paper. For example, quick studies drawn with thick felt-tipped pens or delicate renderings for presentation. Take a minute and note how the three designs (shown on the next two pages) relate to the base drawing (shown above).

Design options developed on base-photo shown on the previous page.

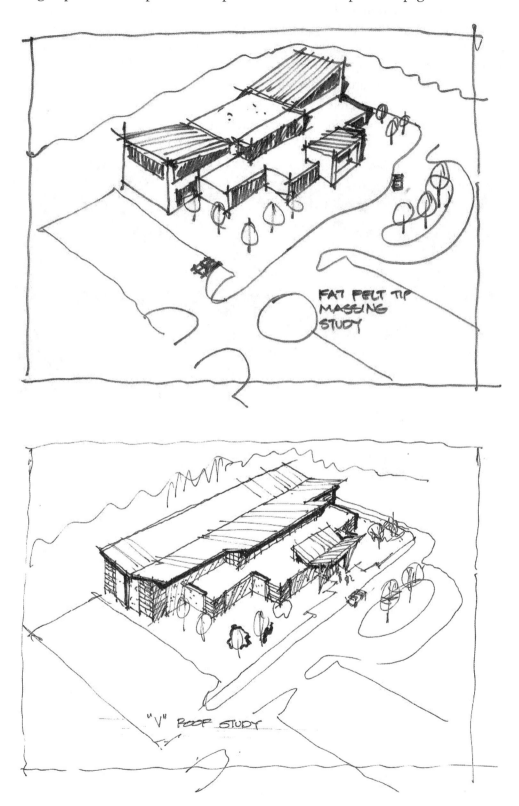

Once you find a design that you like, or you think the client might like, you can then sketch a more refined drawing based on the more loosely drawn overlays shown on the previous page (i.e., they are not meant to be presentation drawings). Sometimes the studious designer will develop, to a point, two or more designs to show the client. These options may be:

- The design the architect likes best
- The design the architect thinks the client will like best
- The design option which costs less to build

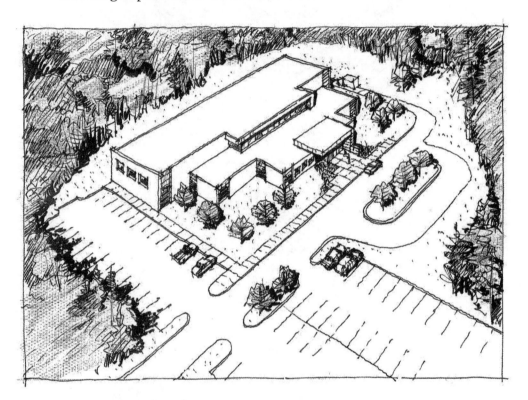

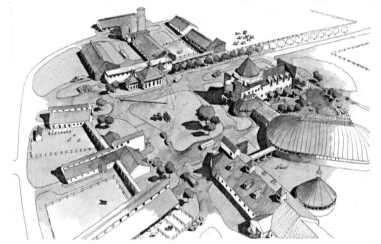

The sketch to the left was not necessarily drawn using the method just described but it could have been. Imagine a photo taken of the campus site plan from this sketch's vantage point.

Hershey Farm Discovery sketch by **Duane Thorbeck** FAIA

Self-Exam:

The following questions can be used as a way to check your knowledge of this lesson. The answers can be found at the bottom of the page.

1. Many architectural drawings omit the third *Vanishing Point*. (T/F)

2. For a one-point (1-point) perspective, you should locate the *Vanishing Point* so no major features are hidden. (T/F)

3. One-point perspectives can be created for floor plans. (T/F)

4. It's okay to copy (or plagiarize) the design of another building. (T/F)

5. It is not possible to find the *Vanishing Point* in a photograph. (T/F)

Review Questions:

The following questions may be assigned by your instructor as a way to assess your knowledge of this section. Your instructor has the answers to the review questions.

1. It is not possible to find the midpoint of a space/surface in a 1-point perspective. (T/F)

2. You can find all three *Vanishing Points* in a photo (by projecting lines back until they converge), but they may be far off the page. (T/F)

3. Once you determine the height of one wall, in a 1-point floor plan, you can start to "connect the dots". (T/F)

4. There are no vertical lines in a 1-point perspective. (T/F)

5. Heads of people align with the *Horizon Line* (for eye-level views). (T/F)

6. _____ _____ is the name of the second "point" in a 1-point perspective, when one needs to accurately establish depth.

7. When the 3rd Vanishing Point is omitted, the perspective lines that would have been defined by it are simply drawn as vertical lines. (T/F)

8. In a 1-point perspective, everything drawn in the cut plane (or main elevation) is to scale. (T/F)

Self-Exam Answers:
1 – T, 2 – T, 3 – T, 4 – F, 5 – F

Notes:

NAME_____ DATE_____

Exercise 10-1

One Point Perspective

Use the image below as a starting point to create the same perspective as covered on the previous pages. Don't forget to make a few copies if you think you might need a few practice runs. Include the following aspects in your design:

1. Add a *Vanishing Point* (VP) more to the right to create a unique view.

2. Add the door and window per the examples above and the floor plan.

3. Also add the following items:
    a. 2'x4' skylight.
    b. Add 3 cabinets to the left wall (2'-0"x2'-0"x3'-0" high).
    c. Sketch a 4'x8' rug centered on the room.

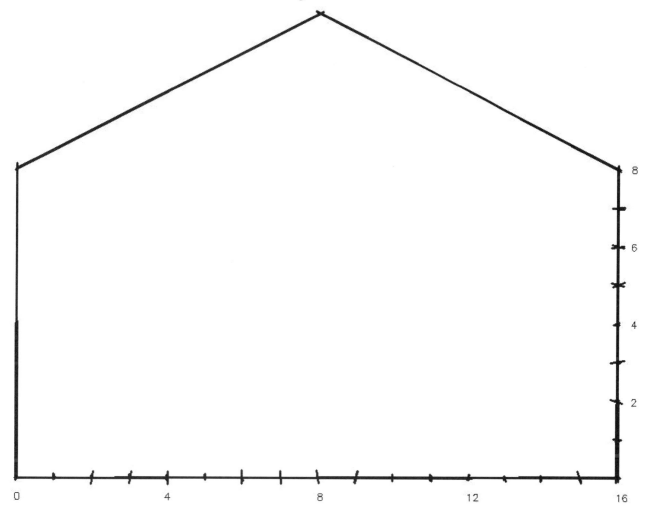

~blank page~

NAME_____ DATE_____

Exercise 10-2

Discover the Vanishing Point
Use a heavy black marker and a straightedge to discover the vanishing point.

~blank page~

NAME_____ DATE_____

Exercise 10-3

One-Point Exercise

Create a one point perspective of your initials like the example.

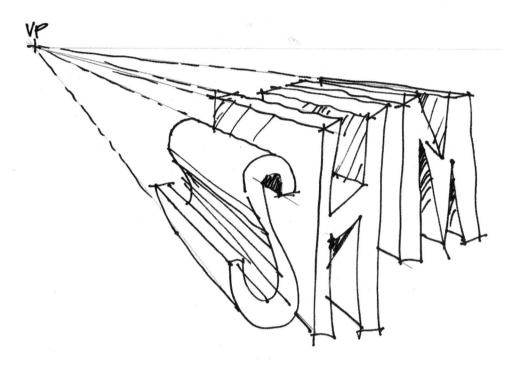

~blank page~

NAME_____DATE_____

Exercise 10-4

One-Point Exercise

Take this section of a public entry space and create a one-point interior perspective. Pick your own vanishing point on the horizon line. Delineate the interior walls, floors and ceiling as you see fit. You may use a straight edge or "freehand" lines. Get the basic "bones" of the space drawn.

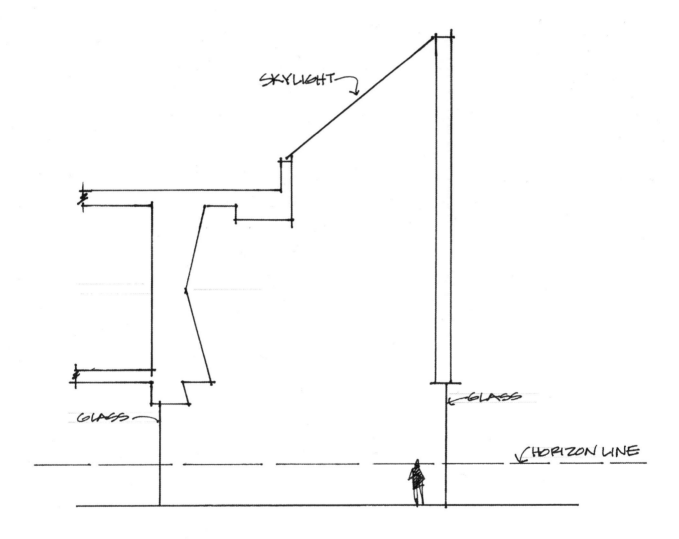

~blank page~

NAME_____**DATE**_____

Exercise 10-5

Discover the Third Vanishing Point

Locate the third vanishing point in the photo provided. There is often distortion in photographs due to the camera lens, so you may approximate the point if needed. In any case, the point should be on this page.

~blank page~

NAME_____DATE_____

Exercise 10-6

Digital Camera Photograph Perspective; *page 1 of 2*
In this exercise you will draw a farmstead. The site plan as shown here has been attached to a table and an oblique bird's-eye type image has been made for your use (using a digital camera and printer). Be creative and sketch in the type of barn and house in your design. Estimate the building heights by eye. Sketch in some light vertical guidelines at the building's corners and then horizontal (i.e., perspective) lines. Sketch in trees, fences and other landscape elements.

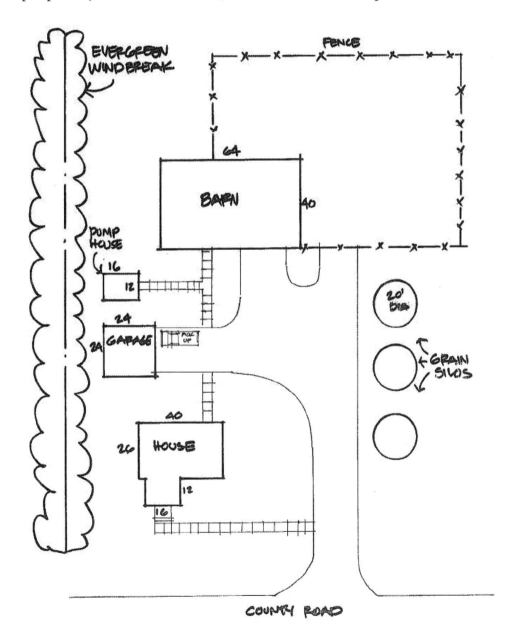

~blank page~

N A M E _____ D A T E _____

Exercise 10-6 (continued)

Digital Camera Photograph Perspective; *page 2 of 2*

Use this photograph of the site plan shown on the previous page to develop your perspective of the farmstead; the photo has been rotated 90 degrees for size.

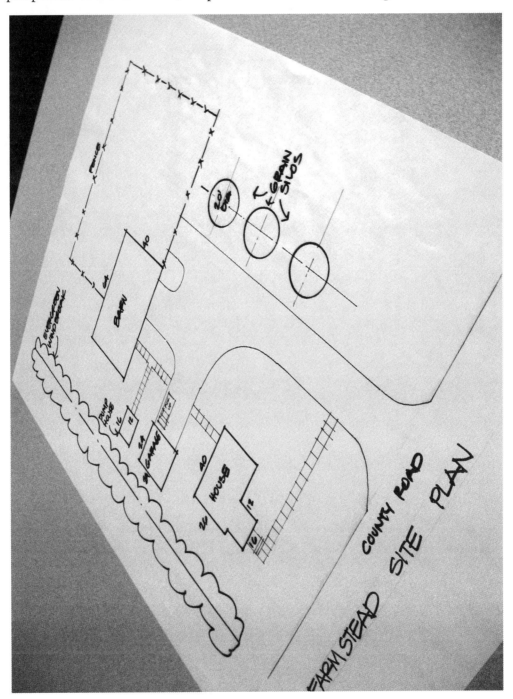

~blank page~

NAME_____DATE_____

Exercise 10-7

Digital Camera Photograph Perspective
Create the same image from this chapter but at the angle shown below.

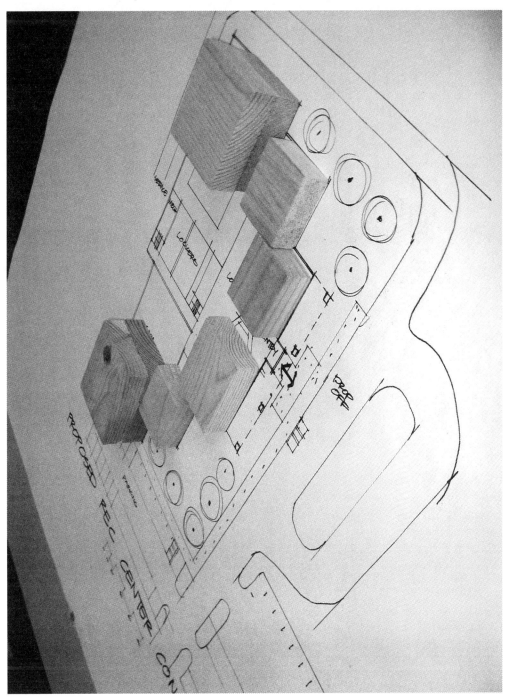

~blank page~

NAME_____ DATE_____

Exercise 10-8

Photographic Fako-Blendo

Using the Fako-Blendo techniques, add a symmetrical addition.

~blank page~

Still Life, Entourage and Reflections

Drawing freehand what you see with the eye can be a challenging, but rewarding, proposition. The exercise of drawing what you see is generally referred to as Still Life or Field Sketching. A still life could be a staged grouping of objects on a table or a grouping of buildings on a given portion of land.

When working on a sketch, the architectural designer has many techniques at his disposal. For example, there are steps one can take to quickly divide a line or a surface (i.e., one side of a 3D box) into equal segments or spaces. Additionally, a 3D drawing can be created that is actually to scale, meaning it can be accurately measured from, called an axonometric. Even when sketching still life scenes or delineating shadows, the designer should be aware of a few fundamental concepts – and that is what this chapter is intended to show you.

Travel Sketches: *Vinland Bridge View* by **Duane Thorbeck** FAIA

Equally dividing a line...

Here is a tip for equally dividing a line… say you need eight equal spaces, such as the third line below. If you start at one end and try working your way to the other end you will almost never end up with equally spaced segments. (It is too hard to judge how big the segments should be.) The trick is to divide and conquer… start with one tick in the middle; it may not be perfect but you will get very close. Next, you can divide each half in half (see the second line below). You continue this process until you have the desired number of segments; this only works for even numbered segments.

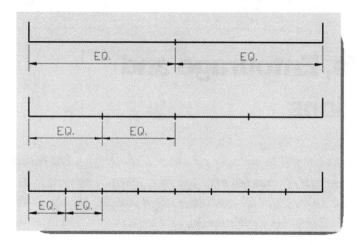

For odd numbered spacing, you use a scale or ruler. Find the number of spaces you want on the scale which is slightly larger than your line. And then position the first and last marks on the scale with the start and end of your line and project down as shown in the example below (the actual scale used does not matter).

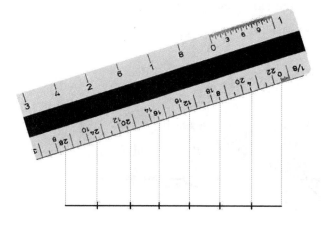

Dividing Spaces

When creating 2D or 3D drawings, you will often have the need to divide a previously created space or surface into smaller areas; for example, make a room in a floor plan exactly half its original size. As you will see in a moment, these methods apply to flat 2D surfaces as well as distorted surfaces which are part of a perspective drawing.

The following technique can be used to equally divide a space into equal pieces. You can, of course, repeat this process to even further divide a space already divided. The graphic below pretty much speaks for itself; you start with any rectilinear face (a simple square is shown here) and sketch an 'X' from which you can project lines from its center point. The center of the "X" is the center of the space in both directions.

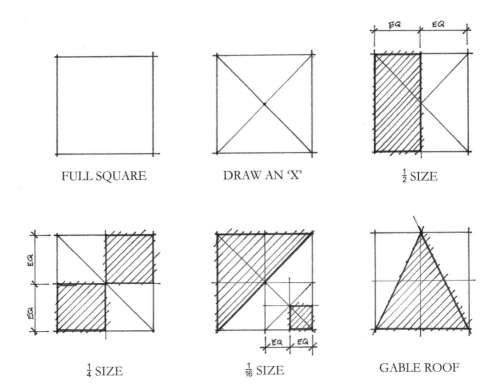

FULL SQUARE   DRAW AN 'X' $\frac{1}{2}$ SIZE

$\frac{1}{4}$ SIZE $\frac{1}{16}$ SIZE   GABLE ROOF

Drawing a Circle

In addition to previously drawn spaces (or squares), you may sketch a rectilinear area as a reference to aid in creating another shape. In a way, you can think of this process as if your square or rectangle were a chuck of wood and you are about to carve away to create another shape from the larger object. This next example uses most of what you learned on the previous page to create a [near perfect] circle. Designers who have been drawing for years are able to create a pretty good circle without this kind of help; however, they would still do it on a major building element that they wanted to be very accurate and maybe even symmetrical about the building façade.

The sketches below pretty much speak for themselves, but a brief outline will be provided to be sure you understand the concept.

1. Draw a square.
2. Draw an "X" to locate the center.
3. Add a horizontal line which passes through the center of the "X".
4. Add a vertical line which passes through the center of the "X".
5. Add two dots, as shown, to divide the diagonal line into three equal spaces.
6. Draw the circle.
   a. The horizontal and vertical lines locate the midpoints of the square – this corresponds to the four quadrants of a circle.
   b. The circle should past just outside the outermost dots on the diagonal lines

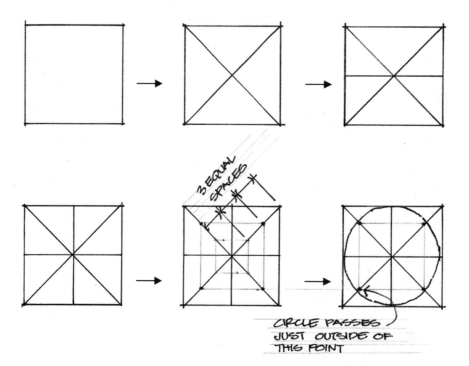

CIRCLE PASSES JUST OUTSIDE OF THIS POINT

Dividing 3D Spaces

Below are examples of dividing a face and inscribing a circle on a three-dimensional object. The steps are identical to the steps outlined on the previous page; you start with the "X" and then add the vertical and horizontal lines. The top example is an isometric box and the bottom one is in perspective (you will learn more about this soon). The bottom example also shows how you can apply the same technique to multiple surfaces (the front and back in this case) and then connect the dots to develop a 3D object – a cylinder in this case! You will have an opportunity to try this on some pre-drawn 3D shapes in the exercise section of this chapter.

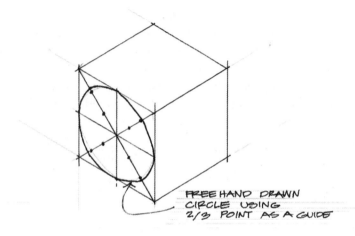

FREE HAND DRAWN
CIRCLE USING
2/3 POINT AS A GUIDE

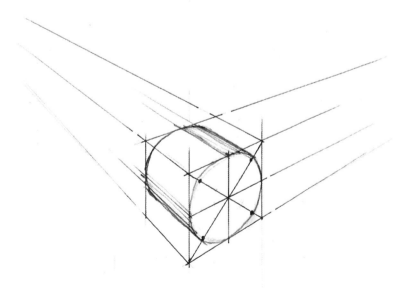

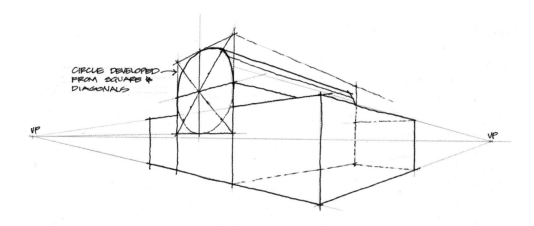

Taking what you just learned, you can easily sketch something such as the example shown above. This is a simple two-point perspective started by developing basic rectilinear shapes and then breaking those shapes and surfaces down by dividing and inscribing a circular element as shown. The extra lines are then erased; or better yet, if you are using pen (which is preferred), you would create a more refined sketch using a tracing paper overlay as described in the Chapter 9.

Still Life Drawing

There are many ways in which to learn and practice hand sketching architectural drawings. One quick and easy way is to use the *Still Life* technique; which involves using something in its natural state/setting or creating a prop of sorts as in the photo below. The interesting thing about the *Still Life* depicted in the photo below, it could just as easily be a group of buildings in a campus setting or an urban area.

The photo above, which will be used as the *Still Life* example for the following pages, was quickly erected using found items: blocks of wood, a coffee cup, an apple, and a chunk of pipe insulation. Notice how the natural daylight softens the shadows and makes them less distinct; using a flood light in a darker room will make the shadows more distinct and crisp, which would be easier to depict in a sketch.

It is possible to simply sit near the *Still Life* setting and sketch it, or it may be more convenient to snap a picture and work from that. You should never just trace over the photo (with tracing paper for example) unless you just plan on practicing hatching and adding shade and shadow.

Once you have your *Still Life* setup, and are ready to get started sketching, you may want to mentally divide the scene into quadrants. This will help you to lay things out with the proper proportions on the paper. This method is helpful to people new to *Still Life* sketching. However, experienced artists rarely do this; at least not on paper (rather in their mind). If you are working from a photo you could even mark the quadrant lines right on the photo.

Start your sketch, add the quadrant lines lightly and rough out the basics. Notice in the image below that the major reference lines and shapes have been laid down first. One major reference line is the angled line across the bottom, which will help to align the vertical block on the left and the flat on the right, as they align (or nearly align) as seen in the photo on the previous page. A circle for the apple has also been added.

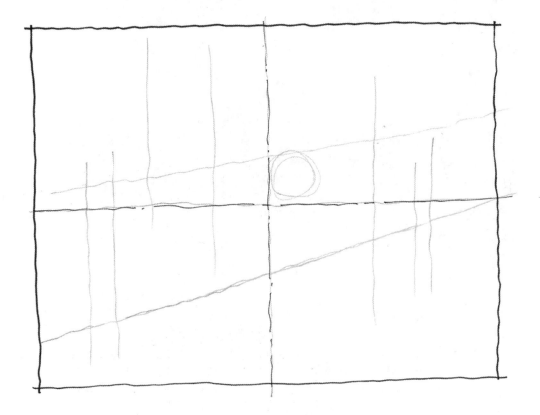

On the next page you can see an intermediate step and the end goal of a loosely sketched still life with shades and shadows added. At this point you are just practicing sketching what you see with your eyes. So at this point (when you get to the exercises), work towards quick sketches in which you focus your energies on line quality.

Still Life sketching can be done with pretty much anything as the subject. As you can see in the sketches below, Architect Alan Anderson spent some time and drew these military jets from different angles.

Airplane sketches by **Alan Anderson**, Duluth, MN

Travel sketch by
Steve McNeill

The opportunities for *Still Life* sketching are endless. Below you see a more refined sketch with blended shades and shadows (using a blending stick or finger) created by a Certified Interior Designer while a student at the University of Wisconsin - Stout.

Still Life sketch by **Anne Porter CID**

Architectural Field Sketching

The idea of *Still Life* sketching can be "super sized" and applied to real-life architectural settings, which is referred to as *Field Sketching*. With this process, Architects can keep their sketching skills sharp – practicing eye-hand coordination, line weights, hatching, shades and shadows, reflections, entourage, etc. This only requires a pen and a sketch book!

Field sketch

To mix things up a little, try creating the same field sketch a few hours later, completely from memory! The image below is a *Memory Sketch...*

Memory sketch

Entourage and Reflections

In the end, buildings are for people, so it makes sense to render your drawings with people in them. Adding people, trees and other "props" brings an otherwise stagnant image to life! The use of reflections in your sketches also adds a layer of realism.

Adding decent looking people, trees and cars to a sketch can be a little tricky. This section will give you a few tips and tricks to help make the process more successful for you. Once you have a handle on adding entourage, reflections, shades and shadows, you will be able to create some stunning sketches and renderings.

Animal Center perspective sketch by **Duane Thorbeck** FAIA

Adding People

Not only do people help to bring your sketches to
life, they also give the viewer a sense of scale. The
simple sketch of people shown to the right can be
created by imagination or you can trace over people
in various poses as found in magazines, newspapers
or digital photographs. In any case, you want to
make sure the people are in the correct perspective
and the proper scale. If you are tracing from a
periodical or a tracing file you can always scale the
image up or down, before tracing it, using a copy
machine. Getting the "models" in the correct
perspective is not as easy; for example, you cannot trace a person pictured mainly
from above in an eye-level rendering.

For eye-level renderings, meaning the angle of the view is as if a person were
standing on the ground, the heads of most people will be at the *Horizon Line* no
matter where they are in the scene. As you can see in the sketch below, some
people are very close while others appear far in the distance, but most of them
have their heads aligned with the horizon. The exceptions are when a person is
sitting, bending over or just shorter than the person they are standing next to.

EYE LEVEL OF VIEWER

If you are tracing people from a newspaper or a magazine, you should be careful not to get too detailed. In fact, you should simplify and slightly alter the sketch so the person is not recognizable; if you traced a famous person (e.g., Bill Gates) and your sketch looked just like him, you could be setting yourself up for a lawsuit!

Some like to be very figurative with the people and trees they add, leaving the primary focus on the architecture, so they simply draw the outline of the people as shown below. These outlines are often left open inside – even when the area all around them is heavily rendered.

Many designers have a book called **ENTOURAGE: A Tracing File For Architecture and Interior Design Drawing** (by Ernest Burden, McGraw-Hill Professional Publishing). This book has a couple hundred pages of people, cars and trees in various poses which can traced and used in your architectural design sketches.

Adding Trees

Trees can be added in much the same way as people; i.e., imagination or tracing.
There are many varieties of trees and seasons to consider; this requires a basic
knowledge of trees for the best results.

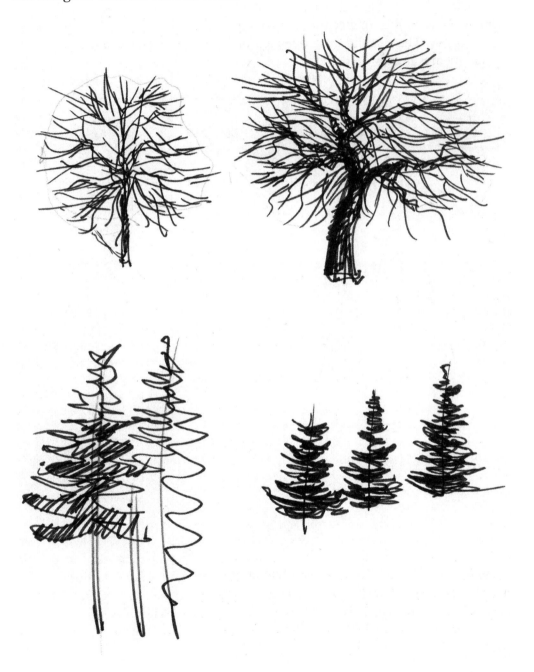

These two pages of trees show a few types and styles of hand sketched trees commonly used in architectural drawings. The use of poché or hatching (or lack of it) can help to indicate fullness or season; just stringy lines with no hatching gives the feel of late fall or winter. Each tree should be slightly different to make the sketch feel more natural – this is pretty easy in a hand sketch as compared to a computer rendering where the same tree is copied around the model.

> **TIP:** You can keep a folder of magazine and newspaper clippings of people in various poses, cars from various angles and trees. This folder can be your own personal tracing file archive. You can scale them up or down on the photocopy machine as needed to match the proportions of your rendering.

This is one of co-author Steve McNeill's travel sketches showing people, trees, benches, etc., in perspective to make the scene very lively!

Adding Vehicles

Not to sound too redundant, but you can also add vehicles in a similar fashion to that of people and trees. Take a look at the reflections section later in the chapter for tips on how to render the vehicle's glass. These vehicles, shown below, were traced from a newspaper advertisement.

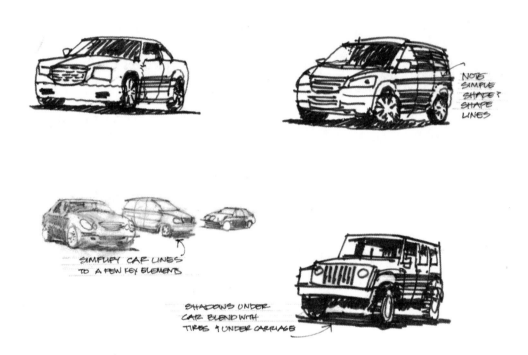

Consistent Shadows

When adding people, trees and vehicles it is important to decide upfront where the sun is coming from and in which direction the resultant shadows are cast; a good rendering will always be consistent in this respect. It is helpful if you can find examples to trace that have the shadows already matching your rendering, but this is not necessary as you can trace the item and then add shadows separately that work. Using a Light Table (i.e., a table with a glass surface which has lights under the glass to make it easier to see through multiple pieces of paper) is helpful when tracing entourage, but you can also use an exterior window on a sunny day; just tape your pages to the window and trace away!

When you are working on "specialty" renderings – that is, when you need people in specific poses – you may need to use your digital camera and photograph people (likely co-workers). You can then print the picture at the proper scale and trace it. You can also take pictures from several angles to make sure you get the correct perspective to trace.

The sketch above is actually of the authors (Stine standing and McNeill sitting) who posed for a rendering of an assisted living facility.

Notice how the use of reflections in the rendering above makes the floor look shiny like marble or terrazzo. The next section begins a discussion on the techniques for adding reflections to your drawings.

Adding "props" to your sketches is sometimes helpful. Notice the large plant placed in the rendering to the right. To make it more realistic shadows were added to the column and floor!

Reflections

Reflections occur throughout buildings and their settings. The most obvious case of reflection is at water. Buildings and landscape elements reflect images that are in complete perspective mirrored about the surface of the water. The perspective continues below the water plane virtually in the same height it appears above it. The example, shown below, illustrates the height of the building corner is the same below (or on) the water plane.

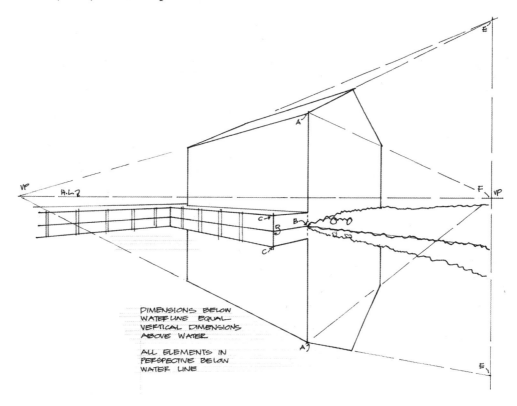

The image above shows, more technically, how reflections are laid out. Before turning the page to see a more refined version of this building, take a felt tipped pen and mark a line along the water's edge in the image above to make sure you understand where it is. The image on the next page serves as an example of how a sketch of the same building would actually look with water reflections. This sketch portrays glass in sunlight with ground level trees, while the water reflects the building, trees and the edge of the water. The surface of the water is often active with subtle waves which can be easily represented by loose horizontal lines used to blur the crisp lines of the mirrored perspective.

This should be clear, but a reflection is a mirrored image and not an image rotated 180 degrees.

Norway Boathouse sketch by **Duane Thorbeck** FAIA

Windows reflect much like water. In the example of the photograph shown below, you see how the upper level of the glass is reflecting the bright blue sky, while the lower level of glass reflects trees and adjacent buildings – which are typically much darker, if not totally black looking.

Just for Fun: Linoleum Block Printing

This has nothing (directly) to do with Entourage or Reflections, but we thought it would be fun to "share" rather than leave this page blank (which would be required to get the next chapter to start in the correct spot).

Linoleum Block Prints create images that use black and white contrast to formulate images. Cutting your own blocks can be a fun way to explore this high contrast imagery that relies on dense tones.

Linoleum Block Printing involves sketching a mirror image design on a smooth piece of linoleum (mounted to a wood block) and then carving the linoleum – leaving your sketch lines untouched (i.e., they remain at the original smooth surface). Next one inks the surface and presses it onto a piece of paper or card front to create images such as the ones shown to the left.

The photo shows an example of two carved blocks and the tools used.

This is a great technique one can use to create greeting and holiday cards – a custom card showing creativity!

Self-Exam:

The following questions can be used as a way to check your knowledge of this lesson. The answers can be found at the bottom of this page.

1. Drawing an "X" within a box aids in sketching a circle. (T/F)

2. *Still Life Sketching* and *Field Sketching* are basically the same thing. (T/F)

3. When dividing a line into an even number of equal spaces, you start in the middle and work your way out. (T/F)

4. *Entourage* helps bring life to your design/rendering. (T/F)

5. Some Architects use _____ sketching, in a sketch book, to help keep their skills sharp.

Review Questions:

The following questions may be assigned by your instructor as a way to assess your knowledge of this section. Your instructor has the answers to the review questions.

1. Field sketching involves mainly drawing farmsteads. (T/F)

2. You draw an _____ to find the center of a box.

3. Dividing a *Still Life* into quadrants helps with capturing proper proportions. (T/F)

4. You can quickly throw together "found" items to create a *Still Life* scene. (T/F)

5. You use a scale/ruler when dividing a line into uneven segments. (T/F)

6. Drawing an "X" only helps to find the center of a flat 2D box and not a 3D surface. (T/F)

7. Using a _____ _____ on a *Still Life* will sharpen shadows.

8. Experienced artists always divide their *Still Life* into quadrants. (T/F)

9. It is not possible to imply the season when sketching trees.

Notes:

NAME_____DATE_____

Exercise 11-1

Entourage

This is a sample of a highly rendered drawing depicting a landscape plaza garden area with many forms: trees, shrubs, pavements, benches, tables and planted beds. Note the use of shadows to suggest depth. Create a landscaped garden on the back of this page, but use the rendering methods for cars, trees, sidewalks, etc., and indicate shadows to portray depth.

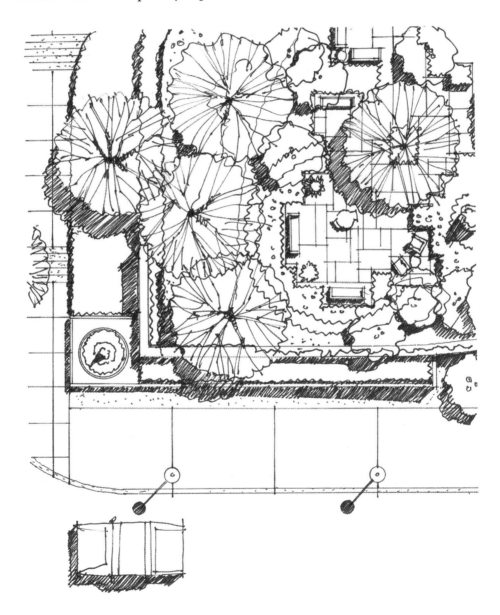

~blank page~

NAME_____ DATE_____

Exercise 11-2

Reflections

Complete the perspective of the waterside building. You may draw it as on a still day or choose to portray water in action.

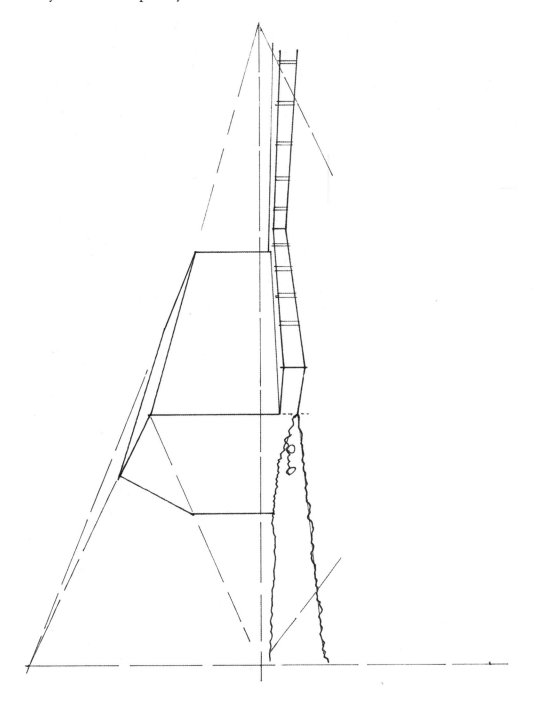

~blank page~

NAME_____ DATE_____

Exercise 11-3

Reflections

Use the hatching techniques you learned in this book to add the reflections shown in the top photograph in the bottom one.

~blank page~

NAME_____DATE_____

Exercise 11-4

Reflections

Complete the perspective of the waterside boathouse. You may draw it as on a still day or choose to portray water in action. Sketch in reflections of the boat.

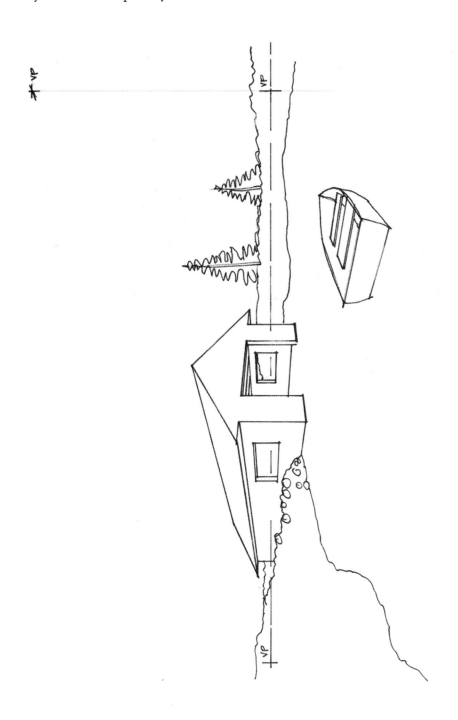

~blank page~

NAME_____DATE_____

Exercise 11-5

Dividing Spaces
Use the squares on the left and practice dividing them into smaller squares; make each one progressively smaller (i.e., 4, 16, 64). And then practice sketching circles in the other three squares.

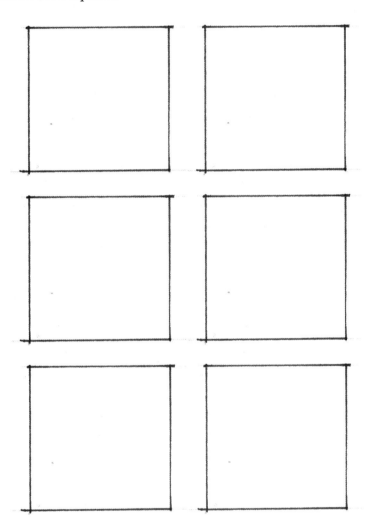

~blank page~

NAME_____DATE_____

Exercise 11-6

Dividing Spaces
Use the faces in perspective below and practice dividing them into four equal spaces. When finished, add a circle over the top of your previous work on this page.

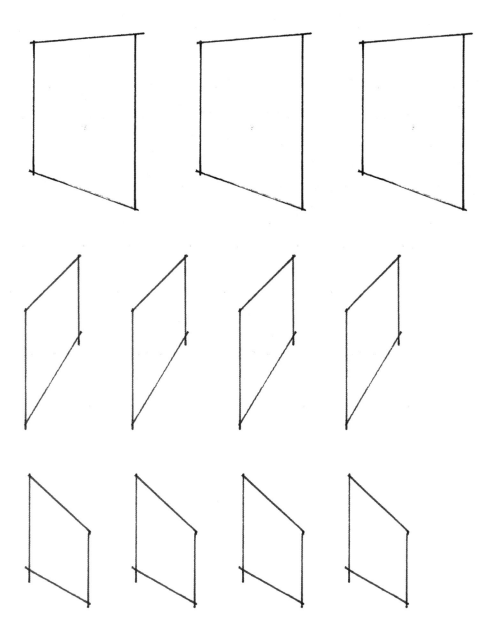

~blank page~

NAME_____DATE_____

Exercise 11-7

Dividing Spaces

Make two boxes ¼ of the original size, and two boxes ½ of the original size. Then add a horizontal and a vertical cylinder to the last two boxes.

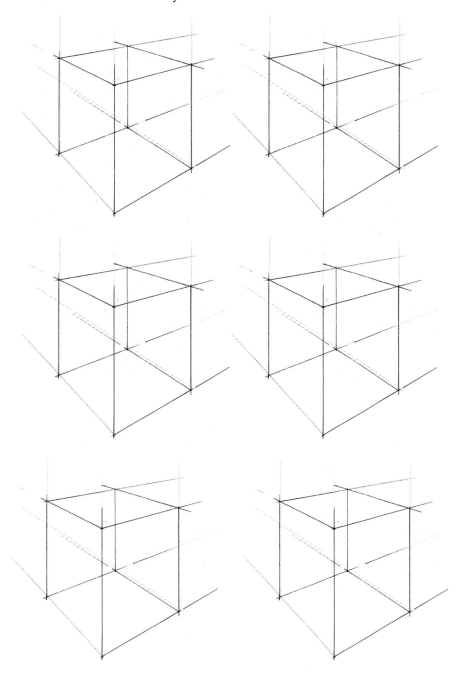

~blank page~

NAME_____ DATE_____

Exercise 11-8

Still Life

Sketch this still life using a pen or pencil. Do not use any straight edges for this exercise. Add the shade and shadows. You need not add the texture or imperfections of the block of wood.

~blank page~

NAME_____DATE_____

Exercise 11-9

Still Life

Sketch this still life using a pen or pencil. Do not use any straight edges for this exercise. Add the shade and shadows. Do not add the texture or imperfections of the block of wood.

~blank page~

NAME_____DATE_____

Exercise 11-10

Still Life

Sketch this still life using a pen or pencil. Do not use any straight edges for this exercise (not that is would help). Add the shade and shadows. Do not add the texture or imperfections of the apple.

~blank page~

NAME_____ DATE_____

Exercise 11-11

Still Life
Draw this still life; add the shades and shadows.

~blank page~

Chapter

12

Project Startup

Now that an introduction has been presented on Computers, SketchUp, Photoshop and hand sketching it is time to apply those skills to a design project. This design project is meant to emulate an interior design studio exercise. These last chapters can be thought of as a studio project with training wheels. The goal is to get everyone on the same page in terms of basic design tools; which are sketching and digital tools. Once this book is completed, the eager design student will have a good foundation from which to continue developing their skills.

Section 12-1
Project Introduction

The design project to be developed by the reader is a fit out of an entire floor in a six story existing brick building built in the 1960's. You will learn more about the building in the next section.

The client is a small, high profile, **public relations firm**. After a number of focus group meetings, which included clients and consultants, and a new strategic plan, the firm decided it was necessary to move from what many considered the "armpit" of the downtown vicinity.

The search for the perfect space is never easy. The firm is quite profitable and considered building new. This would provide associates and clients convenient, free, off-street parking as well as an ideal facility in terms of form, function and infrastructure.

The final decision to renovate an existing 6th floor suite was not easy but was based on several key factors. Many of the firm's clients work in the downtown area. The city is in a colder climate and has built an extensive skywalk system to allow pedestrians to walk throughout the city on the coldest of days without a jacket (see Figure 12-1.1).

FIGURE 12-1.1 Example of city skywalk system

Additional factors in choosing the location included the sustainable aspect of utilizing an existing building which has character and is in a great location relative to the overall layout of the city and is highly accessible; accessible, both in terms of handicap accessibility and in general, due to a skywalk connection and adjacent parking ramp.

The selected space is on the sixth floor, which is the top floor of the building (Figure 12-2.1). The views overlook the city and a large lake. The selected location offers more space and an opportunity to design a high quality, high performance office as compared to other newer buildings or building new.

This fictitious design project will allow you to apply your sketching, SketchUp and Photoshop skills, all along paying close attention to the economy of time in order to derive the best possible design solution, understanding that the client will have to live with your design for many years, and that the client's high profile advertising business demands a complimentary design which will help them to attract and retain clients.

The reader is expected to recreate the designs as presented in the book. This will allow more focus on the tools rather than the inspiration. It would be ideal to develop a parallel design of one's own invention for further practice.

Section 12-2
Existing Conditions

This section will present an overview of the existing building which is the context of your interior design project. The overview will include sketching the basic plan layout in SketchUp. With the SketchUp plan in hand, it is possible to print out the drawing to scale and hand sketch over it.

In an ideal situation, the client will provide you with a CAD or BIM electronic file. The next best thing is to get a copy of dimensioned drawings. These may have been hand drawn or done in CAD, but neither you nor the client has access to the original files. Sometimes, no drawings are available and you have to create these existing condition drawings from scratch.

FIGURE 12-2.1 Existing building from intersection

With a printout of these drawings in hand, or an electronic copy displayed on an iPad or Tablet PC, you can walk through the space and visually verify the accuracy of the documents. Small changes are not always drawn up and documented for future reference. So it is necessary to check things such as door locations and which way they swing. Also, looking for casework (i.e., built-in cabinets and bookcases, reception desks, etc.) and noting finishes. For example, is the ceiling hard (i.e., gypsum board) or is it ACT (Acoustic Ceiling Tile)? Is the floor in a particular room carpet, VCT (Vinyl Composition Tile), CT (Ceramic Tile), Concrete, etc.?

Field verifying the existing conditions and finishes will help to determine if anything can be repurposed, potentially saving the client money and being more sustainable. Maybe an existing office was recently updated by the previous tenants and can be seamlessly worked into the design for your client in terms of size, location and adjacencies (i.e., what has to be close to this room).

When field verifying existing conditions, it is helpful to have drawings which are to scale. Using a tape measure and a laser tape measure you can double check the drawing with what was actually built. When creating existing drawings from scratch, you have to start by sketching the space while standing in it. It helps to use grid paper and try to keep things as proportionally correct as possible. But you do not need to create scaled drawings in the field. Rather, you add the dimensions on the sketch and then use that information, back at the office, to create the drawings.

Surveying existing conditions is somewhat of an art. Making sure you get all necessary dimensions and a number of double check dimensions (i.e., an overall dimension to verify all the ones for a wall which jogs in and out) without needing to make several trips to the project. Also, using known material sizes to visually compare measured results, applying a little common sense. For example, most ceiling tiles are 2'x2' or 2'x4' and floor tiles are often 6"x6", 1'x1', etc. Therefore, you can count the number of ceiling tiles, do the math and compare that to your tape measure reading. This is very helpful as it is easy to sometimes misread the tape measure. Catching a mistake while still in the field can save a significant amount of time.

For this exercise you will be provided with a dimensioned plan which can be used to draw the floor plan in SketchUp. This is one of the first steps you need to do before any design work can begin. Another major step is developing the *Program Statement*, which will be discussed later in this section.

As mentioned in the previous section, the design project will involve the top floor of a six story building. The building is on the corner of the block and has a number of windows with great views of the city and lake on the two sides facing the streets. One side of the building does not have any windows due to the property line location and building codes (Figure 12-2.2); the adjacent property owner could build a multistory building right up to the face of our building. This, plus fire rating rules between buildings, forbids any windows on this face.

FIGURE 12-2.2
Existing building –
no windows on this
side due to building
codes

Starting a SketchUp Model

You will start out drawing the line work for the walls and openings. You do not need to create all the detail such as the doors and windows themselves, or the stairs and elevators. Rather, you can start out by just sketching the walls which define these spaces. Text may be added if needed to remind you that a space is an elevator or stair.

The dimensioned drawing on the next page is what you will work from. The dashed line work at the rear (north) of the building are existing items intended to be removed. The two toilet rooms (northwest corner) are not accessible, so they will be removed and replaced. Keep in mind when renovating an existing building that the space below (and sometimes above) often needs to be accessible to route piping and wires in the ceiling. This can be tricky when that space is actively occupied. Additionally, in multi-story buildings it is often necessary to align the toilet rooms from floor to floor to minimize piping and drainage and clearance issues. None of this will be assumed to be a problem for our project.

The second means of egress is a fire escape on the back side of the building (Figure 12-2.3). This, along with the doors will be removed and a new stair shaft will be added by the building owner in conjunction with this project to bring the building up to code. Notice the windows have been filled in. It would be possible to open a few of them back up on the sixth floor, if needed, except the northeast corner at the service elevator location (see the plan on the next page).

FIGURE 12-2.3 North side of building, existing fire escape to be removed

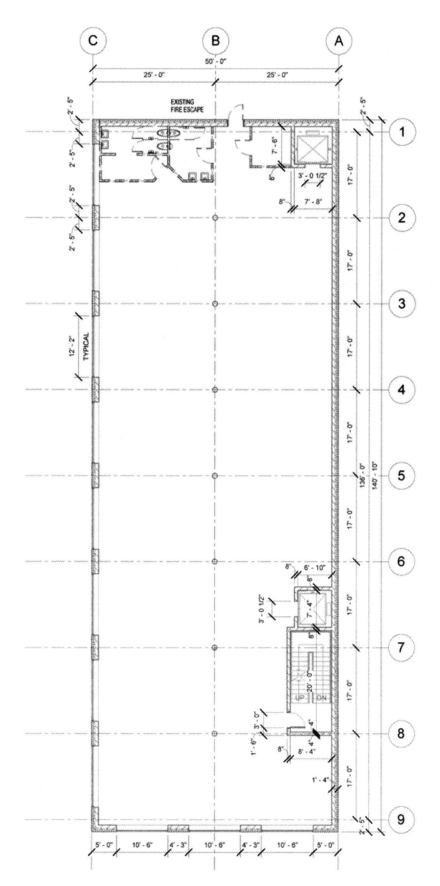

FIGURE 12-2.4
Existing conditions

Now you will draw the existing plan, on the previous page, in SketchUp so you can print it out to scale on a plotter.

1. Using the steps previously covered in this book, create the **2D floor plan** in SketchUp:
   a. Follow the existing drawing on the previous page (Figure 12-2.4).
   b. Set the *Camera* to **Parallel Projection** (see printing notes later).
   c. Switch to the **Top** view (see printing note later in this chapter).
   d. All interior walls to remain are 8″ thick (i.e., existing walls)
   e. All exterior walls are 1′-4″ thick.
   f. Only sketch the openings for the doors and windows.
   g. Do not draw the items to be demolished (shown dashed).
   h. Do not draw the lines for the stairs (i.e., handrails and steps).
   i. Do not draw the grids or dimensions.
   j. Add 12″ round columns.

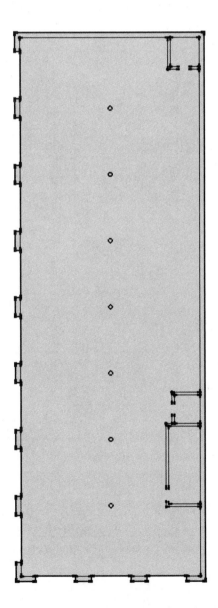

When finished, your SketchUp drawing should look similar to Figure 12-2.5.

Notice the row of columns down the center of the building. These are a major component of the building's infrastructure and cannot be changed in any way. They must be remembered and considered when working on design solutions.

In the image to the right, notice how the outside line of the exterior wall was omitted at each window opening? This is optional, and is used as a way to make all the window openings stand out more in this early stage of development.

All of the door openings are currently shown as simple openings in the walls. We have also left out anything we plan on demolishing: the existing toilet rooms and the door out the back of the building. These "demo" items will need to be drawn later in your CAD/BIM program to document for the contractor what, specifically, needs to be removed from the building. But for now, that is not an issue we need to be concerned with.

FIGURE 12-2.5 Initial SketchUp model

For the simple plan we are working with here it is not necessary to add any text. It is obvious that the two smaller rooms are elevators and the remaining set of walls defines the stair location, none of which can move because we are dealing with an existing building.

2. Save your SketchUp model as **_Office Building Remodel.skp_**.

Printing Your SketchUp Model

The next thing you will want to do is print the floor plan. You have two paths you can take at this point. Both end up at the same situation, that being a printed floor plan which is to scale.

One option is to print the floor plan on smaller paper, maybe not even to scale. This would allow you to do several quick sketch-overs by hand to start thinking about where spaces want to be and their adjacencies. These can start out as bubble diagrams talked about in Chapter 9. An experienced designer can actually visually sketch pretty close to scale – picking up on known dimensions (e.g., the window side, stair width and depth, etc., are all known dimensions to the designer). Having a small printout is handy if you will be traveling or sitting somewhere and you have time to scribble a few ideas while you wait.

This first option allows the designer to start thinking about the big picture aspects of the project. Quickly working through multiple scenarios allows the designer to rule in and out various ideas. Oftentimes the end result is somewhat serendipitous. That is, the final solution was derived by taking elements from several random iterations to come up with an ideal design solution. This final solution might never have otherwise been found if the designer spent too much time worrying about sketching to scale and trying to explore these early design scenarios in CAD/BIM/SketchUp.

Once you study the *Program Statement* (coming up), you should use this method to develop a couple of bubble diagrams.

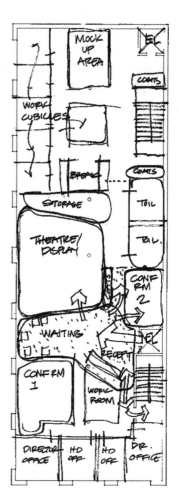

FIGURE 12-2.6
Bubble diagram study

Another option is to print the floor plan to scale and engage in a more formal sketch-over process at your desk. This route can be taken if you, or the client, have a fairly strong notion of what the layout will look like given the *Program* and the space.

Next, you will learn how to create both types of prints.

Printing on a small format printer (not to scale)

The first thing you should do is adjust the settings in the ***Print Setup*** dialog. This tells SketchUp what Printer or Plotter you plan to use, plus the paper size and orientation.

    3.   Select **File → Print Setup** from the menu.

You are now in the *Print Setup* dialog (Figure 12-2.7). Your floor plan is tall and narrow so you will want a ***Portrait*** orientation. The default size is Letter: 8½" x 11". Most small format printers can also print on ***Legal*** size paper, which is 8½" x 14". Some printers will also print on Ledger, which is 11"x17".

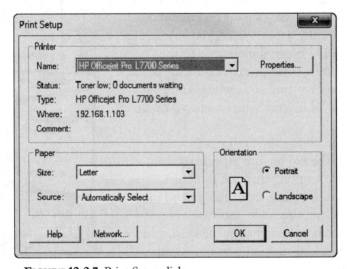

FIGURE 12-2.7 Print Setup dialog

    4.   Select the following in the *Print Setup* dialog:

        a.   *Printer*: (any small format printer you have access to)
        b.   *Size*: Letter
        c.   *Source*: Automatically Select
        d.   *Orientation*: Portrait

    5.   Click **OK** to accept the changes.

Before printing you will temporarily turn off the visibility of the faces as you do not need to see them on the print.

6. Select **View → Face Style → Hidden Line**.

The faces should now be hidden.

With the *Print Setup* options selected, these settings will be the defaults when you open the *Print* dialog box.

7. Select **File → Print** from the menu.

8. Make sure the following options are selected (Figure 12-2.8):

    a. *Printer*: already set based on *Print Setup*
    b. *Fit to Page*: Checked
    c. *Use model extents*: Checked
    d. *Print Quality*: Standard

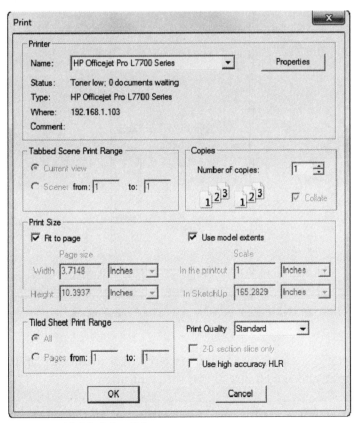

FIGURE 12-2.8 Print dialog

9. Click **OK** to print a copy of your floor plan.

At this point the *Print* dialog closes and your floor plan drawing is sent to the printer. It is a good idea to use the **Print Preview** option found in the *File* menu to visually verify what your print will look like before actually sending it to the printer. This saves time and paper! One common problem is with lines floating way out in space. When using the "extents" option, this will cause the main model to be small as SketchUp is trying to include extraneous lines in the print.

Both your print and the *Print Preview* should look similar to the image below (Figure 12-2.9).

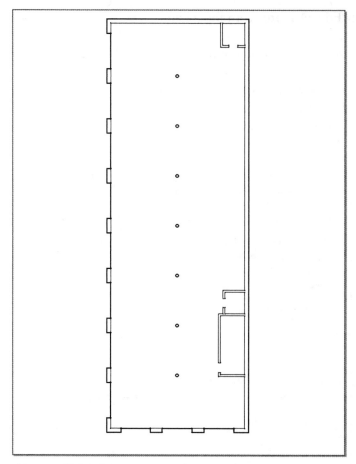

FIGURE 12-2.9 Print preview and "letter" sized paper

At this point you can use tracing paper to sketch over the floor plan printout or print a few copies and sketch directly on the printout.

You may want to write "not to scale" on the printout, or the letters "NTS", so you, or others on the design team, know the drawing is not to scale. It is possible that the printed drawing is really close to a standard scale and could create some major problems in terms of wasted time.

Printing on a large format printer (to scale)

This section will show you how to print to a large format printer, also called a plotter. You will also learn how to print to scale and create a PDF file, both of which could also be applied to the previous steps on creating small format prints.

To actually print to a large format printer, or plotter, you need to have access to one. However, to work through these steps you will learn how to print to a PDF file. This process is identical to actually printing; the only difference is you select a PDF printer driver rather than an installed printer/plotter while in the *Print* dialog. Once you click "OK" to send the print job, you are prompted for the file name and location. Very simple.

Most computers do not come with a PDF printer driver. If you have Adobe Acrobat installed, you will have this PDF printer drive appear in your list of printers. Another option is to download a free driver from the internet – there are several options. However, Adobe does not provide a free option for this feature. One free option is PDF995 (PDF995.com). The free version displays small, self-promoting, company advertisement every time you print to PDF. There are several other options; just do an internet search to explore.

You will need access to a large format printer or a PDF printer driver in order to follow along with the next few steps.

10. Ensure you have set the following options:

   a. Camera → **Parallel Projection**
   b. Camera → Standard Views → **Top**
   c. View → Face Style → **Hidden Line**

In order to print to a specific scale, you must have parallel projection and a standard view selected. Perspective views cannot be printed to scale.

11. Select **File → Print Setup**.

12. Make the following adjustments in the ***Print Setup*** dialog:

   a. *Printer*: select a large format printer or a PDF printer driver
   b. *Size*: 22"x34í (also called ANSI D)
   c. *Orientation*: Portrait

13. Click **OK**.

Next, you will do a *Print Preview* so you can determine what scale will fit on the paper size you have selected.

14. Select **File → Print Preview**.

15. Make the following adjustments to the *Print Preview* dialog (Figure 12-2.10):

   a. *Fit to page*: uncheck
   b. *In the printout*: ¼ (or .25)
   c. *In SketchUp*: 12
   d. *Print Quality*: Large Format

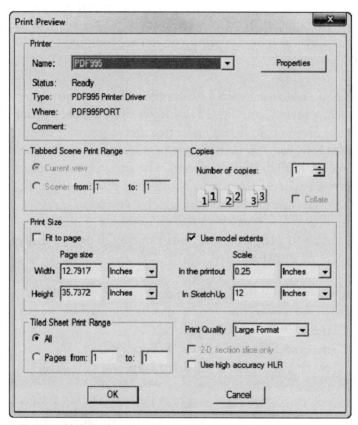

FIGURE 12-2.10 Print preview dialog

Notice, in Figure 12-2.10, that the page size for the printed drawing updated when you specified a scale.

TIP: The page size does not update until you click into another field within the Print *dialog. Note that the Height is 35.7", which is larger than your 22"x34" paper you intend to print on. Therefore the ¼" = 1'-0" scale will not work.*

FYI: If you printed with these settings, SketchUp would tile the drawing onto multiple sheets of paper to print the entire drawing to the selected scale.

Next, you will adjust the settings to try another scale.

16. Change the *In the printout* option to **.125** in the *Print* dialog.

Notice the page size now fits on the desired paper size.

17. Click **OK** to see the *Print Preview.*

The preview image should look similar to Figure 12-2.11.

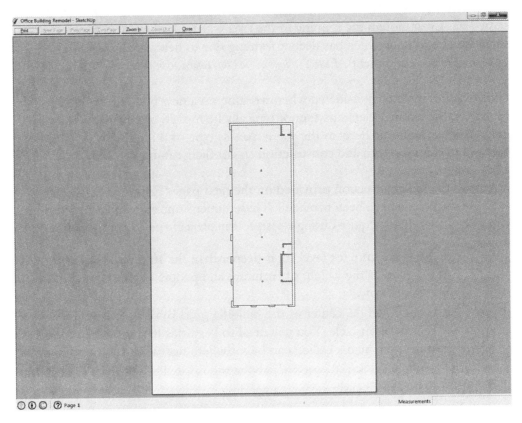

FIGURE 12-2.11 Print preview showing floor plan at ⅛″ = 1′-0″ on 22″ x 34″ paper

18. Click the **Print** button near the top of the application window to enter the *Print* dialog.

19. Click **OK** to print the drawing.

You now have a print out or a PDF that is to scale. You can use your architectural scale on it to read existing building dimensions or sketch proposed items.

Building Section Information

It is important to survey the vertical relationships when remodeling an existing building. Look for things such as the height to the window sill and head (i.e., the bottom and top, respectively). You need to know if a desk will easily fit next to a window. It is also important to measure the existing ceiling heights. When possible, you want to get a distance from the floor to the structure above the ceiling, or from the ceiling to the structure and then add the two dimensions. It is best when you can take an overall dimension without having to add dimensions so as to avoid mistakes. Keep in mind that not all structural framing members are the same size. Even though the framing in the area you are looking at is consistent, there may be an area which has deeper framing due to heavy loads (e.g., bookshelves or equipment). ***FYI:*** *You will not use this information right now.*

Similar issues must be considered when working on a new building design as well. However, the existing elements cannot typically be moved or changed without a great expense and time delay to the client, so this type of thing is closely monitored during design and construction so conflicts can be avoided.

Notice in the building section provided on the next page (Figure 12-2.12) that several dimensions have been provided. These dimensions are similar to what you would typically try to acquire during a visit to the project site. Note the following:

- The floor structure for level six is deeper than the structure for the roof. This is typical as the weight of furniture and people is often much more than rain or snow.
- The beam down the center of the building (grid B) represents the worst case structural obstacle. You will need to keep this in mind when trying to determine how high a ceiling can be, or where ductwork can be routed.
- The window sill is 3'-0" (or 36") above the floor. This means a typical desk (30" high) can fit easily next to a window.
- The ceiling, which is Acoustic Ceiling Tile (ACT), makes it possible to remove a tile and measure to the structure above.

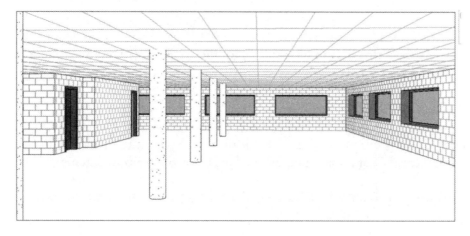

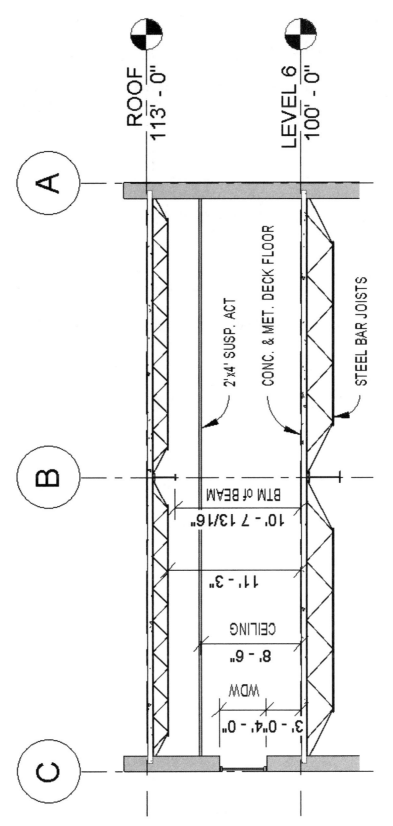

FIGURE 12-2.12 Building section showing existing vertical relationships

Section 12-3
Program Statement

It can be a bit confusing in a design firm when you hear one person talking about "a" program and another talking about "the" *Program*. These are two totally different things. The first is software on your computer, and the second is the topic of discussion in this section.

A ***Program Statement*** is created in the pre-design phase of a project. It is a document identifying the specific requirements of the design. Working with the client or user group, the design team gathers as much information as possible about the project before starting to design.

The information gathered includes:
- Rooms: What rooms are required?

- Size: How big the rooms need to be? For example: toilets for a convention center are much bigger than for a dentist's office.

- Adjacencies: This room needs to be next to that room. For example: the public toilets need to be accessible from the public lobby.

- Equipment: List items required. For example: printer, dishwasher, etc.

Looking at the table on the next page (Figure 12-3.1), the reader can see a simple example of a *Program Statement* for our project. You can think of these as the pieces to the [design] puzzle. It is not possible to start scribbling or sketching anything meaningful until the *Program* has been established.

The process of arriving at a total required square footage is an easier task for an existing remodel. You have a fixed amount of space with which to work. If, after working through the *Programming* process, the clients do not have enough room, they have to make a decision. They can compromise their ideal design by leaving something out, such as a conference room. Or they can try to utilize space on another floor. It may even be that the selected space is not going to work and they have to go back to the site selection process.

When *Programming* for a new facility, the challenge is often to keep the overall building area within budget. For a certain building type, the designer can apply a cost per square foot to the *Program* and see if that matches with the client's budget. If not, the client also has to make a decision on how to proceed: cut back on square footage, reduce the quality of the project, come up with more funds, etc.

This *Program* lists the rooms, how many are needed of each and the required area for each. The client will provide much of the needed information, but the designer plays a big role here. The client might not know they need an elevator machine room, or a telecommunications room. This is where the experienced design professional helps guide the discovery process.

With the project statement in hand, the design team can begin the design process. Although modifications may, and will, need to be made to the *Program Statement*, it is used as a goal to meet the client's needs.

Program Statement

Space	Qty	Area	Subtotal Area	Actual Area
Waiting /Lobby	1	250	250	
Reception Desk Area	1	150	150	
Closet /Coats	2	20	40	
Toilets	2	160	320	
Theatre / Display	1	700	700	
Workroom	1	150	150	
Break/Coffee Rm.	1	140	140	
Storage	1	140	140	
Conference Room 1	1	400	400	
Conference Room 2	1	200	200	
Director's Office	2	180	360	
Head Staff Office	2	150	300	
Mock Up Center	1	150	150	
Work Cubicles	6	100	600	
Subtotal Net Square Feet			3,900	
Circulation, Walls, Stairs and Elevators			3,100	
Total Gross Square Feet			**7,000**	

FIGURE 12-3.1 Program Statement

The *Program* above has an "Actual Area" column in which you can enter the actual area of a space once you have developed a plan. This will provide you with a quick side-by-side comparison.

Some more sophisticated *Programs* will list the required equipment, even having a standard form which is filled out for each room. It might also list adjacencies and other needs the design team can refer back to throughout the design process to make sure all of the client's communicated needs are being met in the design and documentation.

Try entering this information in a spreadsheet such as Microsoft Excel. Use formulas to total up the numbers if you know how.

Self-Exam:

The following questions can be used as a way to check your knowledge of this lesson. The answers can be found at the bottom of this page.

1. Dashed lines often indicate items to be removed. (T/F)

2. SketchUp cannot print drawings to scale. (T/F)

3. What is the measurement between the bottom of the beam and ceiling?

   _____

4. What is the programmed total gross square footage? _____

5. What is the diameter of the existing columns? _____

Review Questions:

The following questions may be assigned by your instructor as a way to assess your knowledge of this section. Your instructor has the answers to the review questions.

1. It is not necessary to worry about existing structural columns. (T/F)

2. The *Program* is established in meetings with the client. (T/F)

3. How many total spaces (not rooms) are required in the design? _____

4. Sixth floor gross square footage of the building: _____ (Figure 12-2.4).

5. SketchUp can print so the drawing fills the page (not to scale). (T/F)

6. Remolding, rather than building new, has sustainable attributes. (T/F)

7. How high are the window sills? _____

8. The toilet rooms are being removed because they do not meet accessibility codes. (T/F)

9. What is the floor construction? _____

10. If the client provides existing dimensioned drawings, it is not necessary to perform any field verification. (T/F)

Chapter

13

Preliminary Design Options

In this chapter you will take the existing conditions plan and *Program Statement* and begin to develop design solutions. This process involves several quick and rough sketches to begin to understand how the client and their clients will use the spaces. Once you have a dozen or so working ideas, you can embark on a slightly more refined sketch or two. At the end of this chapter you will have developed three possible designs which you will present to the client. These designs will be loaded into Photoshop and arranged side by side with added text to identify each option.

Hopefully, a pattern is beginning to unfold as you read this book. Similar to life, one must crawl before they walk, before they run. A professional design is one that has been thoroughly investigated and explored. This process requires problem solving skills more than an artistic flare. However, being able to present one's ideas clearly is closely tied to the quality of drawings placed in front of your audience.

The flow of a typical project:
- **Predesign (PD) Phase**
  - o Survey Existing Conditions
  - o Program Statement
  - o Generally no drawing at this point
- **Schematic Design (SD) Phase**
  - o Bubble diagrams
  - o Visual Listening
  - o Concept drawings
    - ▪ Floor plans
    - ▪ Interior perspective
    - ▪ Simple elevations and sections
  - o Drawings often presented with color
    - ▪ Can be hand or CAD drawings
  - o Major code issues have been considered
    - ▪ Number of exits required
    - ▪ Number of toilet fixtures
    - ▪ Occupant and construction type
    - ▪ Etc.

- **Design Development (DD) Phase**
  - Proof of concept scaled CAD/BIM drawings
  - Furniture, Fixtures and Equipment shown to scale and clearances considered.
  - Major finishes selected
  - All primary drawings have been started
    - Floors plans
    - Exterior elevations
    - Major interior elevations
    - Sections and major details
- **Construction Documents (CD) Phase**
  - Formalized "final" documents used to:
    - Obtain bids from contractors
    - Obtain permits from the government
    - Obtain insurance by/for the owner
  - Fully dimensioned and noted drawings
    - The AIA general conditions, which most projects adhere to, forbid anyone from using a scale to read dimensions off of the printed drawings.
    - Thus, the drawings must have all necessary dimensions added in order to avoid excessive questions by the contractor during construction.
  - Once the bidding stage is over, these documents become legally binding documents by which the contractor and client are bound.
    - The contractor does not have to provide anything more than the documents require without additional compensation and time.
    - However, the contractor may not change or provide anything less than the documents require.
- **Construction Administration (CA) Phase**
  - Formal drawings used to make changes to the Construction Drawings.
  - Changes are due to:
    - Errors in the CD's
    - Unknown conditions
      - For example, a water pipe in an existing wall that nobody knew about – and needs to be moved)
    - Owner changes their mind
      - For example, it is decided that a door is needed into the break room to keep the noise down near the open office area.

It is clear that the design never completely stops until the building project is completely done. For a more detailed study on this, take a look at **The Project**

Resource Manual; CSI Manual of Practice by the Construction Specification Institute (CSI) ISBN: 0-07-137008-4.

This book focuses on the first two phases: **Predesign** and **Schematic Design**.

It is usually counterproductive to try and shortcut or skip one of these phases. Often something significant is overlooked and a significant amount of work becomes void and must be redone.

Section 13-1
Using Imagery to Contextualize Design

Coming up with the initial concepts when starting a new project can be challenging at times. Each designer has his or her own process by which they get their "juices" flowing. This section will present a few ideas on how to conjure up a design vocabulary for the project at hand.

Existing Spaces

When meeting with your client, it is a good idea to take pictures of their current facility and have those photographs as a reference when reflecting upon how they use various types of spaces.

The image below is the office of one of the directors. This image helps one to recall the type of furniture being used, as well as equipment (printer, copier, fax, under-counter refrigerator, space heater, etc.).

Photograph of Director's office at current facility

The photograph to the left is of one of the typical staff desks – these are for the individuals which will be in an open office area. This image can be used to argue that a larger desk is needed to accommodate the equipment and documents needed on a daily basis.

Photographs should be stored in a common location within a project folder so everyone on the team has access them.

Photograph of staff office at current facility

Visual Listening

A great way to get ideas for a new design is to look at other designs. Architects and Interior Designers often spend time paging through design magazines at the beginning of a project to get inspiration. This is one of the reasons we never throw anything away! You never know when you will need it…

Magazine collection

Of course, the intent is not to copy a design as that would be unethical and have serious legal ramifications. However, the design vernacular is what we are looking for. Or maybe a specific design element, be it a furniture style, a built-in casework detail, or trim style, can be gleaned from the pages of a magazine.

The designer can even present some of these images to the client to give them a few options. The design profession will present a very limited set of options to the client so as not to overwhelm. If they do not like any of them, you can take another pass at the next meeting. The client is informed that these images are just to generate discussion and will not be exactly what they will get in the end.

Using images in meetings as just discussed is called *Visual Listening*. Seeing and hearing how the client responds to various styles and options helps the designer understand the client's tastes and draws out little details about needs and desires that might not otherwise be ascertained. Later when sketching ideas, the designer will be able to create a user-centric design – some of which came about from subtle comments in an indirect (or subconscious) manner.

The next few images are examples of how one might find images and then present them in groupings to compare and contrast function and design on a per space basis. The images here are specifically from the **Haworth** website (www.haworth.com). Their **Spaces** sub-page has many of these types of images. Of course, the internet has thousands of options in addition to design magazines.

Executive Offices

With these images one could discuss the idea of glass walls. Would this be too open and not allow for privacy given certain tasks that might need to be done by the occupant of the office. For example, a benefits coordinator in a larger company might need more privacy due to confidential staff medical information. The glass panels and doors certainly make the office feel larger and look more contemporary.

Does the client like the more trendy furniture in the first image, or the feel of the second image which is a cross between traditional and contemporary?
If the client says "I like the glass walls in the second image but prefer the desk in the first image," you can make those notations right on the images. Later, those images can be scanned and saved in the project files for future reference.

While reviewing the second image, the topic of window treatments might come up. Are they needed, and what style if they are?

It is always a good idea to document as much as possible during client meetings. This helps you to remember the massive amount of information that is poured out on you – some of which is not specifically needed this early in the project. Good documentation is also essential when a client comes back several months later, maybe during construction, and insists they wanted something different. Producing the documentation can quickly diffuse what might otherwise be a difficult situation.

Haworth – Berlin Showroom

Haworth – Dallas Showroom

Staff Offices

It is interesting to know that the number one, highest budget item for a business is its staff: payroll, benefits, etc. The psychological effect of the spaces in which they work can certainly affect their desire to be there (in addition to other factors, of course). Therefore, the designer should consider this when engaging in the design of staff spaces. Functional and ergonomically comfortable and adjustable spaces are a must in a high production office area. One must also consider the acoustics, providing surfaces and materials which will help reduce noise levels.

There are many little things often overlooked that an experienced designer will consider: things such as printer noise and distance. Having a printer in an open office area may be convenient, but it might be very noisy and distracting.

Images such as these can help to draw out these types of discussions.

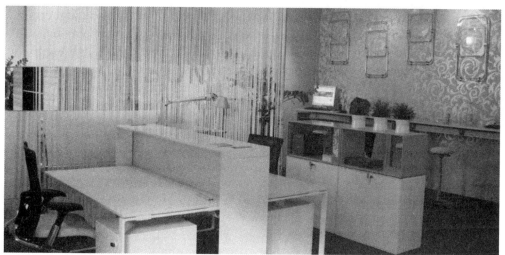

Haworth – Chicago Showroom

Haworth – Dallas Showroom

Lobby Furniture and Conference Rooms

In most companies, the lobby and reception desk provide the first impression when entering. This area often receives special attention and can have a higher budget per square foot than other areas.

When reviewing the images below with clients, using visual listening, one might discuss the style and durability of the lobby furniture. Should there be room for plantings? Will the firm be displaying its work on the walls or maybe artwork? Will these items need special accent lighting?

If the structure and ductwork above allow it, should the ceiling be raised to allow for more volume? Our project does not allow this, but the first image below is a good example of the creation of a two story space with the second level overlooking this space. The lobby has a grand presence and can be very inspiring.

Even though our project cannot have a two story space, it may have a higher ceiling. And, seeing as the suite is on the top floor of the building, it may be possible to add skylights. Skylights would add a nice layer of natural lighting to the space. They would also reduce the need for artificial lighting, thus saving energy and helping to meet any sustainable design guidelines such as Leadership in Environmental and Energy Design (LEED), which is developed by United Stated Green Building Council (USGBC).

Haworth – Toronto Showroom

Additional questions one might want to consider in relation to the lobby are:

- Would there ever be a need to provide after-hours access to the lobby, theater or conference rooms? Sometimes a company might allow staff involved clubs or professional organizations to meet in their space after hours. Maybe a local advertisement club which promotes the advancement of the industry, or a Boy Scouts or Girl Scouts group, etc. This type of space usage is a way one firm might give back to the community. It could be that they allow this in their current space but have not considered how the design might be slightly modified to more easily accommodate this function. The design professional could suggest the arrangement of doors and walls such that the general work areas can be locked down after hours, leaving only "public" access to the lobby, conference rooms, theater and restrooms. Thus, the potentially confidential documents and product designs laying out on staff work areas are safe. This type of discussion can help to exceed the client's expectations in terms of overall satisfaction with the final design solution.

- Another question might be about conference room visibility. Does the client want the conference rooms highly visible from the lobby and reception desk? The image below shows one such example. This looks really cool and makes things feel more spacious and open. However, the client might work with clients who compete with each other. Do you want one to stop in one day and see others meeting with them? Or, maybe the client does not want someone waiting in the lobby and seeing them in a meeting that is dragging on and thus the person waiting is feeling openly (or intentionally) ignored. The design of a space can have very interesting consequences when not fully thought through (and even then things can still come up).

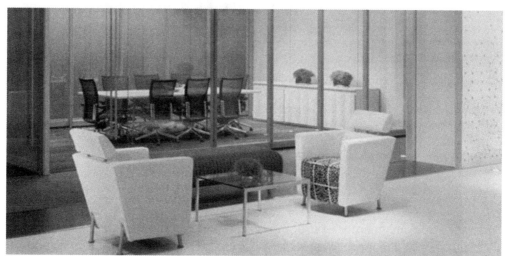

Haworth – Los Angeles Showroom

The method of visual listening can yield highly useful information for both the designer and the client. As previously mentioned, documenting these findings is very important; not the most exciting part of the job, but an absolute necessity none the less!

Section 13-2
Concept Drawings

Now that you have the *Program* in hand, the existing conditions documented, the floor plan printed to scale, and have met with the client a few times, you are ready to put **pencil to paper**!

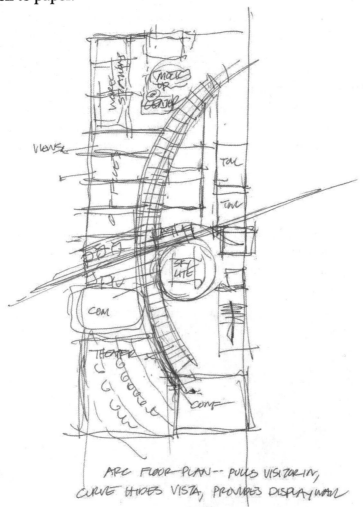

ARC FLOOR PLAN -- PULLS VISITOR IN,
CURVE HIDES VISTA, PROVIDES DISPLAY WALL

The first place one might start is doing several sketchbook drawings. They are meant to be fast and loose. The drawings are not really to scale and may not be understandable by anyone but you. The intent is to lay down several ideas quickly, each floor plan taking only a few minutes – not a half-hour. Of course, this will vary depending on the overall size of the project. These quick sketches will allow the designer to begin to understand how the client works and might utilize the space based on information gathered thus far.

This process will likely yield additional questions by the designer for the client. These can be collected and discussed at the next meeting.

As plans are bring "blurted out," thoughts about vertical form and volume can be sketched as well in your sketchbook or bond paper. The sketches below are thoughts about the lobby (top) and director's office (bottom). These sketches are not meant to be seen by anyone. They are just a form of graphical thinking.

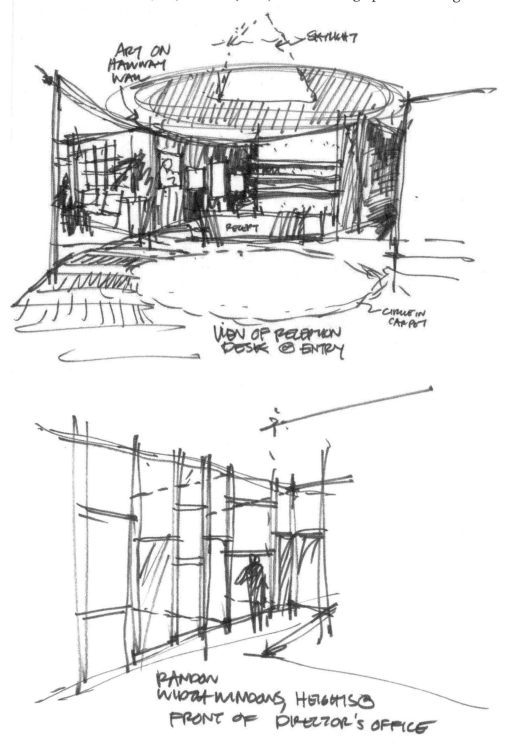

As the design continues to unfold, the thought of adding stadium-style seating is drawn. This would create great sightlines and create an impressive, unique space for delivering presentations. One of the main drawbacks is the space not being very flexible. With fixed raised seating, one could not bring in some tables and have a small banquet dinner, for example. However, this is a question for the client. If we show them this sketch, they can decide: yes, no, maybe?

THEATRE SEATING LAYOUT

The reader is encouraged to take the *Program*, grab a sketchbook and throw down a few ideas. Make sure you include all the spaces. Focus more on proportions rather than actual scale. If Conference Room 1 is 400 square feet and Conference Room 2 is 200 square feet, then one conference room should be twice the size as the other. This type of common sense visual reasoning will go a long way in coming up with more ideas and saving time.

It is a good idea to always have a sketchbook handy, as you never know when a good idea will pop into your head. Another option is to have an Apple iPad handy in place of a sketchbook. There are a number of great sketching tools available for this medium now. Take a look at Autodesk's **SketchBook Pro** for the **iPod** and **iPad**. This is an amazing product for hand sketching and it is under ten bucks!

Developing Design Options

All three designs will have a second stair shaft added to replace the obsolete exterior fire escape. We will assume the stair will be exactly as shown on all designs due to code requirements, how the existing conditions work out at the street level, and the desire not to obscure any existing windows. See Figure 13-2.1 for the stair shaft dimensions; note the walls are 8″ concrete block (CMU). The CMU may be covered with a finish, such as gypsum board, on the office side of the walls.

The three sketches on the page 13-21, Figure 13-2.7, were developed using tracing paper over a scaled printout of the existing conditions floor plan. The solution was based on using each of the spaces listed in the *Program Statement*. It is not necessary to get

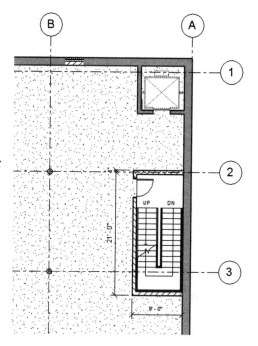

FIGURE 13-2.1
Floor Plan – New Stair

each space to perfectly match the *Program*. It is used as a guide and should be within a close percentage for each room, but does not need to be exact. Keep in mind that any major deviations need to be explained and justified to the client.

Walls

When sketching walls, the experienced designer has an idea of what the wall construction will be but does not have to indicate this or draw it precisely to scale. However, just to ensure the reader understands conceptually what the basic commercial wall construction is, a short conversation will be had about walls at this juncture.

One of the most typical walls on a commercial project consists of 3 5/8″ metal studs (at 16″ O.C.) with one layer of gypsum board on each side, making a wall system that is 4 7/8″ thick.

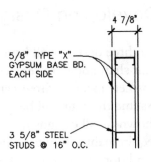

This composition can vary greatly. For example, you may need to add resilient channels to one side of the wall to enhance sound control; they are 7/8″ thick and are installed on the noisy side of the wall.

> **Finishes**: Gypsum board walls can be finished in a variety of ways. The most economical finish is usually paint (one or more colors). Other options include: wall fabrics (i.e., high-end wall paper) which are used in executive offices and conference rooms; fiberglass liner panels which are used in janitor rooms and food service areas; veneer plaster which is used for durability (high-impact gypsum board can also be used); tile which is used in toilet rooms, showers, to name a few. These finishes are nominal and are not included in the thickness used to draw the wall.

Concrete block (often referred to as CMU) walls are often used to construct stair and elevator shafts, high traffic/high abuse areas, and for security; filling the cores with concrete or sand can increase strength, sound control and even stop bullets. The most used size is 8″ wide CMU; 6″, 10″ and 12″ are also commonly used (typically, 6″ for aesthetics and 10″ and 12″ CMU for structural reasons).

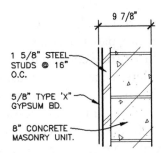

> **Finishes**: Concrete block can just be painted or it can have special finishes such as Glazed Block or Burnished Concrete Block, which cost more but are durable and are available in many colors. In offices, conference rooms and other more refined areas, concrete block walls are not often desirable so they are covered with metal furring channels and gypsum board, especially in rooms where three walls are metal studs and only one would be CMU. The sooner this is taken into consideration, the better, as this can significantly affect space for furniture in a room. (Another major furniture obstacle is fin-tube radiation at the exterior walls.)

Walls often have several **Life Safety** issues related to them. Finishes applied to walls have to have a certain flame spread rating (per local building code). Several walls are usually required to be fire rated (protecting one space from another in the event of a fire); these walls have restrictions on the amount of glass (windows + doors), type of door and window frames (wood vs. steel), and the need to extend the wall to the floor/roof deck above.

While in the early design stage it is only necessary to sketch two general interior wall thicknesses; one that is about 6″ and another at 12″. The first is for most typical conditions and the latter for anticipated special conditions such as a structural bearing wall, stair shafts, special sound control, etc.

Toilet Room Design

When you lay out the toilet rooms, it is necessary to have a basic understanding of the accessibility codes as they will impact the overall shape the space must be. If not properly considered early on, one might have to significantly redesign the project in order to make the toilet rooms code compliant.

One of the codes which impacts virtually all designs is the **American with Disabilities Act** (ADA). Most state codes, and some local codes, will have the ADA code minimums within their regulations, and in some instances go beyond and require more. For example, ADA requires grab bars in an accessible toilet stall, but the Minnesota building code requires this plus an additional vertical grab bar next to the toilet. The requirements of the ADA can be found on the internet and is a good guideline for academic designs; see http://www.ada.gov/stdspdf.htm for more information.

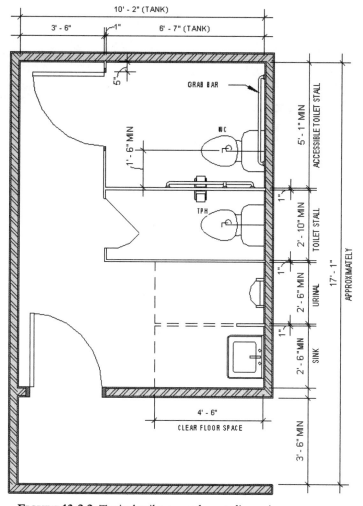

FIGURE 13-2.2 Typical toilet room layout dimensions

Sightlines are typically explored by drawing a line from the adjacent hallway (or space), through the door opening, into the toilet room. Looking at Figure 13-2.4 you can see the sightlines are quite acceptable. This layout takes up a fair amount of floor space but is necessary.

An unacceptable design solution is shown in Figure 13-2.3. The toilet room is much larger and can even have another toilet fixture without the door modification for sightlines; also, the door is right off the circulation path which can be problematic. Notice two lines are shown to visualize the full visual range. Granted, some of this view is obstructed by a person's body as they pass through the door opening; it is still an undesirable design solution.

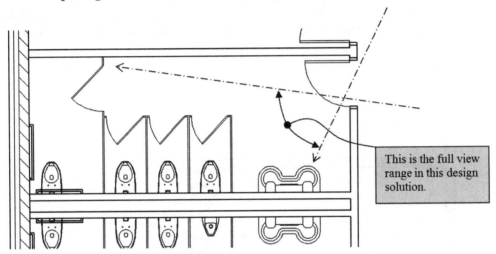

This is the full view range in this design solution.

FIGURE 13-2.3 Dashed lines reveal unacceptable sightlines into toilet room

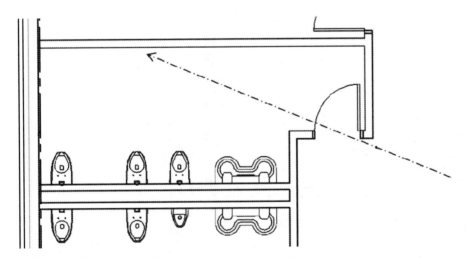

FIGURE 13-2.4 Dashed lines show acceptable sightline

Doors

All the doors, unless noted otherwise, will be 3'-0" wide. This is the typical size for a commercial building. Much of this information is not directly needed for sketching concept drawings, but knowing about it can save you a lot of redesign time.

Most building codes in the US require that a door's clear opening be a minimum of 32" wide. If you look at a typical commercial door that is open 90 degrees, you will notice that the "stops" on the door frame, the door thickness, and the "throw" of the hinges all take space from the actual width of the door in the closed position (see Figure 13-2.5); therefore 36" wide (i.e., 3'-0") doors are typically used.

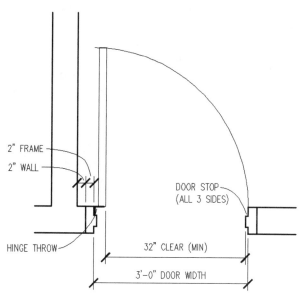

2" FRAME
2" WALL
DOOR STOP
(ALL 3 SIDES)
HINGE THROW
32" CLEAR (MIN)
3'-0" DOOR WIDTH

Figure 13-2.5
Details to know about accessible doors

Door Stops are usually an integral part of the hollow metal door frame. Their main function is to "stop" the door when being shut. However, they also provide visual privacy and can have sound or weather strips applied. Door stops are NOT typically drawn in floor plans.

Hinge Throw is the distance the door is projected out into the opening as the door is opened, which varies relative to the hinge specified.

The **2" Wall** dimension is the amount of wall many designers provide between the frame and any adjacent wall. This helps to ensure that the door will open the full 90 degrees regardless of the door knob/lever/hinges selected.

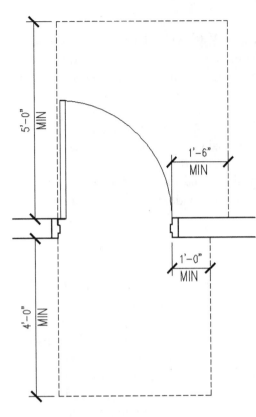

Figure 13-2.6
Clear floor space at accessible doors

Building codes can vary regarding clearances required at a door, but most are pretty similar. Typically, doors that have BOTH a closer and a latch must have sufficient space for a handicapped person to operate the door.

Pull Side of a door that is required to be accessible typically needs to have 18″ clear from the edge of the door (not the outside edge of the frame) to any obstruction. An obstruction could be a wall, a base cabinet or furniture.

Push Side of a door that is required to be accessible typically needs to have 12″ clear from the edge of the door to any obstruction.

Most building codes and ADA (Americans with Disabilities Act) require slightly different dimensions depending on approach (i.e., is the person approaching the door perpendicular or parallel to the wall/door?).

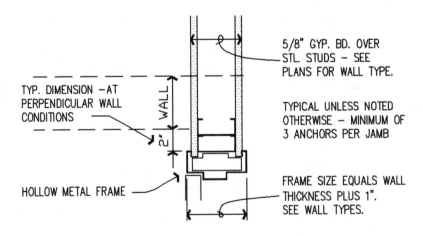

Common Dimensions

The drawings on the next two pages provide general dimensions for a few basic items commonly found in a commercial office space. These things are not usually sketched to scale at an early phase. However, the designer is familiar with them and has the ability to sketch them roughly to scale. If these things are drawn too far out of scale, it might have a serious impact on the validity of the design; that is, there need to be changes because the desks were drawn way too small, or the lobby furniture too big, making the space larger than it really needed to be.

Therefore, seeing as you are sketching over a scaled floor plan, the dimensioned drawings below are offered as a way to spot check your sketches to make sure they are not off too much.

The dashed lines shown in the drawings below suggest the necessary space required around the item to make it functional or meet code (of course codes will vary based on the project location).

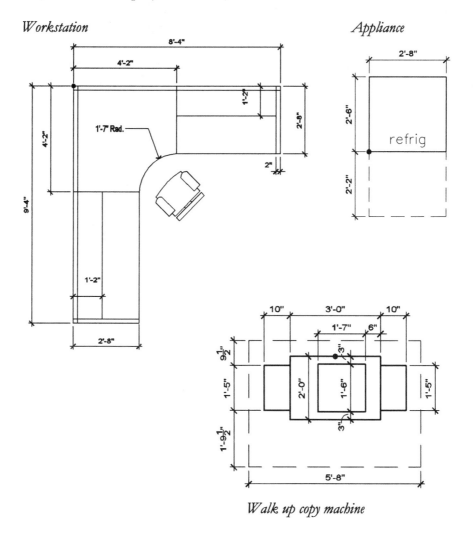

Workstation

Appliance

Walk up copy machine

Lobby Furniture

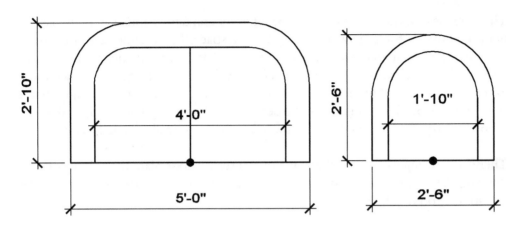

Meeting tables

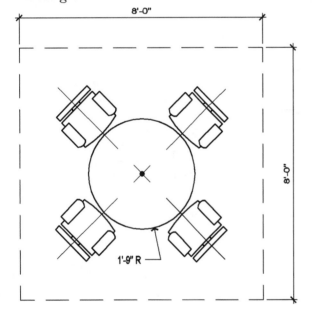

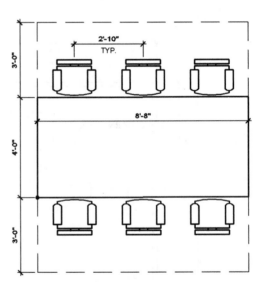

Three Design Options

Once a few decent concepts have worked their way to the surface, from your loose sketching exercises, you will refine them. This process involves working on a larger scaled print of your floor plan. You can use tracing paper laid over the printout or draw directly on it at this point.

At this stage you will want to have an architectural scale in hand to make sure things are working out. That is why the previous pages talked so much about specific dimensions for various portions of a plan. You don't really need to use a straight edge as this can slow things down. However, striking a few light reference lines with a straight edge or parallel bar does not hurt.

The next few pages will present more detailed information about the three design options offered in the book. The three images below (Figure 13-2.7) show the designs side-by-side so the reader can get a feel for the range of variation and similarity between options.

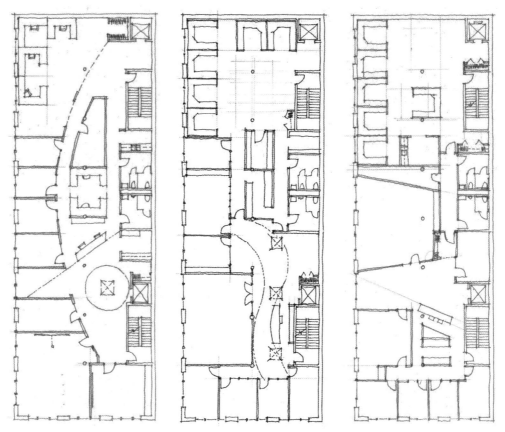

FIGURE 13-2.7
Preliminary Floor Plans – three options

Design Option A – Comments and Observations

The first design to be explored is a conservative, more traditional approach. A talented designer will possess the ability to execute a quality design in multiple styles and not be exclusively committed to one. A common approach to exploring the client's taste is to present more than one style and discuss the pros and cons of each.

Design Option A, as we will refer to this first design, is a simple, average cost design. The walls are orthogonal (perpendicular to the exterior walls – not curved or angled) and generally align with columns.

Here are a few comments (See Figure 13-2.8):

- Most will enter from *Elevator*, some from adjacent *Stair*.
  - *Reception Desk* between Stair and *Elevator* entrance.
  - Three dashed squares represent suggested skylights cut into roof above.
- New Stair shown in northeast corner:
  - Only meant to be used by staff.
  - Used by public in case of emergency for egress.
- Most structural columns buried in new interior walls:
  - Don't forget about columns, they should be the first thing you sketch.
- Occupied rooms all on window walls:
  - *Storage, Stairs, Elevators, Storage Rooms* on east wall, which has no windows.
- Walls and doors are used to clearly delineate public and private (staff only):
  - This is good when working on confidential projects for certain clients.
  - Staff can use *Restrooms* without being seen by someone in the *Waiting Area*.
- Glass walls suggested by single line with vertical mullions rather than double lines as typically shown for a gypsum board wall.
- Tables can be rearranged in the *Mock Up* area.
- Firm partners have the best view, looking south over the city and lake.
- *Break Room* gets exterior window.

Try sketching a plan like this over a scaled print of the SketchUp floor plan. Notice how the moveable items are sketched lighter.

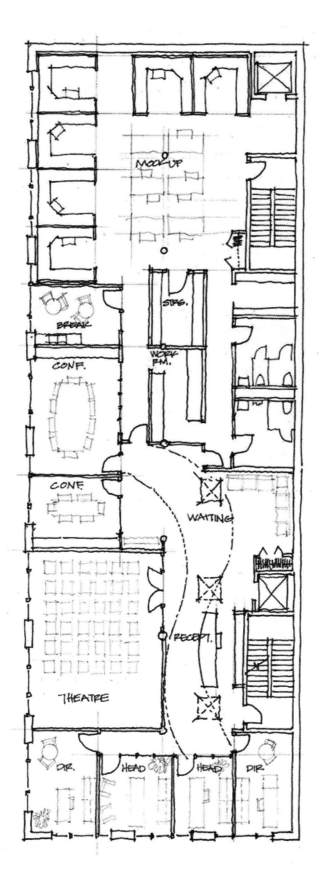

FIGURE 13-2.8
Floor Plan – Option A enhanced

Design Option B – Comments and Observations

This second design takes some of the ideas from the previous one and adds a few new ideas. Not every design option needs to be a totally new idea. Notice the *Toilet Rooms*, the *Director/Head Offices* and a portion of the open office area are the same as Option A.

Option B is slightly more contemporary than the previous in that it has angled elements: the wall and reception desk, mainly.

Here are a few comments (See Figure 13-2.9):

- Columns do not always have to engage a new interior wall.
- Walls and doors are used to clearly delineate public and private (staff only):
  - This is good when working on confidential projects for certain clients.
  - Staff can use *Restrooms* without being seen by someone in the *Waiting Area* and vice versa.
- The visitor approaches the *Reception Desk* from the front when getting off the *Elevator*, but the side (and to the back, slightly) if they take the *Stairs*.
- Angled walls used to create a more interesting *Theater* space:
  - Using angled walls often leads to some spaces being odd and less functional, such as the *Storage Room*.
- Notice how many walls are constrained by where the exterior windows are:
  - The walls either need to hit a wall (preferred) or be on one of the window's vertical mullions.
- This design does not offer natural light for the *Break Room*.

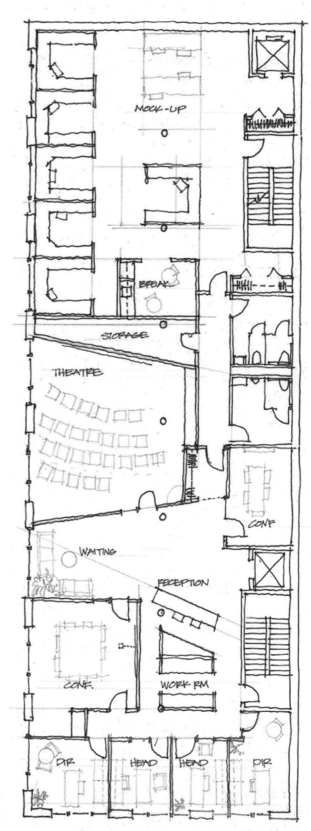

FIGURE 13-2.9
Floor Plan – Option B enhanced

Design Option C – Comments and Observations

The third design is a high impact design, higher cost option. It should be noted that these attributes, high impact and higher cost, do not necessarily make it a better design. An interesting design concept gives the client an opportunity to explore, for themselves, what they would actually prefer for their office. We must try to always keep in mind that our clients do not think about design day-in and day-out as we do. They may see a design option which triggers a remembrance of a space they really connected with and decide to venture down a path they might not otherwise have thought of on their own.

Here are a few comments (See Figure 13-2.10):

- Existing columns do not always have to engage a new interior wall.
- Public and Private spaces not as clearly defined.
- Notice how *Storage Rooms* often fill in the leftover spaces:
    - This makes them odd shaped.
    - An odd shape is not usually the best for efficient storage.
    - You need to know what will be stored in each storage room.
- Curved wall generates interest.

Give it a Try!

Take a shot at sketching these three designs using a scaled printout of the existing floor plan from the previous chapter. Use the existing windows and columns as a general reference when comparing the sketches in this book (Options A-C).

1. Sketch the three design options covered in this section.
2. Use an architectural scale to determine the area for each space and compare to the *Program Statement*.
3. Scan your sketches using a large format scanner.

The last step requires access to a large format scanner. Hopefully your school or firm has one. Many print shops have a large format scanner which can be used for a fee. If you do not have access to one, you will not be able to complete some of the steps that follow in the book. It is possible to take a photograph of your sketch and use it for the steps later in the book; it will not be of the same quality, however.

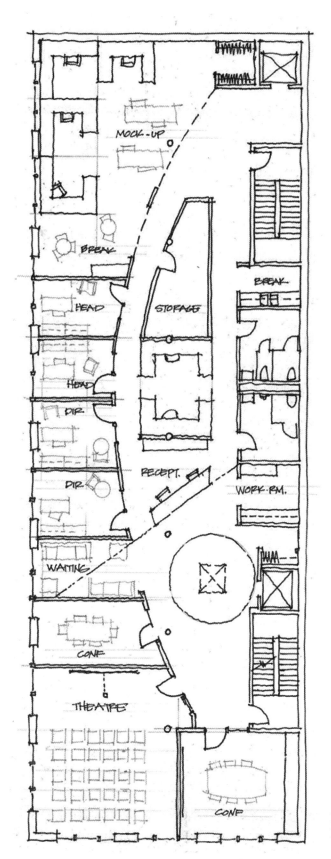

FIGURE 13-2.10
Floor Plan – Option C enhanced

Section 13-3
Preliminary Presentation Boards

This last exercise in Chapter 13 will cover the steps necessary to create a presentation board in Photoshop. This virtual board can be printed to a PDF and emailed, if needed. It can also be printed and pinned to a wall or on foam core for a presentation. Another popular option is to bring your laptop and a projector to the presentation and skip the printing step. This is nice as you can make changes right up until the last minute and not worry about the extra time needed to print and prepare boards.

The process of creating a presentation board in Photoshop is fairly straight-forward. A new file is created with specific dimensions and then images are dropped in and arranged. In this chapter you will also take a quick look at adding text in Photoshop.

Creating a New Photoshop File

1. Open Photoshop and then select **File → New**.

2. Make the changes shown below (Figure 13-3.1)

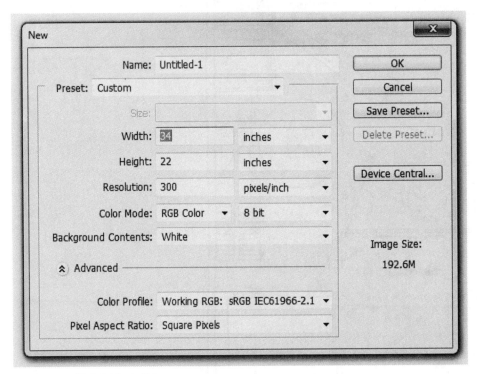

FIGURE 13-3.1 New dialog

The *Preset* drop-down, in the *New* dialog, will default to **Clipboard** if your computer currently has something in the Clipboard. The subsequent settings will then be adjusted to match the item in the Clipboard. In this case, you will change the *Preset* to **Custom** so you can specify exactly what you want. Also, change the *Width* and *Height* from **pixels** to **inches** so you can enter values related to paper size. You may have noticed a *Preset* named **US Paper**, which is great if you want a small format (8½" x 11" or 11" x 17").

3. Click **OK**.

4. Click **Image** → **Image Size...**

Notice in the image below you have your "sheet" size and the *Image Size* dialog confirms the overall size of the image (or sheet).

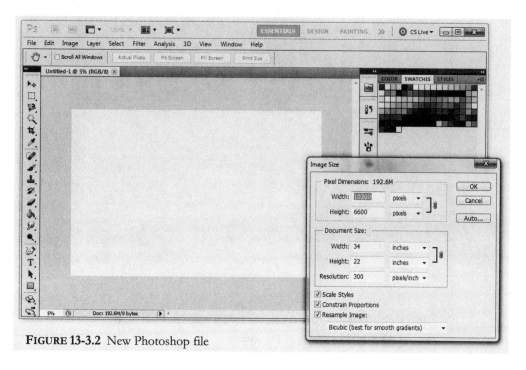

FIGURE 13-3.2 New Photoshop file

5. Click **OK** to close the *Image Size* dialog without making any changes.

Placing an Image

Next, you will place one of the design option sketches you scanned to file in the previous section on the sheet. Photoshop has a tool called ***Place*** which allows you to browse for an image file on your computer (or network) and import it into your current image. A new *Layer* is automatically created for each placement.

6.   Select **File → Place**.

You are now in the *Place* dialog (Figure 13-3.3).

7.   Browse to the location of your scanned floor plan sketches. You can use any image file to try this feature if you do not have access to the scanned floor plans.

FIGURE 13-3.3 Place dialog in Photoshop

8.   Click the **Place** button to begin the *Place* process for the selected image.

The "placed" image is centered on the image by default (Figure 13-3.4). Notice a new *Layer* has been created. Also, the image can easily be moved and/or rotated until the *check mark* is selected on the *Control Panel* (pointed out in the image).

The *chain-link* icon pointed out in Figure 13-3.4 allows you to lock the proportions of the image. Thus, when changing the width or height (located on either side of the *chain-link* icon) the two will remain proportional to each other, and will not get stretched to look odd.

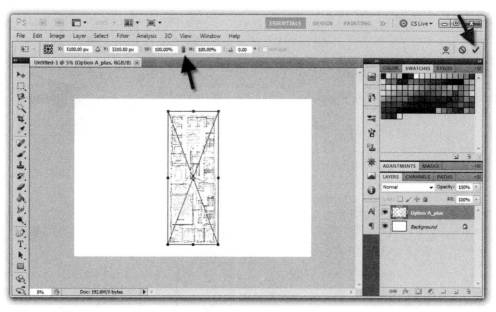

FIGURE 13-3.4 Image centered on "sheet" by default

9. Click and drag the image to the left and then click the **check mark** on the *Control Panel.*

10. Use the **Place** tool and add the other two scanned floor plan options.

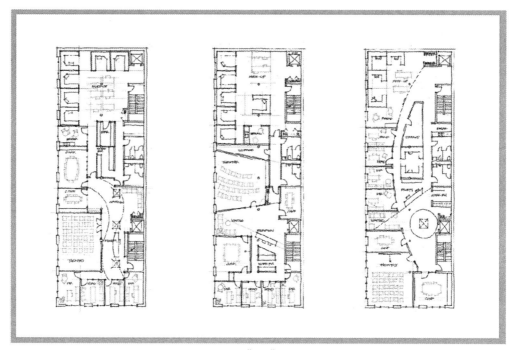

FIGURE 13-3.5 Three designs placed on 22″x34″ sheet

Adding text

The last step in this exercise is to add text below each image.

11. Click the **Text** tool.

12. Click just below the *Option A* floor plan.

13. Type **OPTION A** in all caps as shown below.

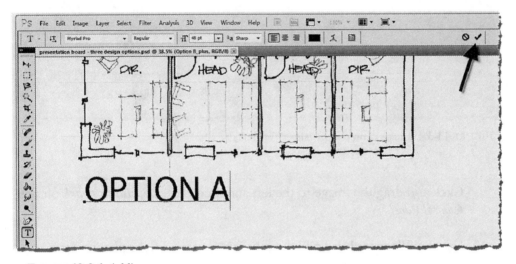

FIGURE 13-3.6 Adding text

Notice the *Control Panel* allows you to change the font and size of the text.

14. Click the **check mark**, on the *Control Panel*, to finish the text.

That is all there is to placing text. Notice another new *Layer* was created to allow you to move the text around later on. Note that the **Text** tool must be active to edit the text in the future. If you do not click directly on the text, you will accidentally begin to create a new text object.

15. Place text under the other two floor plans and name them accordingly.

16. **Save** your file.

You can now print this to a large format plotter or to a PDF file to share with your client or email to your instructor.

Self-Exam:

The following questions can be used as a way to check your knowledge of this lesson. The answers can be found at the bottom of this page.

1. *Predesign* precedes *Schematic Design*. (T/F)

2. Using images to communicate with a client is called *Visual Listening*. (T/F)

3. Use the *Image Size* command to add images to your current Photoshop image file. (T/F)

4. Fixed furniture is sketched heavier than loose items. (T/F)

5. New text is placed on its own _____ in Photoshop.

Review Questions:

The following questions may be assigned by your instructor as a way to assess your knowledge of this section. Your instructor has the answers to the review questions.

1. All design options should represent the lowest cost to the client. (T/F)

2. Using photographs (i.e., *Visual Listening*) in client meetings can help draw out topics that might not otherwise come up. (T/F)

3. Before editing text, you must activate the **Text** tool. (T/F)

4. When you "place" an image, it is automatically aligned to the left. (T/F)

5. Text can be moved when it is on a *Layer*. (T/F)

6. Obsolete item removed from the north side of the building: _____.

7. Minimum width of non-accessible toilet stall: _____ .

8. After typing your text, you click the _____ _____ to finish. (T/F)

9. It is good practice to take pictures of your client's existing spaces to refer back to later; this will help understand how they utilize a space. (T/F)

10. Fully dimensioned and noted drawings are created in the Construction Administration (CA) phase. (T/F)

Notes:

Chapter

14

Develop Interior Perspectives

This chapter will cover the steps used to develop an interior perspective for one of the floor plan options from the previous chapter. The process starts with SketchUp and then moves to a sketch-over on a printout. The results can be very rewarding for both the designer and the client, as it helps to visualize the concept long before things get too formal and more difficult to change.

Section 14-1
Creating a SketchUp Model

The first step in developing an interior perspective is to create a SketchUp model. This process allows the designer to explore the ideal view and establish the major perspective lines. Trying to do all of this manually, by hand, can take a lot more time and it is not possible to turn a little to the right, for example, if you decide the current sketch is not quite right.

The following pages will provide a series of screen shots which will walk you through the process of creating the SketchUp model for Option B.

The goal is to create an image which depicts what a person would see as they enter the *Lobby* from the *Elevator* (Figure 14-1.1).

Drawing angled walls and furniture by hand can be tricky to get in the correct perspective. This is where SketchUp is really helpful.

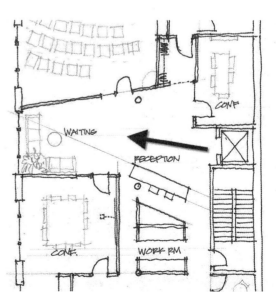

FIGURE 14-1.1 Perspective vantage point

Creating the SketchUp Model

It would be possible to start this model from the existing floor plan previously created in SketchUp. However, you will start from scratch for the practice.

1. Open SketchUp and start a new model using the *Architectural* template as before.

Refer to the following image for dimensions while working through this section. If a dimension is not given, just use an approximate value from your sketched floor plan drawing.

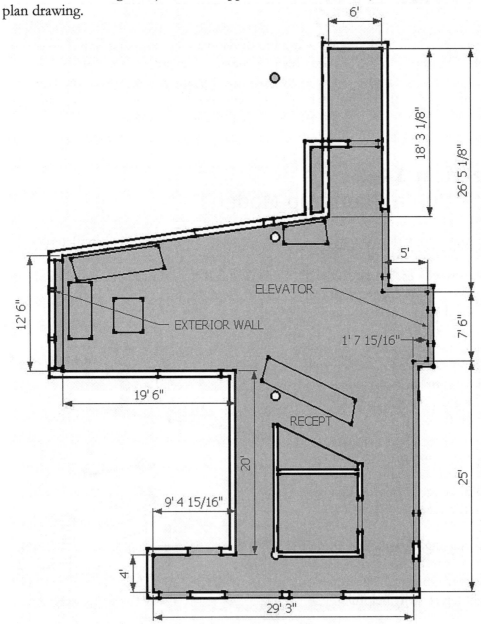

FIGURE 14-1.2 Overall dimensions – to inside face of walls

2. Add *Guides* to define the perimeter of the space (Figure 14-1.3).

3. Use the *Line* tool to sketch the perimeter of the space, snapping to the *Guides* (Figure 14-1.3).

    a. Also add the 12″ diameter columns using the *Circle* tool (see Figure 12-2.4 for additional dimensions).

    b. Refer back to page 4-12 for information on adding *Guides*.

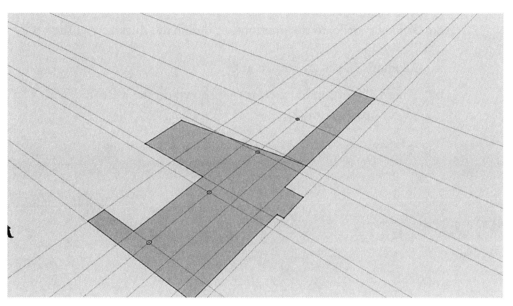

FIGURE 14-1.3 Adding guides and lines at the perimeter

Drawing the *Guides* is optional, but can be very useful. The *Guide* visibility can be toggled on and off via the *View* menu (Figure 14-1.4). When you click *Guide* in the menu list, a check mark will be placed next to it, indicating that *Guide* visibility is on, similar to *Section Cuts* in the image shown.

When *Guide* visibility is on, they will print. So if you do not want them showing up in a print, you need to turn then off before printing. The other option is to just delete them when you are done with them. However, there will typically be a few that you will want to keep.

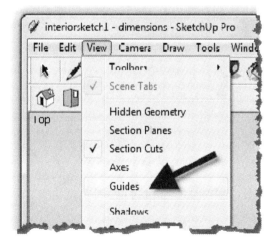

FIGURE 14-1.4 Guide visibility toggle

Next, you will start to define the thickness of the walls around the perimeter of the space. For the most part you only need to model what will be seen in the view you are trying to generate so you can print it out and sketch over it. However, sometimes you are not sure what the best view will be, so modeling a little more than you think you might need is not a bad idea. Additionally, if you want to use SketchUp's *Shadow* feature to define the position of shadows coming through the windows and skylights, you will want to close up the space with faces as much as possible. Otherwise you will have light coming in where an adjacent wall would otherwise be blocking that light.

4. Add **Guides**, parallel to the previous, to define the thickness of the walls.

    a. All interior walls are shown at **8″**.

    b. The small portion of exterior wall shown on the west side, with a window, is **1′-4″** thick.

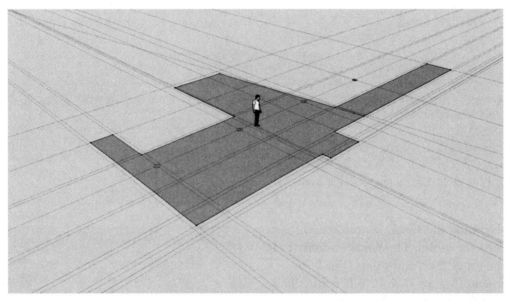

FIGURE 14-1.5 Adding additional guides to define wall thickness

5. Use the **Line** tool to add the outer lines of the walls, snapping to the *Guides* added in the previous step (Figure 14-1.6).

Keep in mind, as you create enclosed areas, they will be filled with a *Face* on what we are considering the floor plane. Later these faces, which exist within the wall thickness, will be extruded upward using the *Push/Pull* tool.

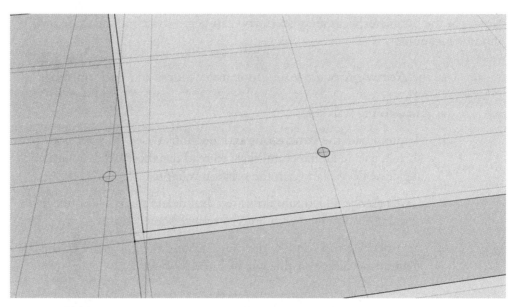

FIGURE 14-1.6 Drawing the line work to define the outer walls

After sketching all the perimeter wall *Guides* and line work, your drawing should look like Figure 14-1.7, shown below. The perimeter lines should be continuous and connected all around so the walls have a separate fill from the floor area of the space under consideration. Hovering your cursor over a face will highlight it and allow you to verify its extents. If a *Face* extends past a line, that means the line must not fully extend to an adjacent line; zoom in and add another line segment to close it off.

FIGURE 14-1.7 Drawing the line work to define the outer walls

Now that the perimeter walls are placed, you can begin to define the door and window locations.

6. Use the **Rectangle** or **Line** tool to define window and door openings.

    a. *Snap* to the wall lines.

    b. Approximate the dimensions and locations based on your floor plan sketch; use an architectural scale to read distances off of your hand sketched floor plan from the previous chapter.

    c. *Guides* can be added first if desired, but delete them when finished defining the opening with lines to reduce screen clutter.

    d. Add all door and window openings around the perimeter of the space; if nothing else, this will be good practice.

FIGURE 14-1.8 Defining door and window openings

Once all the windows are placed, you can begin to develop the elements within the space. It is best to define as much as possible before transforming things into 3D as they become more difficult to modify at that point, and you have to start using *Orbit* more to spin the model to see around 3D elements.

7. Add the following (Figure 14-1.9):

    a. Add the major built-in elements, such as the *Reception Desk*.

    b. Add the interior walls behind the *Reception Desk*:
        i.   Show these walls 6″ thick.
        ii. Note the alignment with the existing column.
        iii. Scale dimensions from your floor plan sketch.

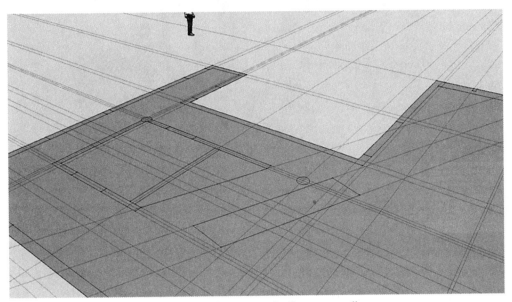

FIGURE 14-1.9 Adding major built-in elements and a few more walls

8. Use ***Push/Pull*** to create 3D walls (Figure 14-1.10; see next page for additional comments). Make walls **13′-0″** tall.

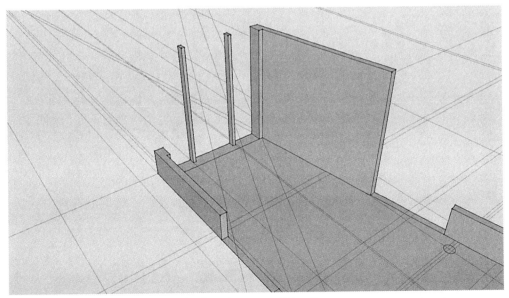

FIGURE 14-1.10 Using the Push/Pull tool to create 3D walls

It is not known what the ceiling will be at this point, so you will model the walls all the way up to the structural roof deck above. As you can see in the image below (Figure 14-1.11), the space is beginning to take shape. Note that you will need to fill in the wall above the doors and windows. This will be discussed in a later step.

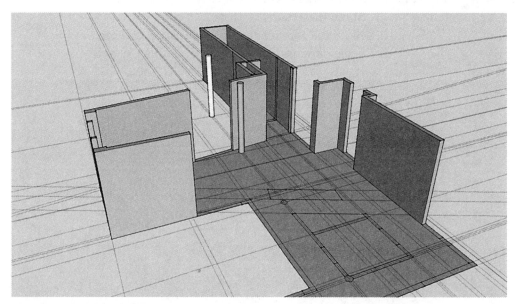

FIGURE 14-1.11 Space beginning to take shape

9. Use the **Push/Pull** tool to extrude the columns and reception desk.

Once you have all the walls extruded into 3D, you can switch to the top view to see an interesting view of the plan. This view has *Perspective Mode* (*Camera* menu) and *Shadows* (*View* menu) turned on

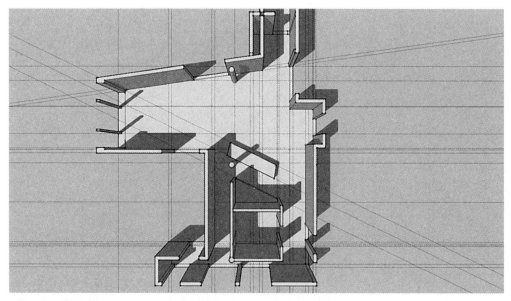

FIGURE 14-1.12 Top view with shadows on

When using shadows, you might set the shadows generically with the intent of making the image more interesting; think of this as artistic license. However, it is also possible to make the daylight be accurate for a given date, time and location. This is great for doing daylighting studies.

If you want accurate daylighting, you need to let SketchUp know where the project is located on Earth. This can be done from **Window → Model → Geo-location** (Figure 14-1.13). You also need to make sure true north is correct; true north aligns with the green axes.

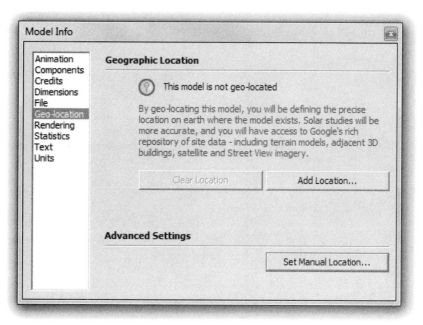

FIGURE 14-1.13 Specifying project location

To adjust how the shadows display, go to **Window → Shadows** (Figure 14-1.14). Here you can adjust the time and date.

Try adjusting the sliders to see the effect it has on the view. Use the *Help Center* to learn more about using *Geo-location* and controlling shadows if you want to learn more.

> *TIP: The time and date sliders may also be controlled via the Shadows toolbar; turn it on by going to **View → Toolbars → Shadows**.*

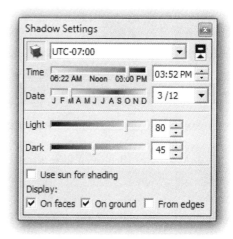

FIGURE 14-1.14 Shadow Settings

The next step is to fill in the walls above the door openings.

10. Complete the walls above doors and windows; use the ***Rectangle*** tool to sketch on the face of the wall and then ***Push/Pull*** the created face back to the other wall face.

The image below (Figure 14-1.15) shows a header above the door with the intention of having a transom above (i.e., a window above the door). Otherwise the wall would align with the top of the adjacent wall.

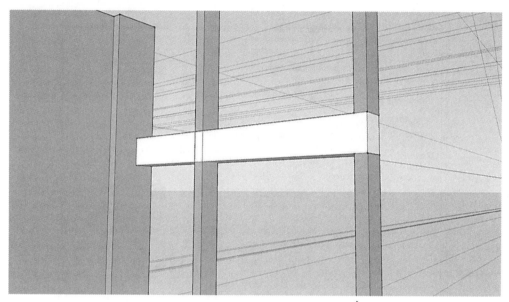

FIGURE 14-1.15 Filling in the wall area above door and window openings.

11. Delete any extra lines that would not otherwise be present on the actual wall; simply **select the line** and **press the Delete key**.

In the case of a sketch-over type hand drawing process, it is not really necessary to delete any extra lines. But in this tutorial it will be good practice to allow the reader to become more familiar and proficient with SketchUp.

If the header in the image above needs to become a full wall, without a transom above, one can adjust the view so the top of the transom is visible and use the *Push/Pull* tool. When pulling the surface up, it will snap in alignment with the adjacent walls.

You will not actually model anything for the doors, windows or glass. This can be more quickly sketched in by hand later. Adding the overall opening is helpful as it locates it in perspective.

Next, you will add a cap to the space. Again, the design of the ceiling may not really be known yet. Here we will simply define the extents of the space, that is, to the roof deck above.

12. Use the *Line* tool to create enclosed areas, which will result in the creation of *Faces* by SketchUp (Figure 14-1.16).

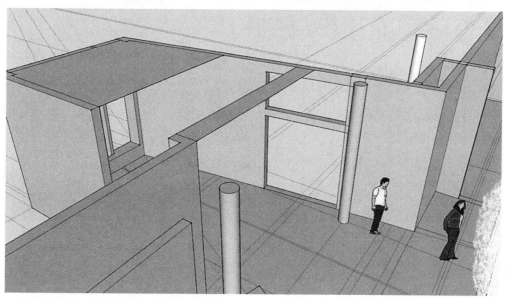

FIGURE 14-1.16 Adding the ceiling plane.

The view below (Figure 14-1.17) gives an idea of how the model is beginning to look from a camera view. You will learn how to set up the camera view.

FIGURE 14-1.17 Adding the ceiling plane.

13. Add any additional people, furniture massing and "2D" line work on the walls to represent artwork (Figure 14-1.18).

FIGURE 14-1.18 Masses for furniture and lines for artwork on walls added

You are now ready to set up the camera view. There are a few specific things you need to know to make this process a little more efficient than just using the *Orbit* tool.

14. Using **Orbit**, adjust the view to look similar to Figure 14-1.19. The item being pointed out with the arrow is covered in the next step.

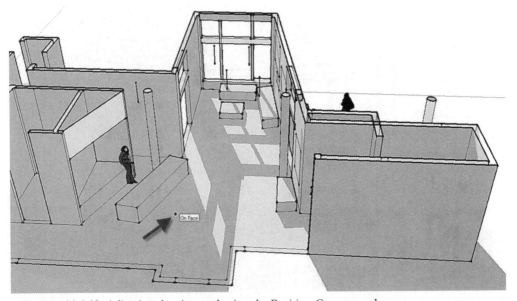

FIGURE 14-1.19 Adjusting the view and using the Position Camera tool

Next, you will use the ***Position Camera*** tool. This tool allows you to pick a point on the floor; SketchUp will then reposition the camera at that point, and 5'-6" above it (which is an average *Eye Height* of a person). The camera will be looking in the direction of the view when the tool was used. That is why the previous step had you adjust the view so your results will be more predictable.

15. Select **Camera → Position Camera**.

16. Pick the point highlighted in Figure 14-1.19.

> ***FYI:*** *You will also see a small person-shaped icon near the cursor. This icon is not able to be captured with the rest of the screen seen in the figure referenced.*

Your model should appear similar to what is shown in Figure 14-1.20. Notice at the lower right, the *Eye Height* of 5'-6" is shown; typing a new value and pressing **Enter** would allow this to be changed (do not change it).

Drag in direction to turn camera   Eye Height 5' 6"

FIGURE 14-1.20 Repositioning the camera

As you move the cursor around, you should notice an icon with a pair of eyes attached to it. This lets you know the ***Look Around*** tool is active; this tool is automatically activated immediately after using the *Position Camera* tool. This tool allows you to, well, look around, but without moving your feet (i.e., the camera).

17. With the *Look Around* tool active, click and drag to make the view look more in the direction shown in Figure 14-1.21, if needed.

   a. Do not use the scroll wheel on the mouse. More on this in a moment.

   b. The *Look Around* tool can be re-activated via **Camera → Look Around**.

Similar to the *Look Around* tool, SketchUp also provides the **Walk** tool. This allows you to move around the model without changing your *Eye Height*. This is used in place of the *Orbit* tool or scroll wheel on the mouse (or zoom) as the *Eye Height* will change using these latter methods.

18. Select **Camera → Walk** from the menu

   a. It is also possible to access these camera view tools from the toolbar: **View → Toolbars → Walkthrough**.

The *Walk* tool is great for navigating through a more complete model. It will automatically look for faces (i.e., walls and furniture) and not let you walk through them. So when you are walking down a hallway, you will not accidentally go through a wall and be in an adjacent room Also, when you come to stairs, SketchUp will adjust the *Camera* up or down automatically!

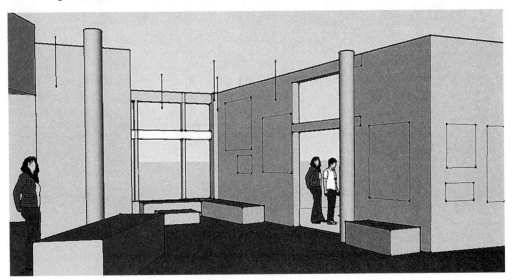

FIGURE 14-1.21 Adjusting the camera view

19. Select **View → Animation → Add Scene** to create a **Scene** tab above the drawing area. This will allow you to return to this view at any time, just by clicking on the tab.

Your model and view are now ready to be printed and sketched over!

Section 14-2
Hand Sketching an Interior Perspective

With the SketchUp model printed it is now possible to quickly hand sketch a few design concepts for the space, looking at volumes, proportions, ceilings, furniture, etc. These first few sketches will likely end up in the garbage. Similar to the initial floor plan sketches, this space requires some brainstorming time.

The image below (Figure 14-2.1) shows a quick initial concept sketch. This was done with red pencil on tracing paper. A pencil or pen of any color would work; you just want something dark so it will show when you lay down another piece of tracing paper. It is a common problem with new designers to not use a heavy hand when sketching and thus have to make several passes to get the drawing to look good. Of course this relates directly to experience and confidence which will come with practice and time (mostly practice).

The photo was taped to a drafting board, using drafting tape dots, and then the tracing paper taped down over that. At times you might have 2-3 layers of tracing paper stacked in order to "glue" together the best parts of multiple sketches.

FIGURE 14-2.1 Preliminary sketching over SketchUp printout

Once a favored concept rises to the forefront, a slightly more refined rendition can be developed. Use a fresh sheet of tracing paper and capture all the major elements in the space. You can begin to depict materials and shaded surfaces (no shadows yet). The image below is a good example (Figure 14-2.2). Notice all the wall surfaces facing the same direction have a shade implied with a loose diagonal hatching. A few materials are being suggested; tile on the floor and something on the ceiling.

FIGURE 14-2.2 Felt tip pen used to create heavy lines

In some cases, the sketch above is all that is needed. Other projects may have more formal presentations to a board or the public in which more refined drawings are needed. In this case a computer rendering might be employed or the hand sketch presented below (Figure 14-2.3). Notice a finer, more accurate line is drawn.

FIGURE 14-2.3 Refined sketch of lobby area

FIGURE 14-2.4 Color added to copy of felt tipped sketch

The sketch on the previous page (Figure 14-2.4) suggests that an intermediate quality sketch with some color added can often be an acceptable benchmark of quality. Most clients can readily understand an image such as this. Notice the sketch has hand drawn lines around the perimeter to help frame and define the edges.

When several new elements need to be added that were not modeled in SketchUp, it may be necessary to find the vanishing point so you can lightly draft in a few major reference lines for the items to be added.

A Second Lobby Concept for Option B

After developing this lobby design for Option B, you decide you want to try another more exciting design to present to the client. The next three images follow the process just described to ultimately come up with the presentation image shown in Figure 14-2.7 (and on the cover of this book).

Your final sketches can be scanned and placed in a presentation using Photoshop or Microsoft PowerPoint. These types of images also make great marketing material when going after future work. When a prospective client sees images like these, it can give them the sense that your firm has the skills to graphically communicate your design solutions to them.

FIGURE 14-2.5 Second design study for lobby – loose sketch on tracing paper

FIGURE 14-2.6 Second design study for lobby – refined sketch of lobby area

FIGURE 14-2.7 Second design study for lobby — Color added to copy of sketch; notice cover of book image has even more color added.

Section 14-3
Photographic Overlay Sketching

This section will take a look at another way to quickly generate interior perspectives – for existing spaces specifically. The process is nearly identical to the previous section, but your underlay is a photograph rather than a SketchUp model. There is no point taking the time to create a SketchUp model if you can just take a picture of the space. The only reason you would want to create a SketchUp model is if any proposed remodeling significantly changed the space.

The photo below is the subject space we will use for this exercise. It is not really from our existing building, but we can imagine it is. It is a good idea to take multiple pictures of the space so you have a few options to choose from.

FIGURE 14-3.1 Photographs of an existing elevator lobby space

Just like with the SketchUp underlay, tracing paper is used to rough out a few concepts. In this case, the photograph captured a one-point perspective. Notice in the image below (Figure 14-3.2), that the vanishing point (VP) has been located by projecting multiple lines back. The VP can now be used to properly define new geometry within the space.

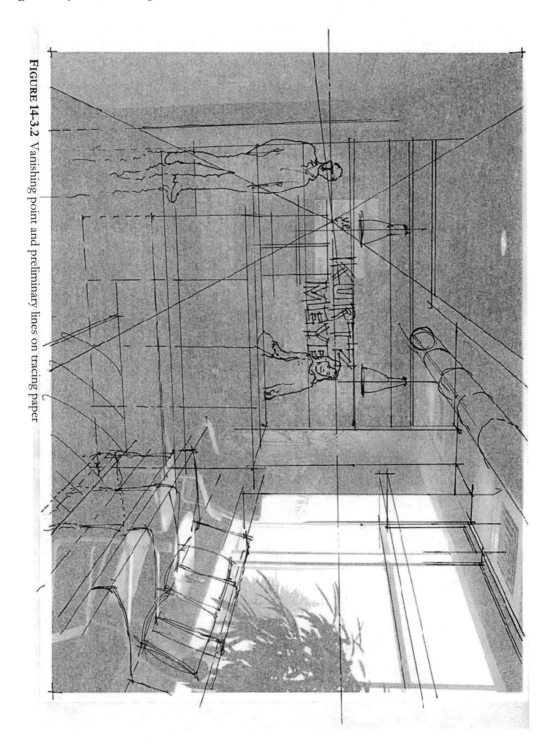

FIGURE 14-3.2 Vanishing point and preliminary lines on tracing paper

The image below shows the tracing paper sketch apart from the photograph. This provides an idea of what has been sketched on the tracing paper.

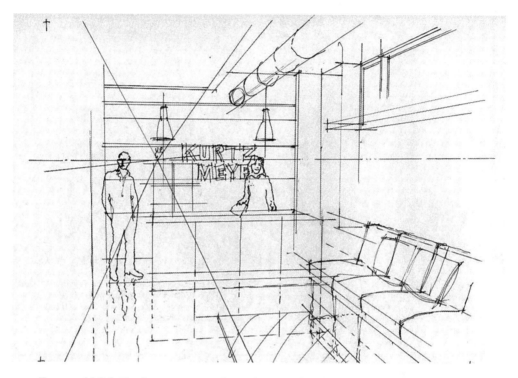

FIGURE 14-3.3 Tracing paper apart from photograph

The next two images show the progression to the final colored image. The color can be added using Photoshop or by hand (using markers and/or colored pencils). If done by hand, you should only color a photocopy and not work directly on the original in case you mess up on the color. This is where Photoshop comes in handy. Because you are adding color to a layer, the original scanned line work is not affected. Therefore, if you mess up the color, or later want to change something, you can *Undo* or use the *Eraser* tool.

There is not too much more that can be said about this process. If you look closely at any small portion of the drawing, you will see rather rough and loose lines. Some might even say they look a little sloppy. But the image as a whole is pleasing to look at and easily discernable. This quality can be had by most, but it takes practice. So carry that sketchbook with you and practice every chance you get.

FIGURE 14-3.4 Refined sketch of elevator lobby

FIGURE 14-3.5 Color added to refined sketch of elevator lobby

Self-Exam:

The following questions can be used as a way to check your knowledge of this lesson. The answers can be found at the bottom of this page.

1. SketchUp saves time getting major elements in perspective. (T/F)

2. Using the *Look Around* tool keeps the camera from moving. (T/F)

3. You may need to find the vanishing point to accurately sketch additional elements in your view. (T/F)

4. Initial concept sketches are done on transparent _____ _____.

5. Command that saves your view in SketchUp: _____.

Review Questions:

The following questions may be assigned by your instructor as a way to assess your knowledge of this section. Your instructor has the answers to the review questions.

1. Accurate shadows require a proper geographic location be specified. (T/F)

2. Enclosed areas, with faces, are needed before extruding into 3D. (T/F)

3. A photograph may be used in place of a SketchUp model. (T/F)

4. Begin your SketchUp model by defining the perimeter with *Guides* or *Lines*. (T/F)

5. Use the *Walk* tool to navigate through your model. (T/F)

6. _____ _____ lists a length without actually drawing anything.

7. When reference lines are needed, you can add _____.

8. SketchUp helps to establish the view prior to hand sketching. (T/F)

9. Tool used to locate the camera within the model: _____.

10. The *Walk* tool prevents you from going through walls by default. (T/F)

Self-Exam Answers:
1 – T, **2** – T, **3** – T, **4** – Tracing Paper, **5** – Add Scene

Final Presentation

In this final chapter the reader will compile a presentation board combined with product and material selections. Additionally, the steps required to create a more refined SketchUp model of a custom reception desk will also be presented.

Section 15-1
Detailed SketchUp Model

It may be helpful at times to create a more detailed SketchUp model. Some do this for an entire project; others just use it to focus on small custom portions of the project. This section will focus on the latter, and will walk through the process of modeling a reception desk. This could also be done for built-in casework, such as cabinets or bookshelves, custom furniture, etc.

You will learn a few new concepts here, such as how to cut a section through your model. However, you already know most of the steps necessary to create the reception desk model. This tutorial will just help you learn to think about what you are trying to model and the various ways in which you can approach the problem given SketchUp's toolset.

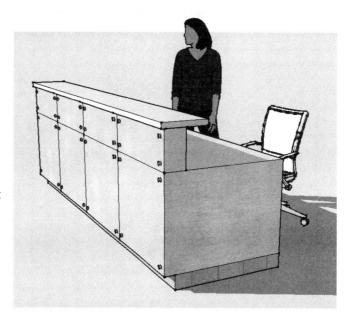

For this tutorial you will start a new SketchUp model. You could work within a project model if you wanted. However, for something detailed like this reception desk, it is easier to work in a separate model and then load it into the project.

1. Start a new SketchUp model.

2. Create a rectangular box (Figure 15-1.1):

   a. Sketch a 10′-0″ x 3′-0″ rectangle on the ground/floor.

   b. Use ***Push/Pull*** to extrude the rectangle 3′-6″ upward.

The rectangle represents the outer extents of what we think the desk will be. The 3′-6″ high is based on the desire to have a 42″ high transaction surface; this is a surface for customers to write and look at paperwork provided by the receptionist. The final desk may extend outside of this box, but we will use this as a starting point. Think of it as a piece of wood you will carve portions away from.

The default person (i.e., *Component*) can remain and be used as a scale reference.

FIGURE 15-1.1 Start with a rectangular box

3. Sketch an outline as shown in Figure 15-1.2:

    a. The three dimensions shown are:

        i. **1'-0"** – transaction surface

        ii. **2'-6"** – typical desk height

        iii. **6"** – thickness of wall supporting transaction surface.

        iv. See Figure 15-1.3 for intended goal.

FIGURE 15-1.2 Sketch outline of areas to be carved out of the box

4. Use the ***Push/Pull*** tool to carve out a portion of the box behind the transaction counter (Figure 15-1.3):

    a. ***Pull*** the surface until it snaps to the opposite end of the box so the section being pulled completely disappears once you let go of the mouse button.

This step also defines the height of the work surface (30″ high).

The next step will be to carve out a portion of the box to define the knee space below the work surface. This often requires brackets to support the work surface, but that will be ignored here – we will save that for the Construction Documents phase.

5. Sketch the **lines** shown in Figure 15-1.4 on the back face of the desk:

   a. 1 ½″ thick work surface
   b. 6″ side walls

FIGURE 15-1.3
Using Push/Pull to remove a portion of the box

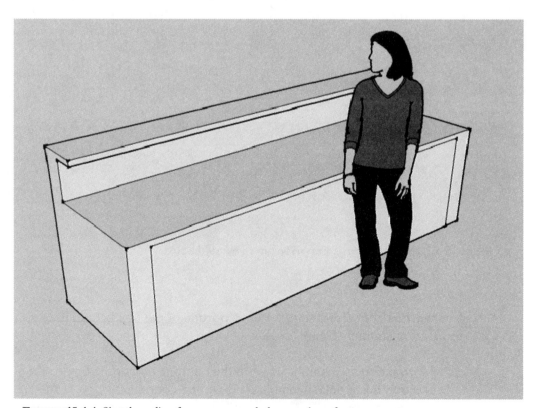

FIGURE 15-1.4 Sketch outline for open space below work surface

6. Use **Push/Pull** to "push" the face back 2'-6".

This modification leaves a 6" wall to support the transaction counter
(3'-0" - 2'-6").

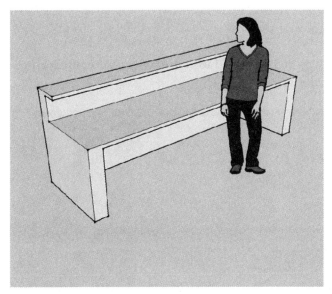

FIGURE 15-1.5 Use Push/Pull to carve out leg space

7. Using similar steps, define a 3" deep and 4" tall **toe space** on the front
   side (or public side) of the reception desk (Figure 15-1.6).

8. Sketch the **lines**, equally spaced vertical lines, as shown in Figure 15-1.6:

   a. Draw one centered and then copy that line 2'-6" each way.

   b. Copy via the **Move** tool while holding down the **Ctrl** key.

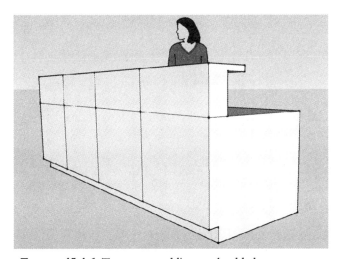

FIGURE 15-1.6 Toe space and line work added

The lines sketched in the previous step will be used to define metal panels. If the desire were to have a more exaggerated reveal, you could sketch the reveal profile and then use *Push/Pull* to create it. However, in most cases a line can adequately suggest a reveal without the extra work.

The next step is to start adding materials. You will have to use *Orbit* to apply materials to all sides of the desk.

9. Use the ***Paint*** tool to add **Metal Aluminum Anodized** to the front and sides of the desk (Figure 15-1.7).

FIGURE 15-1.7 Adding materials

10. Add more materials using the ***Paint*** tool:

    a. Markers\Yellow Green – work surfaces

    b. Tile\Tile Ceramic Natural – base

11. Sketch additional lines and use ***Push/Pull*** to refine the transaction surface as shown in Figure 15-1.8:

    a. Make the front edge extend 1″ out.

    b. Make the sides extend ½″ out.

    c. Adjust the painted faces as necessary.

FIGURE 15-1.8 Defining transaction counter

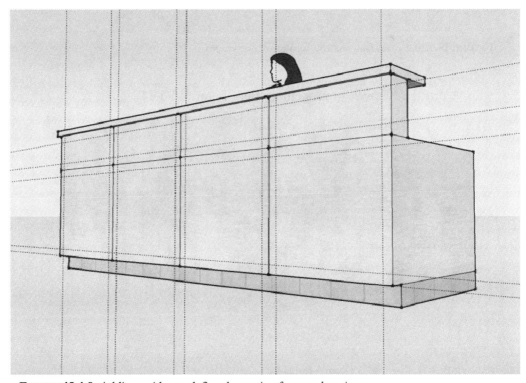

FIGURE 15-1.9 Adding guides to define decorative fastener locations

Next, you will be adding decorative fasteners at the corners of the panels. To help locate them, you will add *Guides* and then use the intersection of these guides to locate the fastener. The fastener will be created as a *Component* so they can all be changed at once if need be later.

12. Add **Guides** 2″ from the edge of the panels as shown in Figure 15-1.10.

    REMINDER: *Use the* Tape Measure *tool.*

13. Create the first fastener off to one side so it does not modify the faces of the panels; once finished, select it, right-click and select **Make Component** (Figure 15-1.10). Make them **2″** diameter and ½″ thick.

FIGURE 15-1.10 Create fastener and turn into component

14. **Copy** the *Fastener* component around (Figure 15-1.11).

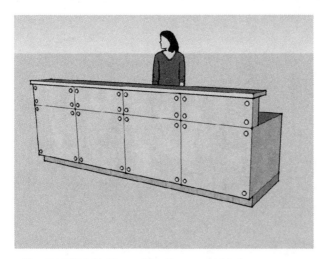

FIGURE 15-1.11 Decorative fasteners added

It is often helpful to use the ***Section Plane*** tool to look at your model in section. This can be done vertically or horizontally. In this exercise you will look at a vertical application. This could also be applied horizontally to a floor plan (i.e., top) view of a more detailed floor plan model.

15. Select **Tools → Section Plane** from the menu.

16. Hover your cursor over the side of the desk, until the *Section Plane* appears as shown in Figure 15-1.12, and then click.

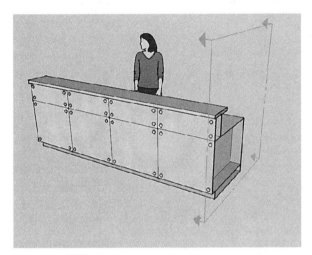

FIGURE 15-1.12 Adding section plane

17. Select the *Section Plane*, and then use the ***Move*** tool to reposition it so you see the desk in section as shown in Figure 15-1.13.

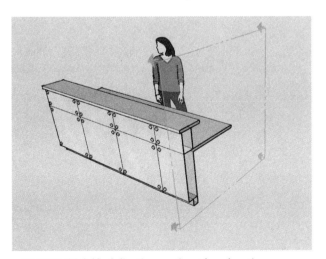

FIGURE 15-1.13 Adjusting section plane location

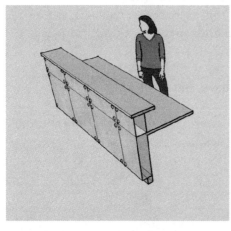

FIGURE 15-1.14
Section plane visibility turned off

18. From the *View* menu, toggle off **Section Planes**.

Notice how the *Section Plane* element is no longer visible, but the model is still in section. This can create a nice presentation drawing. Additionally, toggling off the **Section Cuts** item in the *View* menu restores the entire model even though the *Section Plane* still exists in the model.

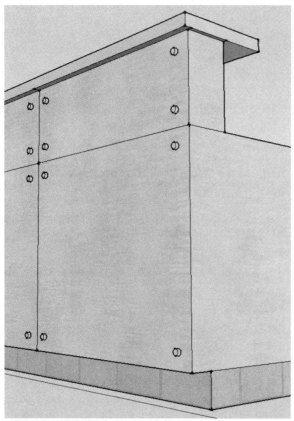

FIGURE 15-1.15
Edit fastener component

It is decided that the 2″ diameter fasteners do not look good, aesthetically speaking. Therefore, you decide to change them to 1″ diameter. Changing one *Component* changes them all!

19. Edit the *Component*; double-click on it.

20. Use the **Scale** tool from the *Tools* menu.

This may take a little trial and error to get it right.

This last step will cover placing furniture in your model.

21. Select **Window → Component**.

22. Type **Haworth** and press **Enter**.

23. Select one of the chairs listed, that are created by Haworth. Place it in your model (Figure 15-1.16).

If you open the *Layers* dialog, you will see new *Layers* created for the chair. The arm rests have their own layer. Therefore, the arms can be turned off, if needed.

FIGURE 15-1.16 Placing components

It is good to remember that some manufacturers have created SketchUp content and made it available on the internet. This can save a lot of time and help to quickly make your models look really great!

This model can now be printed and added to your presentation board covered in the next section. You can use *File → Export → 2D Graphic* to create a raster image file on your hard drive for use in Photoshop. This export feature prompts you for a file name and location.

Section 15-2
Creating Presentation Boards

Most design projects include the preparation of a material or presentation board. This board, or boards – depending on the size and complexity of the project – is used to convey specific materials and fixtures intended to be used in the project.

The process of preparing presentation boards involves the concepts previously covered in this book as well as researching and reviewing several aspects of the design, including:

- Furniture
  - Manufacturer
  - Material: wood, metal, plastic, fabrics
  - Color
  - Quality
  - Cost
- Light fixtures
  - Manufacturer
  - Material
  - Light quality and distribution
  - Cost
  - Work with lighting designer
- Paint
  - Manufacturer
  - Color
  - Quality
  - Cost
  - Alternatives:
    - Burnished Concrete Block
    - Wall Coverings (fabrics, vinyl)
    - Wood panels
    - Stone panels
    - Brick
- Etc.

Flooring samples stored in open shelving

Many design firms have an area or a room which is dedicated to storing materials and creating presentation boards. The two photographs on this page and the one on the next page are good examples of this. The items stored are not uniform in shape or size so theses spaces are never neatly organized.

Baseboard samples

For many products, a representative for the manufacturer will occasionally call on the design firm and update the material in the library. They might also take the time to walk the designer (if they have time) through their new or improved products. Sometimes these product introductions or updates are more formal presentations where lunch is provided (this certainly helps with attendance!) and everyone sits in a conference room. Depending on the topic, these sessions can count towards various professional learning credits.

Plastic laminate samples from multiple manufacturers and a work area.

Furniture Selection

The process of researching furniture can vary depending on the experience of the designer. If they have a product that is "tried and true," they may just go that route. Otherwise, looking through the product catalogues and manufacturers' websites is done to find appropriate items. When an item of interest is found, you can scan the image (if in a catalogue) or save the image to your hard drive (if on a website); to save an image from a website, you right-click on it and select *Save Image*.

The image on the next page (Figure 15-2.1) shows a particular desk option found online. The saved images can then be used in presentation boards or even inserted into meeting minutes to document the furniture ultimately selected by the client.

FIGURE 15-2.1
Researching furniture online

Proposed Break room
tables and seating

Proposed Theater Seating

Material Selection

When selecting materials, such as paint and laminate colors, be sure to write down the manufacturer and model number/name. The image below is a photocopy of the back side of a few of the materials selected for our project (Figure 15-2.2). If you recall, from the Photoshop introduction chapters, the paint colors can be matched in Photoshop if needed, but you need the color information.

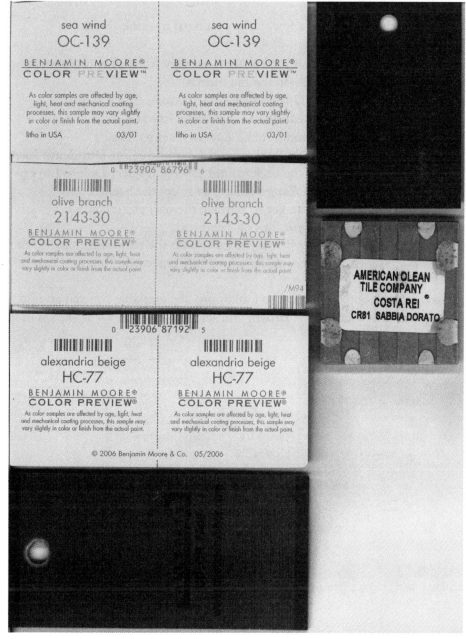

FIGURE 15-2.2
Material names recorded for reference

Colored Floor Plan

At this point the design Option B has been selected and you decided to further enhance the appearance of the floor plan drawing. Figure 15-2.5 shows how color and shadows can be added to make the drawing easier to read. The color could represent floor materials or public versus private areas depending on the specific needs of the project (or presentation). A drawing such as this can be colored using markers (by hand) or digitally using Photoshop.

If using Photoshop, there are a few things you need to think about.

- Removing the background: the steps can vary from what was shown on page 7-16 (this depends on the file format).
  - Saving to a PSD (Photoshop file format) first will help.
  - Set **Image → Mode** to *Grayscale* or *RGB Color*.
    - You cannot make *Layers* if set to *Bitmap*.
  - Right-click on the background *Layer* and select **Duplicate Layer**.
  - Right-click on the background *Layer* and select **Delete Layer**.
  - Use the *Color Range* feature to select the background color.
  - Press the **Delete** key to remove the background color.
  - Create new *Layers* for color and text.
  - Drag the *Layers* below the *Layer* with the hand sketching, so the colors do not cover, or lighten, the line work.

If you want your Photoshop color to look more like markers, you can go into *Brush Properties* (via **Window → Brush**) and select **Wet Edges** – as shown in the two images below.

FIGURE 15-2.3
Creating a marker look where overlaps are darker

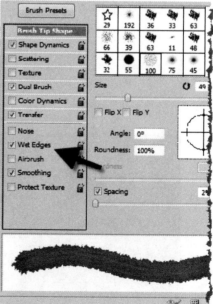

FIGURE 15-2.4
Adjusting Brush Properties

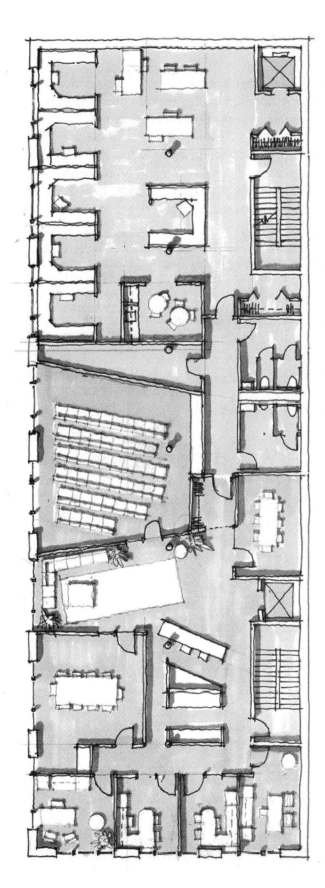

FIGURE 15-2.5
Rendered presentation floor plan

Presentation Story Board

Similar to developing a floor plan, one might choose to sketch a story board (or bubble diagram) for the presentation board. A well-organized board will help make the presentation more concise and speak for itself in many cases.

An example story board for our project is shown below (Figure 15-2.6). The presentation will tell a story, both graphically and with text. The two major focal points will be the project drawings: the floor plan and interior rendering. All other images suggest materials and furnishings for the project.

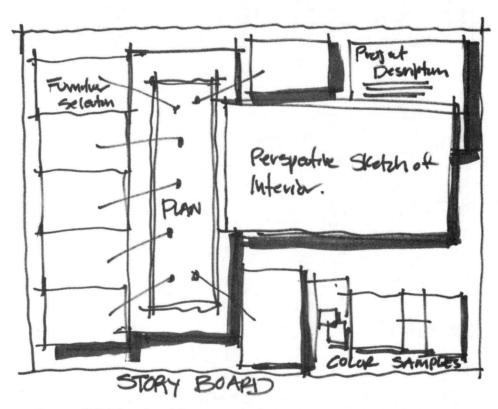

FIGURE 15-2.6 Story board for presentation layout

If you are creating the presentation board completely in Photoshop, you need to scan the selected materials so they can be used in the software. If you are doing parts in Photoshop and taping actual samples (carpet, tile, etc.) to the board, you just need to make sure you leave room for it on the board in Photoshop. You might even consider adding scans of the materials as place holders to help with the overall picture. Once the board is printed the materials can be glued on, directly over the printed out version of the material.

The image below shows the selected materials composed on the scanner with the intent of just using the one raster image on the board (Figure 15-2.7). Another option is to scan each material separately (or cut them out of the overall image) so they can be arranged and rearranged independently.

FIGURE 15-2.7 Scan of materials

Scanning Materials and Drawings

Most office copiers have a scanner built into them. Materials of all shapes and sizes can be scanned on a flatbed scanner. Some bulkier items can be tricky; in some cases the top cover (i.e., Automatic Document Feeder – ADF) of the copier can be removed to allow larger items to be placed on the glass. Be careful not to scratch the glass or press down on it too hard as that might break it.

If you add color to your floor plan drawing, you will need to use a large format scanner.

Whether scanning small or large format, be sure to adjust the resolution so that the printed board has decent image quality. The required resolution can vary depending on the original artwork quality and the capabilities of the printer or plotter to be used. Typically, 200-300 DPI will work. However, you should make a few practice scans and print trials to verify your results.

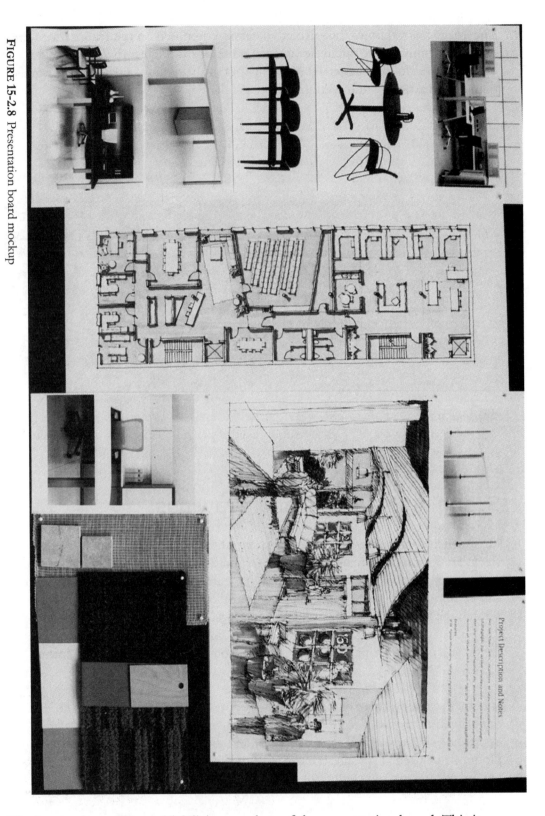

FIGURE 15-2.8 Presentation board mockup

The image above (Figure 15-2.8) is a mockup of the presentation board. This is what you will create in Photoshop.

You should scan the drawings you have created in the previous three chapters and use them to mock up a board in Photoshop. You can use the furniture and materials images located on the CD; however, it would be good practice to find some of your own and use them.

You can use Photoshop to add text to label drawings and things within the drawings, such as room names. You should either use all hand lettering or all computer text. Avoid mixing the two on the same board.

Let the drawings be the focus of the board, not the board itself. New designers sometimes have a tendency to overdo the board with "extras". Just keep in mind this is not a scrapbooking project, it is a design communication tool. There is no need to have drop shadows around images, large background images of a field or gimmicky things such as leaves to suggest green design.

The image below (Figure 15-2.9) shows the final board created in Photoshop. Notice the text label under each image. The text is a "placed" PDF file. The floor plan and interior perspective are scanned images. The reception desk is an export from SketchUp and the furniture are downloads from manufacturer websites.

The board was created as 22″x34″ with the intention of printing it. If you only need to project it on a screen, your size could vary (but this size is still about right for wide format projections). It is convenient that this size can be printed exactly half-scale on 11″x17″ paper. This final image can be sent via email as a PDF file (the PSD file is likely too large to email, plus the recipient would need to have Photoshop). You can use the *Save As* command in Photoshop to create a PDF.

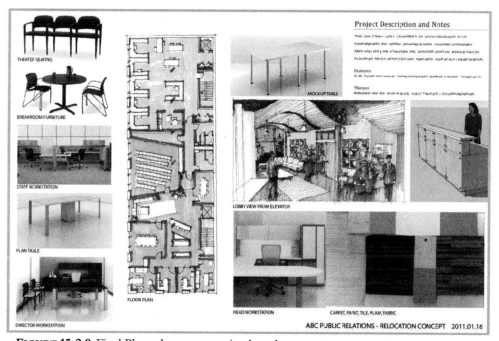

FIGURE 15-2.9 Final Photoshop presentation board

Self-Exam:

The following questions can be used as a way to check your knowledge of this lesson. The answers can be found at the bottom of this page.

1. A Section Plane deletes things in SketchUp. (T/F)

2. Physical material samples can be scanned and added to the digital board in Photoshop. (T/F)

3. In Photoshop, the brush setting "wet edges" has a marker look. (T/F)

4. Some manufacturer content has several _____ in it, which allow you to control visibility of certain portions independently.

5. Height of transaction surface: _____.

Review Questions:

The following questions may be assigned by your instructor as a way to assess your knowledge of this section. Your instructor has the answers to the review questions.

1. Product selection and images can be found on the internet. (T/F)

2. SketchUp guides are useful references. (T/F)

3. The *Layer* order determines if a color covers a scanned sketch or not in Photoshop. (T/F)

4. When a *Component* is edited, all instances are updated. (T/F)

5. *Section Planes* must be deleted when you don't want to see your model in section anymore. (T/F)

6. The height of the reception desk work surface: _____.

7. Product reps typically update a design firm's material library. (T/F)

8. SketchUp tool used to carve out portions of the model: _____.

9. Photoshop can create marker-like coloring. (T/F)

Self-Exam Answers:
1 – F, **2** – T, **3** – T, **4** – Layers, **5** – 3'-6"

Index